D0847301

HEAT PUMPS FOR THE HOME

John Cantor

with illustrations by Gavin D. J. Harper

The Crowood Press

First published in 2011 by
The Crowood Press Ltd
Ramsbury, Marlborough
Wiltshire SN8 2HR

www.crowood.com

British Library Cataloguing-in-Publication Data
A catalogue record for this book is available from the British Library.

ISBN 978 1 84797 292 7

Disclaimer
The authors and the publisher do not accept any responsibility, in any manner whatsoever, for any error, or omission, nor any loss, damage, injury, adverse outcome or liability of any kind incurred as a result of the use of any of the information contained within this book, or reliance upon it. Readers are advised to seek specific professional advice relating to their particular property, project and circumstances before undertaking any installation work concerning heat pumps.

Unless otherwise stated, all illustrations are by the authors.

Typeset by Jean Cussons Typesetting, Diss, Norfolk
Printed and bound in China by Everbest Printing Co. Ltd

CONTENTS

INTRODUCTION

Heat pumps are surprising devices that can extract heat energy from something that appears to be cold – from the air or the ground, for example – and 'magically' use it for home heating. This concept is somewhat perplexing and goes counter to our natural sense of how things ought to work, so it is not surprising that some people wonder if heat pumps really do what they claim. There is, after all, no shortage of gadgets that fail to do what they say on the box!

In this book we want to give you the whole picture, warts and all. Like any other technology, heat pumps can perform poorly if badly installed or used for the wrong purposes, and we cannot expect them always to match the exaggerated promises of salesmen. But the basics are straightforward. The science is completely sound. The engineering principles are well-established. And we know from hands-on experience that heat pumps will deliver low heating bills, if they are installed properly. This book aims to demystify a subject clouded in hype and misunderstanding.

The book is aimed at anyone who wants to improve their understanding of modern heat pumps, such as householders, planners, plumbers, students or architects. Armed with the content of this book, the informed homeowner or designer should be able to judge whether a heat-pump installation might be appropriate in a given situation and how its performance might be optimized. It is written with UK readers in mind, but the practical information will be equally useful to readers from elsewhere.

How To Read This Book

Although heat pumps have a wide range of applications in all sorts of circumstances, there is no getting around the fact that they are not a one-size-fits-all technology. Heat-pump installations tend to be very case-specific. That is, they are sensitive to what might seem at first small details regarding the site, usage factors, operation and so on.

Let's suggest an analogy. The difference between a domestic heat-pump system and a 'normal' central-heating system is a bit like a sailing boat compared with a motorboat. A motorboat is brutally simple. You just rev up the engine and blast away. There's no finesse and one size does (more or less) fit all. With a sailing boat it's much more subtle and fine details of hull design, trim and setting the sails and rudder correctly make all the difference between slicing swiftly through the water and merely limping along. Heat-pump installations are rather like this and small details can make the difference between outstanding and mediocre performance. But we don't want to imply that you have to spend all your time adjusting a heat pump's 'rigging': once it's set correctly, it should operate automatically throughout the seasons with no attention. Indeed, they promise to be a fit-and-forget technology.

To get a handle on these small-details-that-make-all-the-difference, involves at least some understanding of a fair sprinkling of different ideas, some of which might be new to you. Most of these ideas can be grasped immediately, but others seem to go against our normal intuition and can take more than usual effort to enable you to become comfortable with them. We'll try and help you as much as possible in these cases and usually it doesn't take long before you will be saying, 'Aha! Why didn't I get that all along?'.

Once you have got a reasonable grasp of the basic ideas, you can put them together, a bit like a jigsaw-puzzle and then you will have a good idea of the potential for heat pumps and in what kinds of situations they would be suitable. It should then be possible for you to evaluate a real situation and decide what kind of heat-pump installation, if any, would be right for the job. Or, to look at it another way, you could look at a proposed installation and be able to say with some confidence if it's likely to be a winner or if another technology would actually be a better proposition.

For these reasons it is difficult to lay out the book in a linear sequence, because to some extent all the bits depend on each other. The 'whole picture' perhaps won't be apparent until you get towards the end. So to put the details in context, we shall start with a section illustrating how heat pumps are currently being used and what they can offer. Then we get down to the nitty-gritty, looking at the 'ideal' heat pump, how the thing is supposed to work and compare it with the constraints of real life. Then we go through the details of a house's heating needs and how they can be matched to the right kind of installation. We will, when appropriate, remind readers that a heat pump is not always the right answer! We deal with economic issues and environmental aspects later in the book, and readers who don't want to grapple with the technicalities can jump straight there. Finally, for the heroic survivors we have added a more detailed account of what goes on inside your heat pump in the Appendices.

Acknowledgements

Over the last thirty years I have had countless in-depth conversations on the topic of heating and heat pumps. I would like to thank all those people, too numerous to mention, who have increased my knowledge, shaped my perception and made this book possible.

In particular, I would like to thank my mentor, Peter Harper, for his book-writing wisdom and help with the Introduction, and Gavin Harper (no relation to Peter), without whom this book would not have been written. For my wife Sabrina, whose frequent; 'What do you mean by this?' was exceptionally helpful, and for Adelyn's epic formatting and proof-reading stint, with technical support from Tomos.

For recent brain-picking, I would like to thank Robin Curtis, John Williamson and Rob Gwillim.

For material in the case studies: Will Pierce and Leanna at Flintshire County Council; Steve Macken; Phil and Kate Thomas and family; Tim and Angie Carver.

Many thanks for photos from Mark at Newark Copper Cylinders, Kensa Heat Pumps, Drexel and Weiss, Dimplex, Worcester Bosch, AFT Trenchers, Clina UK, Paul and Brenda Leeke and Will Anderson. Last, but far from least, Andria Thwaites for her wonderful cartoons.

John Cantor

CHAPTER 1

HEAT PUMPS IN CONTEXT

What is a Heat Pump?

A heat pump is a device that can transfer (pump) heat in the opposite direction to its normal direction of flow. Rather than 'producing' heat (like any other heating method) it *moves* it. In fact, your fridge is a heat pump and it 'pumps' heat out of your food and then ejects the heat to the room via the warm grille at the back. But in the context of this book, the technology described is used to replace a conventional home heating system.

The heat delivered is not free because you do need some energy input to operate the system, but intriguingly heat pumps can produce far more useful heat energy than the energy input needed to drive them. Indeed, this is usually the motivation for installing one. Moreover, the net CO_2 emissions in a correctly configured installation are usually lower than those of conventional fuels, like oil or gas, that they might displace. For this reason, they are classed as a 'low carbon' technology and a recognized form of heating worldwide.

Why Heat Pumps?

Heating is expensive, both in money and environmental terms. Heat pumps can potentially reduce the amount of energy input required, so can reduce both cash and environmental costs. That's it, in a nutshell.

Until relatively recently these 'costs' have not been considered a matter for concern: fuel has been cheap and the phrase 'environmental impact' didn't even exist. With the twin problems of climate change and peak oil now looming, any approach that can reduce consumption of fossil fuels deserves attention, and heat pumps are definitely one of them.

Our options are either to generate energy from the natural forces of the waves, wind or rivers, collecting energy from the sun, or by reducing our needs through insulation and minimizing waste. Clearly a mix of strategies is needed.

Heat pumps are sometimes categorized alongside renewables like wind, wave, solar and hydro, but heat pumps are only partly renewable since, at the present time, the energy input that is required is rarely from a renewable source. On the other hand, unlike most other renewables, they can operate on-demand at any time.

Heat pumps are also classified as a low-carbon technology and as such attract funding from the Renewable Heat Incentive (RHI). This should be in operation by the time this book is published and should dramatically change the economic viability of heat pumps. Whilst at this moment in time the final manifestation of the scheme is a little unclear, it seems likely that it will be instrumental in the rapid expansion of the industry.

The RHI will pay you for having a heat pump and the rate will relate to a 'deemed' quantity of heat that your house should need, assuming some basic energy-saving measures have been adopted first. The payment will be greater than the cost of the electricity to run the system. The reason for such a generous offer is, in part, a means to assist the country to meet its carbon-abatement targets.

Looking to the future, the scenarios presented in the Centre for Alternative Technology's *Zero Carbon Britain* and David MacKay's *Sustainable*

HISTORY OF HEAT PUMPS

Before the development of refrigeration there were no known ways of making things cold, other than the slight cooling effect due to the evaporation of water. The only ice that was available was stored from the winter or shipped from cold regions, as it was in very large quantities from northern America in the early 1800s.

About half a century later, scientists had generally agreed on the true nature of heat and that 'cold' was merely a lack of heat. They also developed ways of making fluids evaporate so as to cause very large reductions in temperature. Refrigeration and air-conditioning were born and have been under development ever since. The applications for heating were installed somewhat sporadically in the early days since, whilst heat pumps were known as a possible method of heating, they were rarely cost-effective, so there was little incentive to build them.

Some examples of early development:

- John Sumner carried out some pioneering work with ground-source systems in Norfolk in the 1940s.
- A revolutionary project, installed in the early 1950s at the London Festival Hall, took water from the River Thames and then returned it back slightly colder, thus extracting energy from this vast body of water. The system was driven by gas engines, but was sadly short lived.
- At around this time there were several examples of heating applications using the technology normally used for refrigeration.
- In the 1980s, when oil was becoming expensive, air-source heat-pumps were being manufactured in the UK by Eastwood Heat Pumps in Nottinghamshire. The enterprise was not long-lived; this was due in part to the relatively low cost of newly exploited North Sea gas, but also because these units were not wholly compatible with most UK buildings, which were poorly insulated and draughty.
- Meanwhile, in Norway and Sweden, the industry flourished due to differing circumstances. The abundance of hydro-electricity made the heat pump a viable proposition and they have already, due to necessity, embraced the need to insulate their houses.
- America and many other countries have, in their own ways, pioneered this technology and adapted it for use in their specific circumstances. For example, many American systems use ducted air distribution, since this is more suitable for cooling, as required by many particular regions.

Energy – Without the Hot Air, suggest that heat pumps will play a large and vital part at a time when electricity becomes the predominant form of energy.

The Future of Heat Pumps

Over the years, heat pumps have undergone small developmental improvements, as have many technologies, from the bike to the boiler. The laws of physics cast limits on what is attainable, as evidenced by the internal combustion engine that has only improved modestly over the last 100 years (unlike electronics that improve in quantum leaps). It is unlikely that we will see any dramatic breakthrough with heat-pump design, just modest step-by-step improvements.

HEAT PUMP EFFICIENCY

Heat pumps have been around for many years. This rather mystical device promises to deliver 3kW of heat for every kW of electricity consumed. This figure seemed to creep up from 3 to 4 around the first years of the twenty-first century. However, the recent field studies carried out by the Energy Saving Trust indicate that most of the UK's installations are falling well short of expectations.

Some think that even the original forecast of 3 could be optimistic, but there is no doubt whatsoever that there are many systems running with figures of 4. Experience on the continent, where the technology is more customary, tells us that they achieve on average 3.5kW for every 1kW input with a well-installed ground-source system.

Where things will improve, however, is when manufacturers produce heat pumps in ever-greater numbers and manufacturing techniques evolve, so that things become more cost-effective. The area that currently requires the most attention, however, is that of the end-use of the equipment. From planning to installing, this is where we still have a lot to learn, as we hopefully realize what works well and what doesn't.

Another important prerequisite for sustainable heat-pump installations is a trained and capable workforce, familiar with installing the technology in a range of installations. In other countries where the heat-pump installation industry has more experience, they have already learned from past errors. In the UK, the building industry is in a period of transition, whilst it embraces demands to reduce energy. This challenges our traditional methods. The heating industry is still learning how to adapt to the many changes it encounters and as such there are occasionally poor installations that perform badly, attract negative publicity and give the industry as a whole a bad name. In countries where there is a much greater market penetration of heat-pump technology, few installations fail to provide both financial and environmental benefits.

With present awareness of the need to conserve energy resources, it seems that heat pumps will have many roles to play in the future. There is no doubt that the heat pump is here to stay.

Planning an Installation – Things to Consider

Prior to deciding if a heat pump is right for you or not, one should be aware that there are many ways of reducing your energy expenditure. Most of these will involve capital outlay and the principle of 'opportunity cost' may be important here, since there is rarely an unlimited budget. If you spend on one option, you cannot afford another, so a choice between different options must be made. For example, you could choose between high-specification external thermal insulation and a new boiler, or a heat pump and cheaper insulation (assuming each option costs the same). The choices must be weighed up with respect to predicted savings in the long- and short-term.

Since there are many routes that could be taken, it is useful to consider things in this order:

1. Minimizing your energy demand.
2. Producing heat more economically and environmentally.

Reducing energy demand is always the best starting point. There are many factors that may affect your energy needs, such as the number of occupants in the house, their ages, how warm it needs to be, whether it is occupied all day and so on. Your overall energy strategy should start with trying to minimize the overall energy requirement. All the basic rules of energy conservation should be observed and there is plenty of advice about this available. Insulation is nearly always a prime option, even if it is very expensive. It should last indefinitely and should not require any attention. But there is sometimes a limit to levels of insulation that can be achieved, e.g. losing wall space due to internal insulation might be unwelcome and external insulation might be impractical.

Once your heat needs have been assessed, the method of heating (potentially a heat pump) can then be considered. Some people install a heat pump for environmental reasons and as an investment for the future, others are more concerned with their immediate running costs, so different people will have different concerns. Generally though, everyone will want the highest energy efficiency for the least installation upheaval and cost.

The following list suggests some initial questions to consider:

- Will a heat pump be suitable for my house and lifestyle?
- What different heat pump options do I have?
- What will a system cost to install?
- What are likely long-term running costs?
- How disruptive will the installation be?
- What CO_2 savings will I achieve?
- What else could I do instead?

We hope that this book will answer these questions.

CHAPTER 2

UNDERSTANDING HEAT

Before we consider any notion of 'ambient energy', we need a clear and simple understanding of energy and temperature. We need to address the obvious question – how can heat be extracted from something that is cold?

The sun's surface is almost 6,000°C and many parts of space are close to –273°C. Given this, the temperature at the Earth's surface varies by a remarkably small amount. But as warm-blooded humans, we have a rather distorted sense of heat and temperature. This is because we are 'programmed' at birth for survival, since our body needs to be kept almost exactly at 37°C (98.6°F).

On a winter's day, at zero outside, one might instinctively judge a warm living room to be many times hotter than the outside, but in reality the energy content is only 7 per cent greater (0°C and 20°C is actually 273° and 293° Kelvin, respectively).

Zero centigrade is only a label that scientists gave to a convenient temperature datum – the freezing point of water. In reality, temperatures could go down to –273°C (–460°F). At every temperature above this, there is heat. So, surprisingly, the ground immediately below our feet holds lots of heat, it's just at a temperature a little too low to be of apparent use.

This more scientific understanding of temperature levels (the Kelvin, or 'absolute' scale) should make one realize that there is a lot of heat in our surroundings, even when they appear to us to be very cold. So the idea of extracting some heat from this should not seem so implausible.

Unlike the air, ground temperatures are much more stable. Indeed, at a 2m depth it changes very little over the year and is unaffected by sudden cold snaps. In mid-winter, this sizeable store of heat can be tapped using a heat pump. There is some confusion as to the origin of this heat, since these systems are commonly termed 'geothermal'. The amount of heat flowing upwards from the Earth's core is very small. The vast majority of the heat in the Earth's surface layer actually comes from the sun.

The energy received from the sun peaks at 1,000W (1kW) for every square metre surface that is directly facing towards the sun. Surprisingly, the peak radiation intensity (facing the sun directly) is hardly any stronger at the equator than it is in Northern Europe. But as one travels further towards the Earth's poles, the sun's reduced angle relative to the ground causes less and less sun to be available, and at low angles, the rays also lose energy since they travel through more of the Earth's atmosphere.

The energy input comes from the sun's rays, which fall on the ground and are converted into thermal energy. The warmed surface then radiates due to its temperature (*see* the absolute zero chart opposite) resulting in heat energy loss. This happens day and night and is most

Description	Celsius	Kelvin	Fahrenheit
water boils	100°C	373°K	212°F
hot bath	40°C	313°K	104°F
warm room	20°C	293°K	68°F
water freezes	0°C	273°K	32°F
	-18°C	255°K	0°F
arctic	-40°C	233°K	-40°F
absolute zero	-273°C	0°K	-459°F

RIGHT: Putting temperatures into perspective.

BELOW: The ground-heat battery.

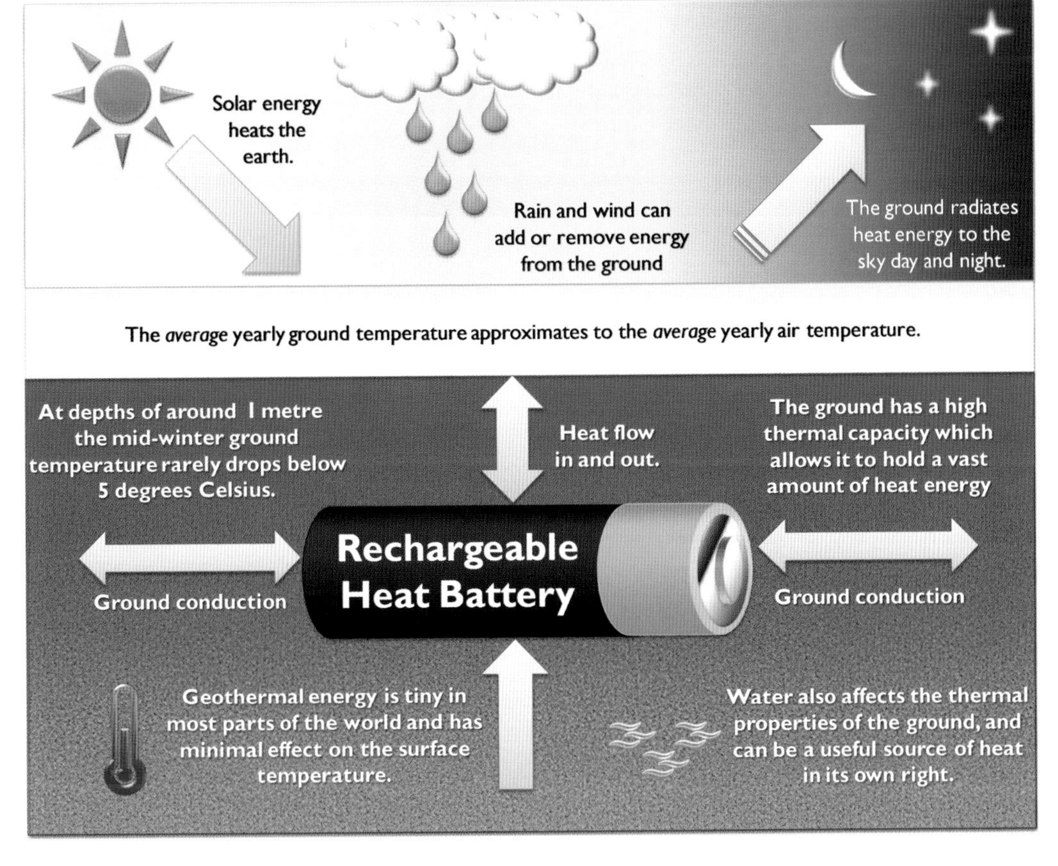

THERMAL ENERGY STORE

The ground can be seen as a giant thermal battery that is constantly being charged and discharged as a result of the many energy flows in and out. The ground's temperature tends to balance out several metres below the surface and averages around 10°C in the UK.

noticeable during clear, frosty nights, where the ground's heat radiates unhindered to the cold, night sky. Any surfaces 'seeing' the sky at this time can drop in temperature considerably.

The action of rain is a complicated cycle, but in simple terms some of the sun's rays convert water to water vapour. This forms clouds that eventually cause rain. At a local level relating to a heat pump, this rain could either heat or cool the ground depending on the time of year. However, the net effect of rain is generally positive, due to the increase in thermal capacity and thermal conductivity of wet ground. This improves the heat pump's efficiency.

The amount of 'geothermal' heat coming up from the centre of the Earth is tiny; in most places it is only 1/20th of a watt per square metre. This is negligible compared to the *average* radiation from the sun, which is in the order of 100W/m^2. Since the actions of the wind, the rain, ground conduction and below-soil water movements tend to even things out, the solar aspect of a potential ground source has a smaller effect on its temperature than one might think

The Ambient Thermal Resource

The outside air temperature averages in the region of 10°C and in very general terms, varies from around –10°C in winter to +30°C in summer. This makes it *not* an ideal heat source, since the air is at its coldest when the heat demand is at its greatest. None the less, it can prove to be a viable and effective heat source.

Air weighs approximately 1kg/m^3 and it has a fairly low thermal capacity. You need to process about 1m^3 of air every second to get sufficient heat for a small domestic heat-pump system. This is no problem since air is abundant and the energy required to move it through a heat-exchanger is relatively small. Water is a better proposition since it has a thermal capacity about 3,500 times that of the equivalent volume of air. However, few of us have a river or underground spring to hand.

The thermal capacity of the ground itself is in the order of one half that of water. This is still exceptionally high and we do happen to have a lot of it about. This vast thermal store below us can be used to our advantage with the help of heat pumps. The advantage is that the heat is still there, even if there is an extreme cold snap above.

It is worth mentioning here the extreme weather of winter 2010. This will have challenged any type of heating system. Clearly, the air source may struggle to supply adequate heating during extended cold spells. The ground tends to retain its heat, but if the heat-demand is exceptionally high and the 'cold' is penetrating from the surface, then even ground source may struggle during such extremes of temperature. However, as we see later, it is often acceptable to use alternative supplementary heating methods to assist the heat pump, since the total cost of this short extreme period is a small proportion of the annual total.

Whilst one would normally consider the ambient heat resources to be potentially endless, maybe we should touch on the question – if everyone had a heat pump, would the ground freeze, or would the air get very chilly around air-source heat-pumps? First, the small amount of heat used within houses is tiny compared to the vast heat gains and losses that go on outside in our immediate surroundings every day. However, extracting heat from air could cause some localized cooling in certain conditions, but this is unlikely to be a big problem if units are sited sensibly. If very large areas of housing were all using borehole technology, then the ground could, in time, cool significantly towards the centre. David MacKay tackled this question using some very elegant maths in his book *Sustainable Energy – without the hot air.* He concludes that we could exhaust the ground if we fitted ground collectors to all the existing houses in densely populated areas (remember, most of these houses will still be standing well into the future). However, time is on our side, since it would take a while before heat pumps become so widespread. Simple means could be devised to re-charge the ground using the plentiful heat of the summer, so issues of large-scale adoption should not be insurmountable. One would also hope, and expect, that our heating demands would reduce as time progresses. Furthermore, the ground below London, for example, is apparently several degrees warmer than in the surrounding countryside. This heat is due to activity above – think of all those tonnes of waste hot-water going into drains. What's more, the London Underground has a serious overheating problem due to energy used by the train system. This is a very localized hot-spot – a drop in the ocean – but you would think it not beyond the whit of planners and engineers to capitalize on this resource.

Geothermal or Not Geothermal?

A heat pump can be used to extract heat from a borehole. This is sometimes referred to as a 'geothermal borehole'. However, the vast majority of the extracted heat comes from the Earth's surface, so is it really geothermal energy?

Geothermal energy is generally considered as heat originating from the Earth's core. It is possible to utilize this heat in areas of the world where the Earth's crust is relatively thin. It is a practical proposition to capture steam from the ground in a few places around the globe, and Iceland generates all of its electricity in this way. Cornwall and Aberdeen are potential sites for hot dry rock, where water is pumped down and steam comes up (now referred to as Enhanced or Engineered Geothermal Systems, EGS). However, there are only a very few places in the world where this is possible.

Southampton or Bath may be 'marginal' areas where it may be possible to drill down into the ground, pump cold water down and get hot water up. It would be expensive to install the infrastructure and only viable on a very large scale.

For the rest of us, there is only a modest increase in temperature as you drill down into the ground. There is only about 2°C rise per 100m depth, so we cannot gain much unless we drill very deep. The actual quantity of heat rising from the ground is tiny and only in the order of 1/20th of a watt per square metre.

You could easily argue that 'geothermal', meaning 'thermal energy from the ground', makes no distinction about the original source of that heat. It is still 'heat from the ground'. We would rather use the term 'ground-source heat-pump' for any extraction system using either horizontal or vertical boreholes and leave the term 'geothermal' for the proper stuff that comes from deep in the Earth's core. However, it seems that the term 'geothermal' will continue to be used by many for ground-source heat-pump systems.

CHAPTER 3

THE PRINCIPLE OF HOW A HEAT PUMP WORKS

You don't actually have to know much about how heat pumps work to be able to own one, but a basic understanding helps before considering buying one. We need first to define the use of the word 'efficiency' in this book, since the term is often used rather loosely.

We are mostly concerned with 'energy efficiency'. A fast car might be efficient at being fast, but not fuel-efficient. We are not only concerned with the amount of heat, but also with the amount of energy used to achieve it. Efficiency is, therefore, always related to what heat you get out compared to what energy you need to put in to operate the system.

Our normal understanding of heating is associated with the burning of gas, oil or solid fuel. The flame produces heat for direct use in the house. With electric heat, the fuel is burned at the power station to produce the electricity, which is then turned back to heat in your heater, kettle or toaster. It's relatively simple. Nuclear energy is just another way of producing heat to drive electric generators in power stations. All of these processes are fairly easy to understand.

Heat pumps are different.

Heat pumps transfer heat from a cold place to a hot place. They work against the natural flow of heat and therefore require an energy input. Fortunately, this energy input to enable the heat transfer is only a small proportion of the total heat energy output.

The concept of a heat pump is at first not easy to grasp, in many ways it seems counter-intuitive, but it can be understood by all if given a little thought.

But to understand heat pumps we need to appreciate some more simple fundamental principles.

Energy cannot be created or destroyed.

Heat has to go somewhere. It may not be obvious, but when your hot cup of tea has gone cold, the energy has not disappeared, it has been transferred to the room. The room has actually heated up by a minuscule amount. Conversely, when your ice cream melts, it gains energy from its surroundings and the room cools by an immeasurably small amount. Energy can be converted or transferred, but it cannot appear or disappear.

Such simple concepts about energy become second nature once you have thought about them; they are the foundations to learning the next stage. There are various ways that the heat-pump concept can be explained, and different people like to think of it in different ways. Let us continue with some simple and intriguing school science.

Can this process be reversed?

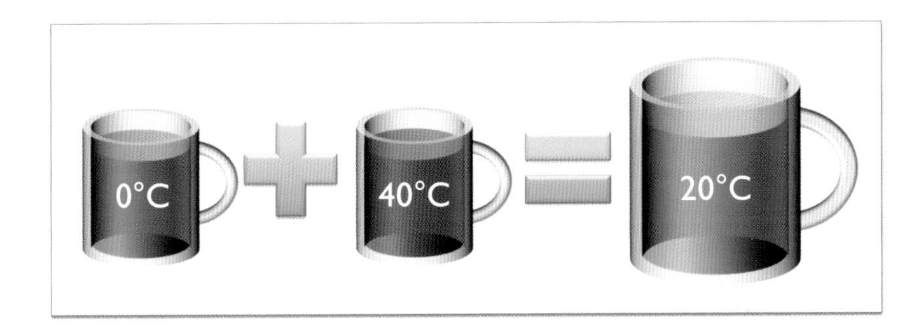

If you take one cup of hot water and mix it with a cup of very cold water, you end up with a cup full of lukewarm water (note, there is no ice in our 0°C cup of water). In this example, the mix ends up at room temperature (20°C). All very straightforward and expected... heat cannot be created or destroyed.

If you have one cup of water at 20°C (about room temperature), could you separate it to produce one cup of hot water and one cup of chilled water?

Answer... 'About as easily as you could separate-out white and red paint from a pot of pink, i.e. not very easily!'. But the total energy content of the hot cup plus the cold cup is exactly equal to the energy in the big lukewarm cup, so there is no reason why this should not be possible. You simply need to shift some heat from one to the other.

The only way of getting back to one hot cup and one chilled cup would be to use a heat pump: start with the two cups at room temperature, now use a heat pump to transfer heat from one to the other. One goes up by 20°C, the other goes down by 20°C. The good news is that the energy required to make this heat transfer possible is far less than the energy used by any conventional method of heating up a cup from room temperature to 40°C. The chilled water, which is an unavoidable by-product of the process, can simply be thrown away.

The crux of the process is in fact the 'making cold'; this is where the gain of free heat energy comes from.

We all have a heat pump to keep the milk cold! Let us consider a fridge. You cannot produce 'cold' without making heat somewhere else. It's a bit like a seesaw: as one temperature goes down, the other temperature goes up.

In our household fridge we only use the 'cold' and don't consider the heat that comes out the back of it.

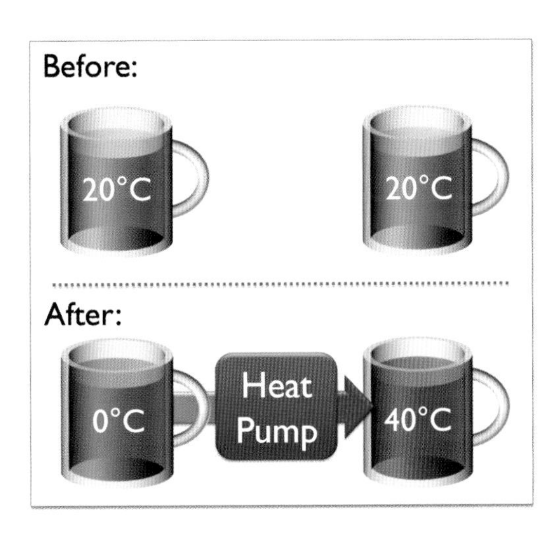

Using a heat pump to transfer heat.

UNDERSTANDING HEAT

It is not immediately obvious that 'hot' and 'cold' are not simply two states that somehow cancel each other out. It was not until the mid-1800s that scientists agreed that there is actually no such thing as 'cold' (as such), simply a lack of heat. It was established that the molecules that things are made of are vibrating at a rate depending on their temperature. Down at absolute zero (–273°C), molecules would theoretically stop vibrating.

It was no simple task for scientists to devise a mechanism to 'make cold', or rather to remove heat. Experiments were conducted as early as 1740, but it was not until the late 1800s that the 'vapour compression refrigeration cycle' was demonstrated commercially. Surprisingly, this principle is the exact same one that is used in the best fridges and heat pumps today, and involves the evaporation and condensation of a fluid.

With the heat pump, we are mostly concerned with the heat.

A final point to our science lesson – one of the best ways to think of heat is to consider it as the speed or rate of vibration of the tiny molecules of which matter is made. The hotter the item, the faster the molecules vibrate. This is a form of energy that every thing has, unless it's at absolute zero (–273°C) where the molecules are theoretically stationary.

Just to clinch the concept, let us consider a house. Imagine the air in a room having molecules vibrating at an average intensity. If we want the room to be a little warmer, then we need to add a little more energy so that the molecules vibrate a little more. This could be achieved in several ways, for example by adding energy from a fire.

A little thinking 'outside the box' and you realize that outside the building the surroundings are also vibrating, albeit at a slightly slower rate. What if we manage to slow down the rate of vibration of a large volume of the ground outside the house, therefore cooling it down? Could we then make something else's (the house's) molecules speed up in the process? This is the principle of the ground-source heat-pump.

No heat has been created or destroyed – it has merely been transferred from one place to another.

With a ground-source heat pump, we are

UNDERSTANDING THE HEAT PUMP CONCEPT

It is always useful to use simple analogies to explain scientific principles. The following may help to give a better picture of the heat pump process.

A *water* pump can move water in the opposite direction to its natural flow, such as up out of a well. Water would normally flow down into the well due to gravity.

A *heat* pump is a device that 'pumps' heat in the opposite direction to that which heat naturally flows. The term 'heat pump' is therefore very descriptive – heat is literally 'pumped' out of a fridge.

One analogy compares temperature differences to heights. A heat pump is like driving a car up a hill. The larger the temperature difference, the steeper the hill and the more power you need. This, like many analogies, only works to a point. None the less, it can serve a purpose.

Useful Heat Output = Extracted Heat + Energy Input

Equation to calculate useful heat output.

A THOUGHT FOR THE PERPLEXED

Many people say that you cannot get *out* more than you put in – you can't get something for nothing.

Heat pumps claim to get three to four times more heat out than the electricity used to run them.

How can that be?

Both statements are true.

If you consider the whole energy cycle of your house, including the garden, then everything equates, the values balance as expected. It all adds up to 100 per cent. However, if you consider the house only, then your clever heat pump has managed to collect (or extract) heat from your garden. Your garden has lost energy – energy that your house has gained, so the total energy in the house is a sum of any energy (electricity) used to drive the heat pump plus the heat extracted from the garden. In those terms (which are the only important terms to the house owner), the efficiency is, in practice, 300–400 per cent.

SANKEY DIAGRAM

A 'Sankey' diagram is a style of diagram commonly used to visualize energy flows.

Heat to house (7kW) = heat from garden (5kW) plus electrical input (2kW).

It's not magic, just simple, well-understood science.

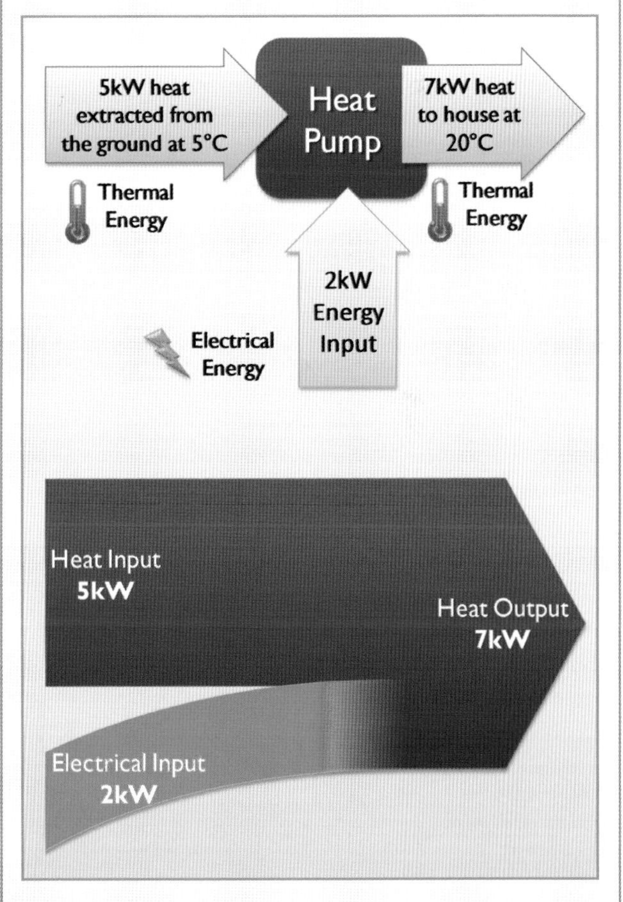

Box diagram and Sankey diagram showing a typical home heat-pump.

reducing the energy of a very large mass of ground, by a fairly small amount. In the case of an air-source heat-pump we do the same, reducing the temperature by a small amount, but to a large mass of air. In the process we are increasing the energy in our house.

To actually extract heat from one place and transfer it to another (for example, from the ground or the air outside into our living-room) will require an energy input. The good news is that the total useful heat delivered will usually be several times more than the energy input required. If it wasn't for this advantage, this book would not be written and the process would have little practical use.

The energy required to drive the system (usually electricity) will also end up as heat in the house. The equation on p.17 describes the process for a typical heat-pump system.

Heat-Pump System Configurations

There are two sides to every heat pump: the **source** and the **sink**.

The **source** is where the heat is extracted from; this is the 'cold-side' of the system.

The **sink** is where the heat is distributed and emitted for use; this is the heat-output side or 'load' side of the system, such as the radiators, under-floor heating or hot-water cylinder and so on.

Heat pumps are often described by listing the source, then the sink, with a 'to' in between. For example, 'air to water' describes a system that extracts heat from the air to produce hot water (for radiators or tap water).

Thus the main categories could be listed:

- Air to air.
- Air to water.
- Water to air.
- Water to water.

OPERATING TEMPERATURES

The following is the most important statement in this book:

The smaller the temperature difference between the heat source (e.g. the ground collector) and the heat sink (e.g. the house radiators), the higher the energy efficiency of the heat pump will be.

in other words, the warmer the source and the cooler the sink – the better.

Energy Efficiency Rating – Coefficient of Performance (COP)

If high energy efficiencies are to be achieved, then this fact must be considered at all times.

The working temperatures within our heat pump are dictated by the application. For example, if we are heating hot bath-water by taking heat from the air on a winter's day, then the energy efficiency would be low. However, a swimming pool being heated in the summer may be not much warmer than its surroundings, so the efficiency could be extremely high.

This shows how the energy efficiency of a heat pump will vary greatly due to its application. In a similar way, the fuel efficiency of a car will vary significantly depending on the slope incline that it is being driven up.

The graph shown opposite is an approximate and general graph to show the relationship between the source temperature and the sink. For example, if you extract heat from a river at 5°C to heat water to 40°C, then the coefficient of performance (COP) is likely to be in the order of 4 (temperature 'lift' 35°C).

Graph showing variation in COP depending on temperature lift.

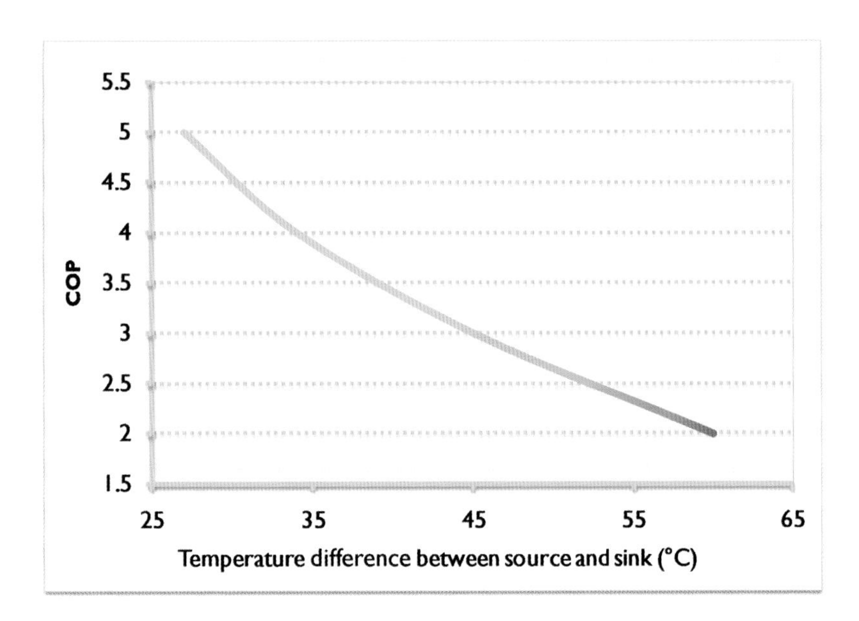

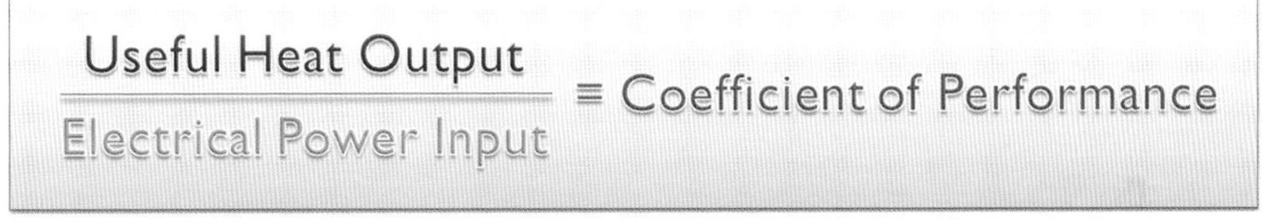

Equation to calculate coefficient of performance.

A more detailed account of COPs can be found later in the book.

It is important to quantify how efficient a heat pump is – the equation illustrated above is used.

This is a vital piece of fundamental knowledge and gives a value for a functioning heat-pump at any one moment. However, the coefficient of performance is a meaningless figure unless the working temperatures are also known.

We can see an example of this in the diagram (*see* page 20), which illustrates a simple coefficient of performance for a typical heat pump. We will explain the vapour compression cycle later, so read ahead and the diagram should make more sense.

Standard Methods for Displaying COP Figures

The next chapter covers the different types of heat pump but the next paragraph considers the COP ratings of common ground- and air-source

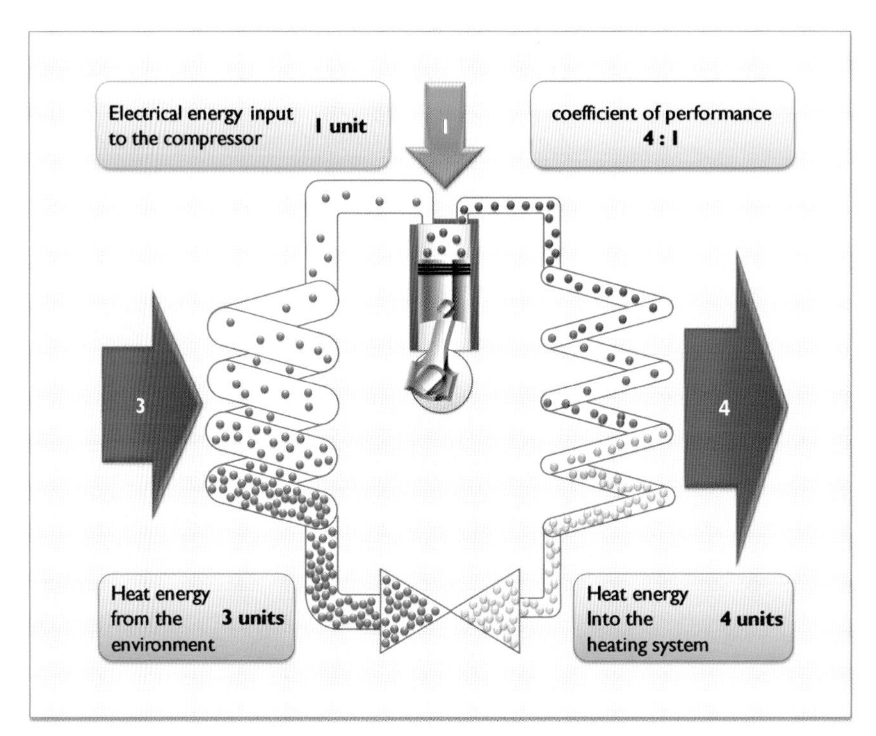

Coefficient of performance explained.

units. Brine is the name given to the fluid used in the ground-source pipes.

For a typical ground-source heat-pump: two example COPs are stated for the same heat pump at two different operating conditions:

COP = 4 (B0/W35).
COP = 2.8 (B0/W50).

The 'B' refers to the liquid brine's 'return from ground' temperature. The 'W' refers to the heated water 'flow' temperature (outlet to heating). (B0 denotes brine in at 0°C, W35 denotes heating flow at 35°C, W50 denotes heating flow at 50°C.)

It is also important to note that these figures may or may not include any necessary circulation pumps. Generally, if the circulation pump is included within the heat-pump box, then it is included in the energy-input assumptions.

For a typical air-source unit:

COP = 4.5 (A7/W35).
COP = 2.8 (A2/W50).

The 'A' refers to the entering air temperature (outside ambient temperature): A7 denotes air in at 7°C, W35 denotes heating flow at 35°C, and so on.

As can be seen, COP figures given at the favourable conditions of air at 7°C and water heated to 35°C (A7/W35) are somewhat optimistic, since air temperatures will be considerably lower when most of the operating hours are clocked-up and the heated water temperature is likely to exceed 35°C.

The COP is a useful measure of the efficiency at any one set of working temperatures. However, both the source and sink temperatures will vary over the year, so high COPs can be expected in the summer and low ones in the winter. A simple arithmetic average figure may not be representative, since most heat is delivered in the winter. We have produced some charts giving typical COP values at various working conditions, which can be found in the Appendices.

Seasonal Performance Factor (SPF)

The seasonal performance factor attempts to compensate for this and is a measure of the total heat delivered by the system divided by the total energy input over one year. The input should also include any pumps or power used by integral top-up electric heating elements.

Few people are familiar with this meaning of the term SPF, so we usually refer to COP in cases where either term would do.

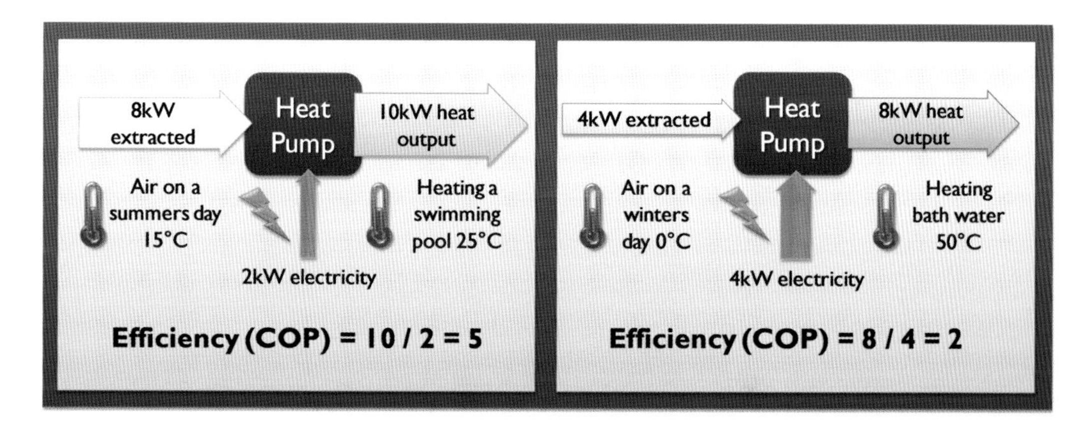

Example COPs with different input and output temperatures.

CHAPTER 4

METHODS OF PUMPING HEAT

There is more than one method of transferring heat from a cold object to a hot one. These are namely:

- The vapour compression cycle.
- The absorption cycle.
- The Peltier semi-conductor device.

The Vapour Compression Cycle

All heat pumps currently on the market use this principle. If a gas is compressed, it heats up. This will be known by anyone who has pumped up a bicycle tyre – the pump gets hot. When gas experiences a drop in pressure, it cools down. A simple heat-pump can be made using the principle of compression and expansion of a gas. However, the energy efficiency and effectiveness of such a system is poor. It is only used somewhat crudely, but very effectively, for cooling within aircraft.

A far more efficient heat-transfer method involves the change of state of a fluid from vapour to liquid and liquid to vapour. When something changes state, there can be a large exchange of energy, for example, to boil a kettle dry and convert all its water into steam will take several minutes. During this time a lot of energy is required to make the change of state from liquid to vapour. Likewise, a lot of energy can be released when a vapour returns to a liquid. This is, in part, the reason why a scald from a kettle spout is so severe. The energy involved when a substance changes state, such as from liquid to vapour, is called the 'latent heat'.

To enable heat transfer using this system, an appropriate fluid must be selected that has a boiling point at a suitable pressure within the range of temperatures that your system is to operate. Water is an option, but will only work at high temperatures. It is ideal for steam engines but not practical for any form of heat pump or refrigeration. Cigarette-lighter gas, on the other hand, would work quite well.

The vapour compression cycle was the method used when refrigeration was first invented and it is the same principle that is used in almost every fridge and heat pump today. The main reason for its widespread use is that it offers the highest energy efficiency.

The vapour-compression mechanism involves two heat-exchangers. One is the evaporator, where the fluid experiences a reduction in pressure – thus it is encouraged to evaporate. In doing so it drops in temperature and heat energy naturally flows in from its surroundings.

The other heat-exchanger is called the 'condenser', where high-pressure refrigerant

Vapour compression cycle.

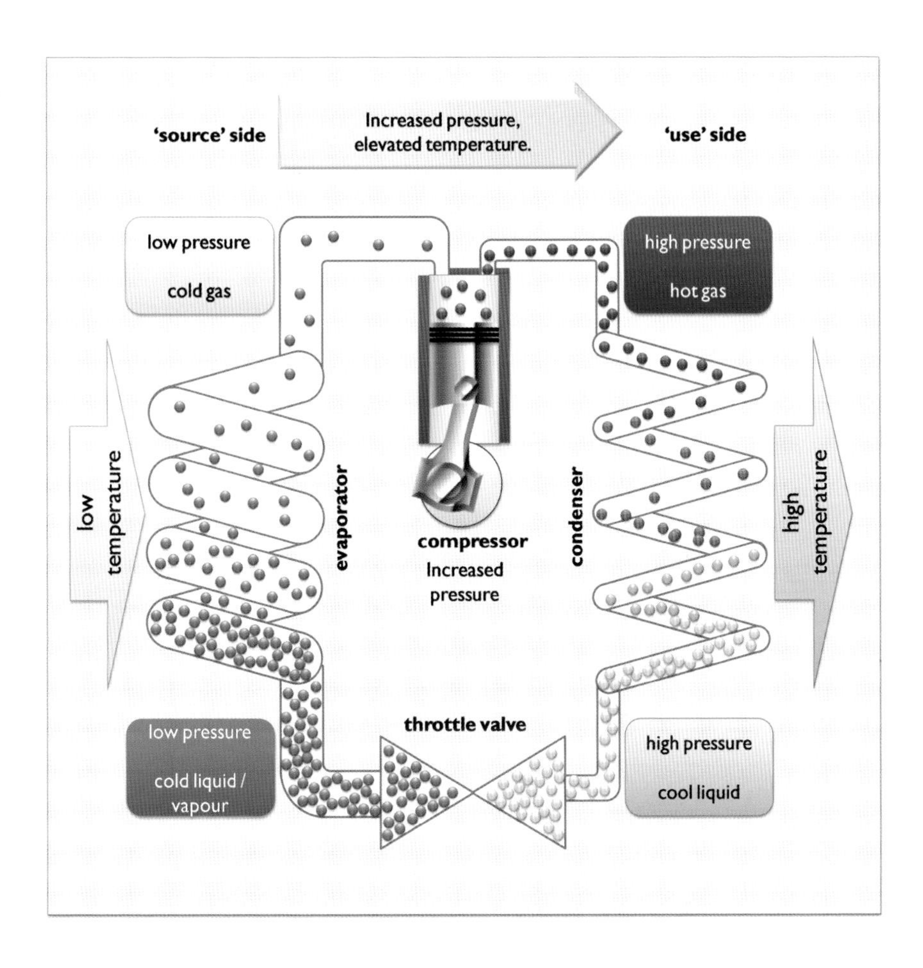

changes from a vapour to a liquid. This is the 'hot' or heat-output side of the system.

To enable the pressure differences, a compressor is used. This is a bit like a glorified bike pump that takes the vapour from the evaporator and forces it into the condenser. The resulting increase in pressure causes heating and as heat is taken away to warm the building, the vapour condenses. In doing so, it releases its latent heat.

The power input to drive this process is the motive power required to drive the compressor. In most cases this is from an electric motor and the power is supplied by main's electricity.

We have included a more detailed account of what goes on inside a normal heat pump in the Appendices.

There are some alternative drive options to the electric motor.

Internal Combustion Gas-Engine

Mains gas, or possibly fuel oil, can be used to power a heat pump. The engine would be the same as that used in a combined heat and power (CHP) unit.

A car-type internal combustion engine can be used to drive a compressor and large-sized units are currently on the market. However, as a technology, there are some challenges, the biggest being that internal combustion engines require a great deal of maintenance when used for extended periods (car engines are at rest for the vast majority of the time). An engine-driven heat pump would require many oil changes per year and would not last very long.

Stirling Engines (Hot-Air Engines)

This is another possible power drive that can convert heat into motive power, which could be used to drive a heat-pump compressor.

Stirling engines, or hot-air engines, work on the simple principle of the expansion and contraction of a gas at different temperatures. In its simplest form the hot-air engine works by heating a cylinder of air, which then expands and drives a simple crankshaft to turn a shaft. As this happens, a displacer piston pushes the hot air into a cooler cylinder. As this cools, it contracts and thus 'pulls' on the drive piston, continuing to rotate the shaft. The displacer piston acts again to divert the air back to the hot cylinder, where it expands and on goes the cycle.

All that is needed is a temperature difference between the two cylinders and the motor should run. A small model can be made and, if you are lucky, you will produce enough energy to overcome friction and possibly power a small fan. Whilst development has been slow, the Stirling engine has much promise. It can be completely sealed and can use a gas with better properties than air. If completely sealed, it can be engineered to operate continuously without wearing out. It will require a great deal of development, but with the advances in materials and manufacturing techniques, it could be the way things go in the future.

The Absorption Cycle

The absorption system was used in the domestic gas (flame)-powered fridges that were fairly common in the 1960s. This technology is silent, apart from the odd gurgle, since the only moving parts are the fluids inside. They are unfortunately not very energy efficient, so for home-use they are now virtually extinct. They have, however, found their niche in caravans and mobile homes, since one unit can easily be powered off multiple inputs, namely bottle gas, mains electricity or 12V battery, and the silence is a plus if you are sleeping in close proximity.

These small absorption devices have no moving parts, apart from the fluids inside them. The working fluids are usually water, ammonia and a little hydrogen, so environmentally they are relatively benign. Ammonia, whilst very nasty if inhaled, does not have a significant wider effect on the atmosphere.

The actual process is based on the principle that ammonia is readily absorbed into water and its affinity to water depends on the water's temperature. Thus, if an ammonia/water solution is heated, ammonia vapour is driven out of solution. This ammonia can be encouraged to condense if it is cooled to room temperature. If the weakened water/ammonia solution left behind is cooled to room temperature, then its properties change and it will readily absorb ammonia vapour. So, if the components are arranged appropriately, the ammonia can be re-absorbed by the cooler water solution. At the same time, this causes liquid ammonia to evaporate, thus causing 'cooling'.

Large cooling systems can use the absorption principle and may use different refrigerants. They are not particularly energy efficient, but to balance this, the gas fuel powering them is relatively clean. It seems unlikely, however, that this method would be viable for heat-pump systems, but we should be open to developments in this area. It may be possible that phase-change materials, giving long-term storage, could be developed along similar lines.

The Peltier Junction

The peltier device has only been with us for the last twenty-five years or so. The principle works by passing an electrical current through a special silicon semi-conductor. One side of the 'chip' gets cold, the other gets warm. Magic! This sounds like the ideal heat pump. Unfortunately, the transfer of heat back through the device from the hot side back to the cold makes the energy efficiency much lower than the vapour compression system. The device has however found its niche. The small, portable picnic boxes use this technology, since the working part is very compact and the energy transferred from such a small box is small, so the energy efficiency is not the highest priority. One added bonus is that you can, on some models, reverse the polarity at a flick of a switch and now you have a box to keep food warm.

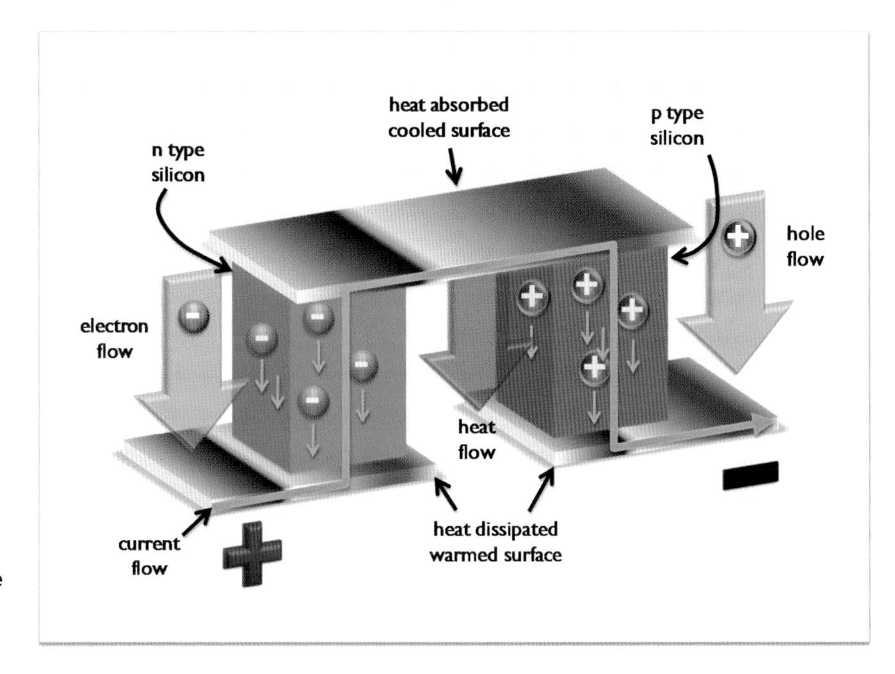

RIGHT: A single Peltier junction.

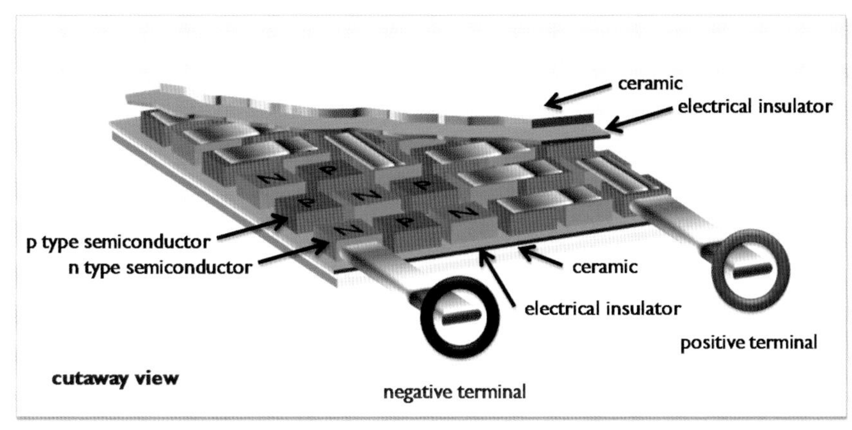

LEFT: A Peltier heat pump.

CHAPTER 5

EXTRACTING HEAT THE SOURCE

Heat can be extracted from a variety of places:

- Outside air.
- The ground (either horizontal trenches or vertical boreholes).
- Surface water, river, stream or lake.
- Ground-water, e.g. underground springs.
- Waste heat, heat recovery.

These have a range of advantages and disadvantages – these are set out in the table below, but are discussed in more detail in the following section.

Outside Air

This is the most abundant and readily available

Source	Advantage	Disadvantage
Air	Abundant everywhere. Easy to capture	Energy content lowest during times of highest heating demand
Ground	Energy output stable even on coldest days	More expensive and potentially disruptive to install
Surface water	Can be cheaper to exploit and less disruptive than ground source	Open-loop type may cut-out in mid winter. Source should be nearby
Groundwater	Potential for very high energy efficiencies	Source not commonly available. Source should be nearby
Waste heat	Not affected by outside temperatures. May be easy to exploit.	Available heat limited, and may not match heat demand.

Advantages and disadvantages of different heat sources.

Inside components of a 'split' air-to-air reversible heat pump.

heat source. It is all around and obtainable everywhere. Its thermal capacity (ability to hold heat) is fairly low, so large quantities must be drawn through a suitable heat-exchanger to be able to extract sufficient energy.

Air-source (air to air) heat pumps can be seen in any city, in affluent residential areas and in all hot countries. They are commonly known as air-conditioners for cooling buildings, but for many years such rooftop units have been available as 'reversible heat pumps'. So at any time when heating is required within the building, the system can be reversed.

This system was first designed as an air-conditioner; it takes in outside air at, say, 30°C (a hot day) and blows out even hotter air to the atmosphere. In this mode it is dissipating heat that originated from inside the building, hence cooling it.

In heating mode, the outside (ambient) air could be at any temperature between minus 15°C and plus 15°C. The air would pass through the outside heat-exchanger and exit at maybe five or so degrees colder. In this mode, heat is being extracted from the outside air and this energy is transferred into the building via the heat pump.

Air-source reversible heat pumps are often optimized for cooling, and the energy efficiency

Outside components of a split air-to-air reversible heat pump.

This Dimplex air-source operates down to –20°C outside temperatures.

On test at the Centre for Alternative Technology, this interesting air-to-water heat pump is new to the market and uses CO_2 as the refrigerant, so promises low environmental impact.

The fine fins of the air heat-exchanger will collect ice in cold weather. This is periodically (and automatically) melted by briefly reversing the system.

A close-up of the fins after defrost.

in reverse mode (heating) may not be as high as it could be, particularly at low outside air temperatures. However, many research and development departments around the world are working hard to improve efficiencies. So we are seeing a slow improvement as time passes, as with all other technologies.

There are, however, many air-source systems that are designed specifically for heating. These tend to be air-to-water types and are considerably more energy efficient. They are often physically bigger, since a larger heat-exchanger gives better efficiencies.

Air-source units have a continuous stream of outside air passing through them and it is quite normal for water to condense as the air passes over the heat-exchanger. This actually helps the heat-transfer process. However, one of the problems with any air-source heat-pump is that the condensed water will turn to ice on the heat-exchanger fins when the entering air is around 6°C or colder. This would block the airflow, but it is not an insurmountable problem, since a defrost mechanism is engaged to melt the ice. This may happen every hour during the worst times, but the energy required to melt the ice is relatively small. The defrost process may take up to five minutes and the total loss due to necessary defrosting could lead to an average reduction in the energy efficiency in the order of only 5 per cent with a good model, but this could be as much as 10 per cent on others. Defrosting is one area where improvements are currently being made. Mechanisms vary and, generally, more expensive units are likely to have more refined and more efficient defrost mechanisms.

As air temperatures drop, so does the energy efficiency of the system, but surprisingly many high-quality air-source units will operate down to temperatures as low as –15°C, albeit at relatively low efficiencies. However, at such temperatures there is little moisture in the air, so defrosting can be less of an issue.

A normal air-source heat-pump consists of a

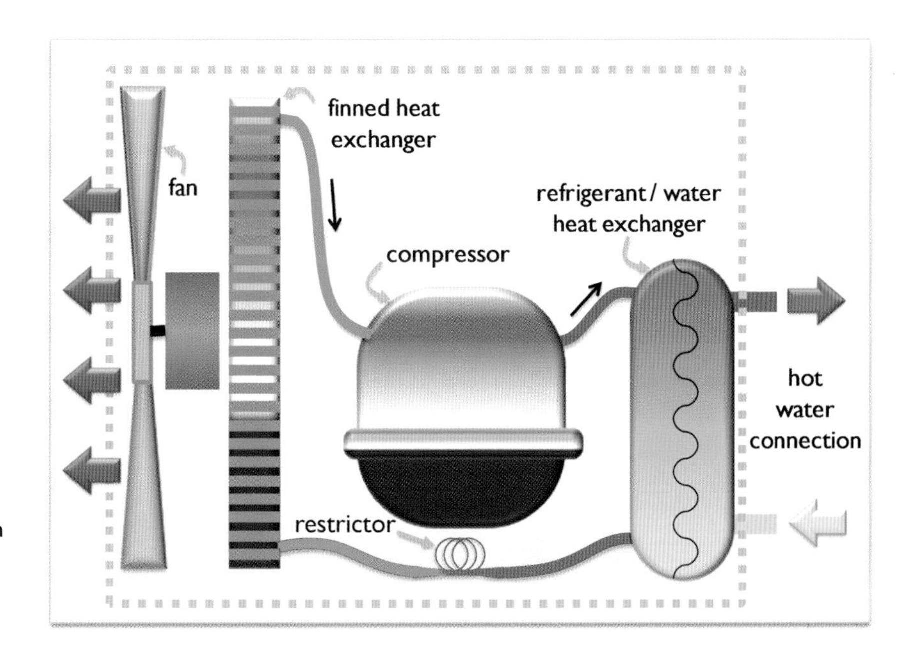

Simple diagrammatic representation of an air-to-water heat-pump.

finned heat-exchanger and a suitable low-energy quiet fan. The unit's casing also contains the compressor and other equipment.

Although very quiet, units need to be located away from sleeping areas, where noise could be a problem. They also need to be positioned carefully such that they do not impose noise on the neighbours. Furthermore, too many units in close proximity could result in localized cooling and therefore a drop in efficiency. It is mostly for the above reasons that building regulations approval is required before installing an air-source unit.

Being out in the elements, the air-source unit is likely to deteriorate more quickly than a ground-source system. Again, the quality has a big impact on longevity. Cheaper units tend to be less protected from hard rain.

Snow could be a problem unless the unit is raised on a stand, or a well-designed cowl is used. Such cowls are often fitted to the more serious air-source systems, especially when used in areas prone to snow. The primary function of a cowl is, however, for noise abatement. In extreme weather conditions, carefully clearing snow might be a necessary task, since the defrost mechanism would not be able to cope with it.

Laying trenches in a field for a large horizontal trench system.

The Ground

Most ground-source heat-pumps are designed to take heat from a buried plastic pipe known as a 'closed loop', containing an antifreeze solution. This solution is often referred to as 'brine' (the actual solution is not salt water, but commonly a glycol or similar chemical). This would be referred to as: brine to water. 'Brine' or 'water' source heat pumps are mostly identical, apart from being set up and optimized to operate at a different temperature ranges.

We have already seen that it is possible to use the 'ground-heat resource'. Now let us look at the methods we can use to extract this heat from the ground.

Horizontal Trenches

Horizontal trenches are fairly self-explanatory and are laid within the top 2m or so of ground. Trenches can come in a variety of forms and contain straight or coiled plastic pipes that extract the heat.

In very general terms, the near-surface temperature ranges from around 0° to 20°C over the year in our climate. At 3m depth it is a stable 10°C. At 1m depth, this may stray up to 15°C in summer and drop down to around 5°C in winter. These figures will vary plus or minus 1.5°C, depending on the geographical location.

We have already seen that a warmer source will deliver better energy efficiency. However, as we extract heat from the ground, this ground will inevitably get cooler, thus a trench drops in temperature as it is used, thereby reducing the energy efficiency. For this reason, a very large trench is required. Indeed, the bigger the better is the general rule with respect to trench sizing.

The graph (opposite) shows how the trench temperature varies over the season as heat is extracted. The recovery time is very site-specific.

Graph showing temperature variations at various depths.

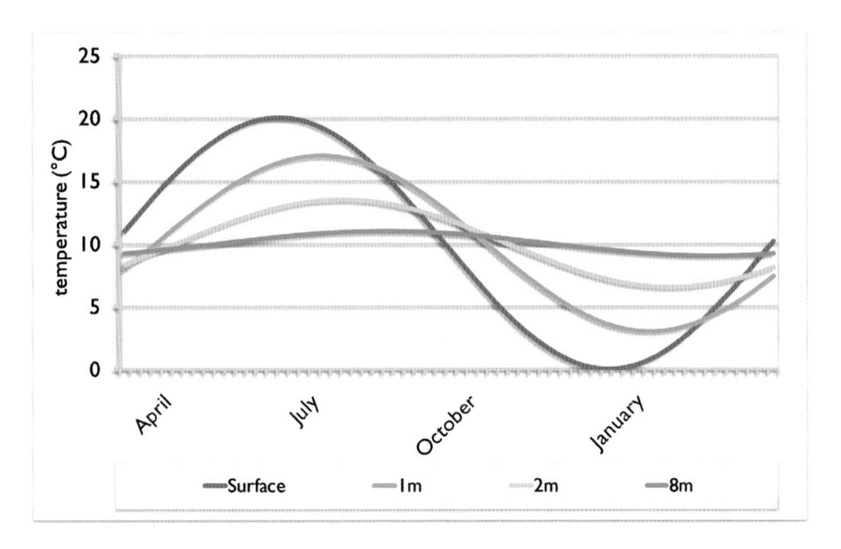

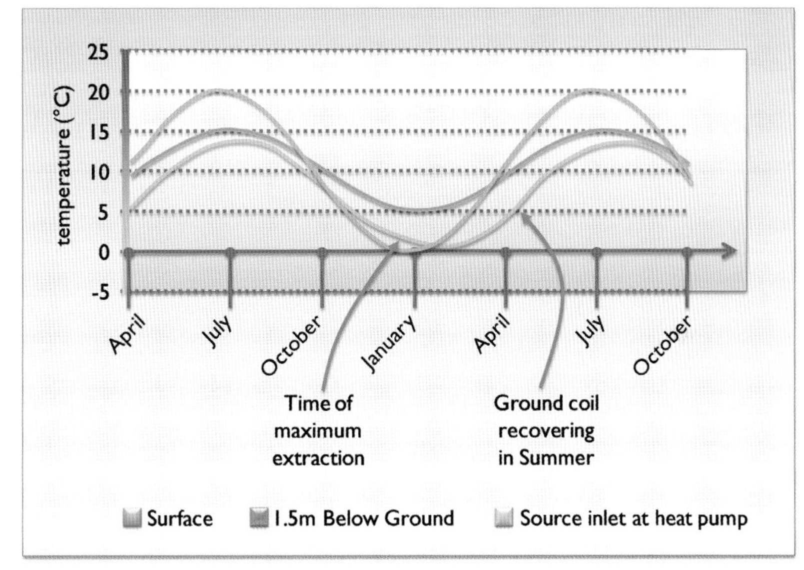

Graph showing working trench temperatures.

If, for example, moving ground-water is present, this could cause the trench to recover in weeks rather than months and the graph would look quite different.

There are many trench configurations, which depend on a number of factors:

- How much land is available.
- The make-up of the ground.
- Access for and availability of machinery.
- Preferred method of installers.

How Much Land is Needed?

The thermal properties of the ground vary – this is a topic that can become very complex. However, we can also view things in simple terms. It is sufficient to say that the ground consists of varying sized solid particles that can both

METHODS OF MAKING TRENCHES

Trenches are normally made using an excavator. Often referred to as 360s (because they can rotate a full circle on their base), such track-laying vehicles are superior to earlier tractor-derived diggers. They vary in size from very small to very large, and the machine would be chosen to suit the job in hand. In general, a small machine takes longer and may struggle making deep trenches, but it may ultimately make less mess. A big machine is usually much quicker and often more practical. Digger drivers invariably take pride in their work and are familiar with the ground types in their local area, so they are the experts in the matter.

ABOVE: **A five-ton excavator digging a trench.**

BELOW: **This little machine has tracks that retract, so can get down narrow paths.**

OPPOSITE TOP: **A large machine makes for light work, and can save time.**

OPPOSITE BOTTOM: **AFT100 tractor-mounted trencher. (Courtesy AFT Trenchers Ltd.)**

An alternative method is to use a trenching machine. This looks a bit like a giant chainsaw and can create a neat and tidy narrow slot. Only large machines will give a deep enough trench. This method will only work in suitable ground types and could be halted by the presence of very large stones. In the right conditions these machines can nip along at a good pace.

store and conduct heat. There may also be a significant amount of air present and if you consider dry sand, for example, a third of its volume could be air. Air is an insulator and has a very low heat-capacity, so is undesirable. Water can displace these air spaces and improve the conduction and thermal capacity dramatically. The migration of water can also play a significant part in the heat-transfer process.

Most data used for typical ground-source heat systems use figures for the expected heat (in Watts) available per square metre of ground (W/m^2), or per metre of pipe in a borehole (W/m).

We have produced this graph (*see* page 34) for interest. It shows how different ground types vary in both 'heat capacity' (the amount of heat a substance can hold) and 'thermal conductivity'. (*See* Appendices to convert MJ to kWh.)

As can be seen, wet sand could have over twice the thermal capacity of dry sand. This means that for comparable heat quantity extracted, a ground trench would need to be twice as big in dry sand, as opposed to wet.

The actual size of trench will need to reflect the thermal capacity of the ground, whilst the pipe density (e.g. number of pipes in a trench, or pipe spacing) may need to take into account the thermal conductivity.

In reality, the sizing of the trench and ground coil doesn't quite work like that. In an ideal world, all ground collectors would be very large but this is a costly and unworkable strategy. As with anything, a compromise is sought between cost and pay-off and it may be difficult to justify the cost of the very large collector required for dry sand, so some drop in efficiency may be accepted in these cases. Conversely, if the ground has excellent properties, one could get away with a relatively small collector. However, you may choose not to trim down the size of

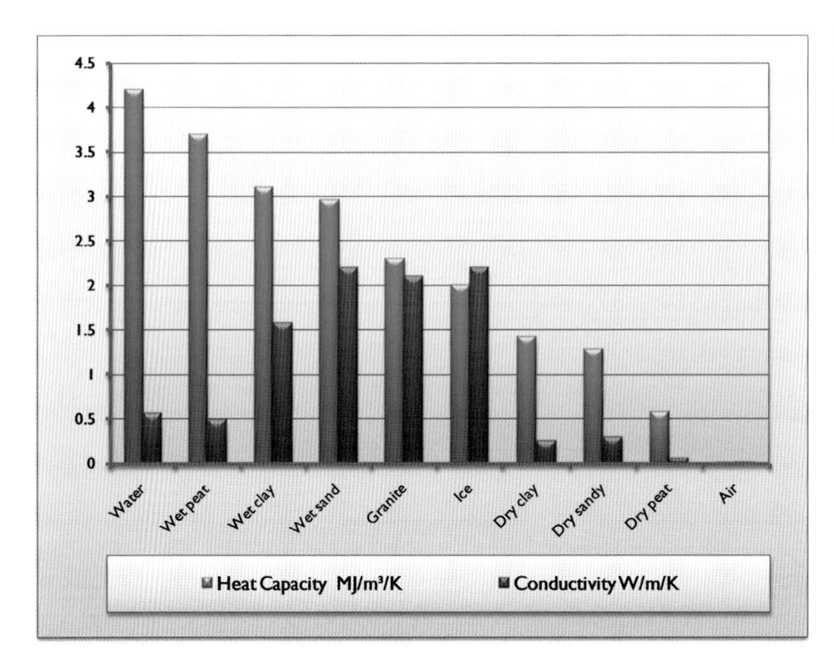

Graph showing thermal properties of different ground types.

trench, but to enjoy the long-term benefits of a standard-size ground collector working in ideal conditions.

A contentious issue is the build up of ice around collector pipes. A lot of heat can be extracted whilst ice is forming (assuming that water is present in the ground). This means that you can install a relatively smaller collector. Some argue that ice build-up around a pipe increases the heat transfer, since ice conducts better than some ground types (*see* graph). However, there is a counter-argument to this, since the continued action of water repeatedly freezing can cause small ice cavities. This could later manifest as air pockets around the pipe, which would decrease conductivity.

Whenever a ground collector strays to sub-zero temperatures, it will be operating below that for ideal energy efficiencies (the lower the source temperature, the lower the COP of the heat pump). In temperate climates, better COPs can be achieved when the brine circulates at above 0°C, but for cold countries there may be no option other than to operate in the sub-zero zone. Many designs aim for higher collector temperatures, with the contingency that one can stray into sub-zero for a short period if the heat demand is, for some reason, greater than expected (like the winter of 2010).

There are now a very great number of installed trenches extracting heat from different ground types, giving manufacturers and installers experience to draw from when they make their assessments.

To give a rough idea of sizing: for a typical house in the UK, one might expect to need at least 10m of trench per kW (heat output) of heat pump. Trenches would need to be 3m apart. Thus a typical 7kW heat-pump may need a total of around 70–100m of trench, occupying anything up to 300m^2 of ground. Manufacturers have detailed methods of designing this aspect.

The heat-pump size (kW) is not the only factor to consider here. The total heat extracted throughout the year might be a more important consideration. Very roughly, a typical heat pump may sit idle for between two-thirds and four-fifths of the time (running for, say, 33 per cent to 20 per cent of the time). This results in a considerable time for the ground to replenish its heat. Heat pumps that are relatively small and run alongside a back-up heater could run for almost half of the year, so they need well-sized collectors. This is also the case of a domestic system that is also heating a swimming pool in summer. The total energy extracted from the ground over the year would be relatively large, so the collector must be sized accordingly.

As a tip for those of you who are pacing out your garden to see if you have anything like enough space, consider a temporary space for the spoil that will be produced and also consider the practical space required by the digger driver to operate in. It is always a surprise how much soil comes out of a trench and it has to be put somewhere before being used for back-fill.

Pipes in narrow trench awaiting protective layer of sand. This one has a single 'hair-pin' loop of pipe.

Straight Trench with Single or Multiple Pipes

A single pipe is a simple method, but requires a lot of digging for just for one pipe. For that reason it was found cost-effective to lay multiple-pipes in one trench. Multi-pipe trenches may require more total metres of pipe (per kW of heat) than single-pipe trenches, but the trenches could be a little smaller, so on balance, the extra cost of pipe may be relatively small compared to the cost of the whole ground-work operation.

In rural areas where there is plenty of space, it may be possible to use a mole plough to position pipe into the ground. This technique would only suit certain ground types, but could slash installation times dramatically. Mole ploughing is commonly used to put electrical cables in the ground, but heat-pump collectors need to be much deeper. This method will only work using

Four pipes laid in the bottom of a 1m-wide trench.

LEFT: **A pipe being 'cut' into the ground using special equipment. (Reproduced with permission of the Gough Group, NZ.)**

BELOW: **A coiled 'slinky' pipe ready to enter a trench.**

a large and powerful machine with a plough specifically designed to go deep enough. Finding a system to provide sufficient depth is not easy at present.

Coiled Pipes

Also known as 'Slinkies', this is a convenient way of getting pipe in to the ground and was developed in the USA by IGSHPA, Oklahoma. It performs similarly to a multiple-pipe trench, but it is fairly straightforward to install. The coils are made up and 'tied' such that you have one manageable item that is relatively easy to position in a trench. The coils may be laid either vertically in a narrow trench, or horizontally in a trench about 1m wide.

Deep, narrow trenches (typically 2m deep) are easier in some instances but one needs to know that the ground will hold up without collapsing. Wide trenches are sometimes a better option. One further issue here is the likely requirement for sand to protect the pipes, since the narrow

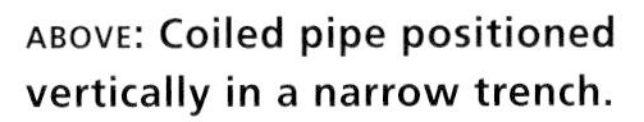

ABOVE: **Coiled pipe positioned vertically in a narrow trench.**

RIGHT: **Horizontal trench with 'slinky' coil laid flat.**

trench may require a lot more sand to protect the pipes from sharp stones and so on. The horizontal slinky can, however, be more sparing with sand and if very large stones are present, then a wide trench might be your only option.

Slinkies that are laid flat would ideally end up 1.5m from the surface, but health and safety regulations can make this difficult to achieve. The performance of either vertical or horizontal type is effectively the same, assuming that the average depth is similar.

Compact Collector

It is a mistake to think that you can get much more heat out of the ground by using a collector with a larger surface area. There is only so much heat in so much ground. However, if the ground properties are good, and especially in the unlikely event of moving ground-water, compact collectors or a close-coiled slinky can be a good option. There are no hard and fast rules here. If land space is limited, then a compact ground-collector may be one way of partly making-up for the lack of ground. It is not a cheap option and is relatively uncommon in the UK.

Large, Horizontal Trench

This method is commonly used in Germany and the UK. The procedure is quite simple: dig a very large, wide trench, lay pipes in a similar manner to under-floor heating and cover over. This method involves a lot of earth moving and requires a large excavator. However, such machinery is often present on a new building site and this operation can be relatively quick and practical.

Pipe/Trench Depth

There is some controversy relating to the ideal

A sizable machine makes light work of this large trench.

The pipe is protected by carefully covering with sand before the subsoil is replaced.

trench depth. Some argue that a deep trench will take longer to recover during spring than a shallow one. However, most run-hours are clocked-up in the middle of winter and at such times a relatively deep trench will retain a higher temperature than a shallow one. This is again a compromise and very deep trenches are simply too expensive to make. The general depth used for this type of trench is between 1 and 1.5m.

Heat pumps evolved in the UK during a decade of relatively mild winters. If long, cold winters are to become common, then the size and depth of trenches might need to be re-assessed.

Proximity of Trench to House

Ideally the collector trench would be fairly close to the heat pump, for example in the garden next to the house that is being heated. However, in remote rural situations, it may be advantageous to locate the trench some distance from the house; a wetter area might look beneficial due to its potentially better ground properties. The pipe run to and from the trench must be designed carefully otherwise a large and energy-hungry pump may be needed to circulate the liquid. Every pipe causes a restriction to flow, but if it is big enough in diameter, the pressure drop will be reasonable.

To give an example, let us consider a specific heat-pump where the maximum allowable length of a 32mm diameter pipe run to the trench is 20m. However, if a 50mm pipe is fitted, it could go 170m for the same circulation pump size. Therefore it is vital that the pipe diameter is correct. Such long distances may be unviable, since the pipe and the glycol within it add to the installation cost. Your heat-pump installer will know what pipes are possible and what is required.

For sites on a slope, there can be problems if the proposed trench is at a significantly higher level than the heat pump, but such issues may not be insurmountable. A trench at a lower level poses no such problems.

Manifolds

Some ground pipes consist of just one big single loop of fairly large diameter pipe. This tends to be preferred by some Swedish manufacturers and could be ideal for small installations. Others tend to go for multiple pipes, which can have advantages as they can be smaller in diameter and are easier to manage. Smaller pipes also have a larger area compared to the internal volume, so if nothing else, small-bore pipe-collector systems tend to require less antifreeze solution in them than larger pipes systems.

When multiple pipes are used they must be arranged in parallel circuits, so some sort of manifold is required to join them all up. Circuits can typically range from four to ten or more, depending on the many variables. One very important aspect of the design is to ensure that the total pressure drop around the ground loops is not too high. This ensures that the pump

Looking into the manifold pit of a large system.

LEFT: There are different ways of manifolding. Great care is needed during assembly so that they are 100 per cent leak-free.

BELOW: This small two-loop Kensa system fixes to the outside wall of the house.

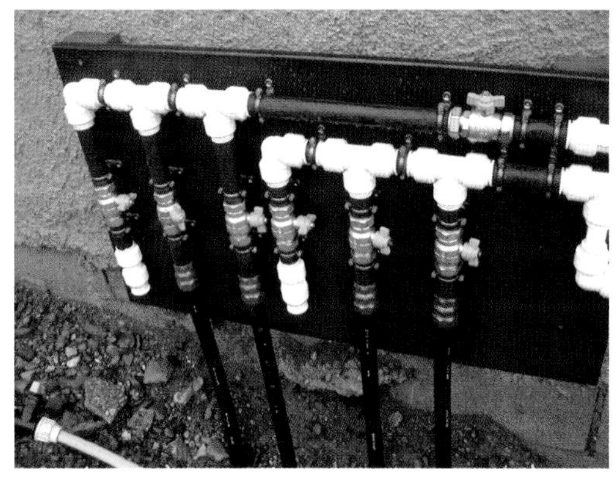

energy is relatively small. Manifolds themselves should be big enough so as not to cause a pressure drop.

One small additional advantage of many multiple circuits is in the very rare circumstance of a pipe leak. Such leaks are almost unheard of but, should one happen, blanking off one zone out of six, for example, may result in only a relatively small drop in performance.

The pictures show typical manifold arrangements that would be used with multiple ground loops (or boreholes on a big site). This is usually located outside the house and often below a manhole cover. Plastic manifolds are ideal for the job.

Direct Expansion Systems (DX)

Direct expansion systems are occasionally used in normal ground-source situations, but are relatively rare. Instead of circulating a glycol solution around the ground, the refrigerant is effectively in direct contact with the ground within plastic-cated copper pipes, and no source circulation pump or glycol is needed. Theoretically they promise high energy-efficiency. However, once fitted and with the refrigerant pipes buried, there is no way of removing the heat-pump unit without involving the expertise of a refrigeration engineer. In the very rare event of a punctured ground-pipe, the results could be disastrous.

A direct expansion heat pump. (NEURA GmbH.)

Vertical Boreholes

A specialist drilling rig is needed to make a vertical hole in the ground. This is typically 60–100m (200–300ft) deep. Drilling a hole is no easy business and not without risk, since one can never be certain of exactly what is below the ground, especially in the UK where the geology is so varied. However, the drilling industry is extremely experienced and very well-established.

Most heat pumps use the 'closed loop' system, where a pipe loop in the form of a 'hair-pin', or 'U' tube, is dropped into the borehole. This is then 'grouted' in by injecting a bentonite slurry from the bottom of the hole. This seals the pipe in and allows a good thermal contact between the pipe and the surrounding ground and rock.

Houses may typically have two medium-sized boreholes. A low-energy house may have only one. Sometimes a multiple of shallower holes are used. The variety of depths and the number of boreholes amounts to the same thing and the choice is often a matter of cost and practicality. Drilling multiple bores radially from one point is an option and, in rare cases, the ground might be suitable for the pipe to be 'pressed' in using hydraulic force. As time passes, the operation to install a vertical collector should be getting easier and cheaper. Having said that, currently the cost of boring for a single property is sometimes prohibitively high. This is less of a constraint with large housing projects, where multiples of scale can make this ground source a neat and practical solution.

Boreholes are sometimes the only option if land-size is limited. The end product is rather a neat and unobtrusive pair of pipes emerging from the ground. They are completely buried, so are effectively as invisible as the trench system

A fairly compact drilling rig, National Trust, Beddgelert.

The 'U' pipe fitting that is fusion-welded to the 40mm pipes at the bottom of the borehole.

and the disruption to the garden is considerably less. It is worth considering that the borehole is there for life, so can extract a huge amount of heat over its lifetime.

The actual rise in temperature due to 'geothermal' heat (from the Earth's core) is actually very slight. Go 3m down and you reach a constant temperature. Go 100m down and the temperature rises only a degree or two. The net gain in terms of degrees Celsius that your heat pump 'sees', when comparing the vertical or horizontal trench system, is very slight; it is often a matter of cost. If drilling was easier and cheaper, then it certainly would be the favoured method because you could afford to put a lot of pipe in the ground and get very good temperatures, especially in the grips of winter.

If heat is also rejected to the ground by a reversible system, then the borehole is likely to be a better option and in the case of using passive or 'free' cooling, boreholes may be the only effective solution.

Boreholes that are used for water supplies are generally quite different to ground-source (geothermal) boreholes. It is rarely practical to pump water from a borehole for use in a heat pump on a domestic scale. There are several reasons for this:

- The energy used to pump the water up can be excessive.
- The quantity of water would probably exceed normal abstraction allowances.
- The borehole pump would run for too many hours, so maintenance could be high.
- Regulations may forbid this type of operation.

Having said that, the 'standing column' system is used very successfully in some parts of the USA. These use a normal borehole to provide both drinking water and 'geothermal' heat. These systems pump up water, pass it through a heat pump and then send it back down the same borehole. The risk of contaminating upper and lower strata water makes it impractical for all but a few countries. However, the 'standing column', as pioneered by John Logan in Maine USA, can give excellent results. The clever part is that they 'spill' 10 per cent of the water to waste, such that there is a slow and steady flow of water from the surrounding ground towards the borehole. This ingress enhances the natural conduction into the well and has proven to give good results. Experience indicates a 20 per cent improvement on energy efficiency compared to a normal ground-source system. However, it is unlikely to be accepted in densely populated countries; that said, systems have been installed in some parts of Scotland, where the geology is suitable. Any system that pumps ground-water would need approval from the Environment Agency or the Scottish Environment Protection Agency.

Surface Water, Rivers, Streams and Lakes

Water has a relatively high specific-heat capacity, meaning that a small amount of it contains a lot of heat. It therefore acts very well as a heat source for a heat pump.

The temperature of surface water approximates to average air temperature; this can seem surprising, since it often feels colder, but it is clear that on very cold days, a river or stream is likely to be considerably warmer than the air.

There are two types of system that can be used to extract heat from surface water, rivers, streams and lakes, commonly referred to as open- and closed-loop systems. In an open-loop system the water itself is pumped through a heat-pump unit; in a closed-loop system a secondary fluid (antifreeze solution) circulates in a closed loop.

Open-Loop Systems

Surface water can be pumped directly through a heat pump, if the unit is designed to cope with potentially corrosive and oxygenated water. This method is commonly referred to as the open-loop system and has some disadvantages:

- The water must be over approximately 5 or 7°C (depending on the model).
- The water must not corrode the heat pump's internal heat-exchanger.
- Maintenance is required to deal with fouling or clogging.

The above points make the open-loop an option to be chosen with caution. Surface water is likely to drop below 6°C in mid-winter, so the unit could stop and a back-up method of heating would be required.

There is also the possibility that power needed for the pump to raise and filter the water, and pass it through the heat pump, may be relatively high as compared to the closed-loop system. However, if the source is easily accessible and not deep in the ground, then this system can offer the highest energy efficiency. It may, therefore, be worth overcoming the above-mentioned issues.

Closed-Loop Systems

The normal ground-source system is a closed-loop system, and this may be a safer method of extracting heat from surface water. Here, a plastic pipe is used in which a secondary fluid is circulated (like trench systems) to transfer heat from the flowing water into the heat pump's internal heat-exchanger. There are issues, however:

- Plastic pipes are vulnerable to mechanical damage and may degrade due to sunlight.
- There needs to be a significant quantity of antifreeze fluid within the pipes, which is a potential pollutant.

The closed-loop system is most likely to be viable for lake systems. The plastic collector-pipes can be dropped to the lake bottom, if suitably weighted. Great consideration is needed to ensure that the collector pipes will not be damaged, such as by persons with no knowledge of the system punting on the lake or dredging it.

One advantage to using a lake in this manner is the possible cost-saving by not needing to dig trenches. However, finding a suitable method of securing the pipes can end up being costly. The temperatures at the bottom of the lake are likely to be similar to those of a good trench system. All in all, this can be an excellent proposition if a lake is available.

DX Systems

Back in the 1980s, some direct expansion (DX) heat-pumps were installed that had a simple copper coil within a river or stream. This coil contained the working fluid (the refrigerant) that enabled the heat pump to work. Even at water temperatures approaching freezing point (0°C), a useful amount of heat could be extracted from the water as ice formed around the pipes. This method does have risks associated with it; in particular, the danger of mechanical damage or corrosion resulting in the loss of refrigerant, which could be catastrophic in this situation, since water ingress into the compressor would probably render the whole system irreparable. Not only would the heat pump be destroyed, but the river could also be polluted by spillage of a small amount of oil from the compressor. Again, these issues are not insurmountable and oil-traps could be designed to contain oil spills. It is clearly not a system that the Environment Agency would (or should) approve of easily.

Springs and Ground-Water

Water that naturally flows out from the ground is an outstanding heat source. The ground temperature in the UK varies from around 9°C in the north of Scotland up to 12°C in Cornwall. Ground-water can emerge from springs at these temperatures all year round. This is truly a 'pot of gold' as a heat source.

With temperatures in this region, you can pump directly through a suitable heat pump and realistically achieve the unlikely COPs of up to 5 (with a well-insulated building). A surface spring, as could be the case in hilly areas, is excellent, since the energy requirements to pump the water can be very small. But be mindful that any need to pump the water up from depth will start to eat into that promised high COP.

A small temperature-logger is very useful for assessing if a supply appearing at the surface is proper ground-water; if it is being diluted with surface water, this will show-up as variations in the temperature. The assessment of a water supply can be made either in summer or winter, e.g. if water is recorded in mid-summer at only 11°C, then it is likely to be around 9°C in winter (given that the mean temperature is likely to be in the order of 10°C). It is harder to assess potential ground-water in autumn or spring, since ground-water or surface water could be similar, by chance, at such times.

One of the biggest problems with open-source systems is corrosion and silting of the equipment and some water purity tests would be recommended. However, some heat pumps are designed specifically for such water.

The spiral stainless steel heat-exchanger from Dimplex is used as the evaporator in some of their units and can be used with untreated water.

In situations where the water is particularly corrosive, it may be safer to use the closed-loop plastic-pipe array within a gravel bed and arrange the spring water to run over the pipes. Very careful design is required to avoid freezing and eventual silting. Excellent results can be achieved from such a system, if it is designed well.

Spiral stainless steel heat-exchanger for untreated water. (Courtesy of Dimplex Ltd.)

Waste Heat–Heat Recovery

The drive to conserve energy and reduce fuel costs has pushed us to consider recovering and making use of this otherwise wasted resource. Heat is sometimes available from exhaust ventilation air or waste washing water. This could be a suitable source for a heat pump.

First, the temperature of the source should be assessed. If the temperature is high enough, then a 'passive' heat-exchanger should be used (without heat pump). This method simply allows natural conduction/convection from the warm waste medium to where the heat is needed. The passive method is effectively free heat, apart from any necessary fans or pumps, which consume a very small amount of energy.

An example of a 'passive' method is mechanical heat-recovery ventilation (MHRV), where extracted air from bathrooms and kitchens passes through a heat-exchanger. The fresh, incoming air passes in very close proximity to (but without actually coming into contact with) the exhaust air before it enters the living areas.

Spring water passes through coiled pipes in gravel 'envelope'. This method can achieve 'brine' temperatures of 7°C, resulting in excellent efficiencies.

The energy efficiency of different models can vary dramatically, but they can pick up as much as 90 per cent of the energy that would otherwise be lost to the building. There are few working parts is such systems – they are inherently simple.

In many cases, the waste heat is not hot enough for such 'passive' use. This is where a heat pump comes in, since it can 'elevate' the temperature to make it useable.

It might be possible to take the heat from waste water from a shower-block to pre-heat the cold inlet to the main hot-water cylinder. This system would have fouling issues relating to dirt in the water, but it could achieve a COP of 3.5.

Taking heat from exhaust ventilation air at 20°C to heat a domestic hot-water cylinder up to 60°C is a more established method and may give a COP between 2.5 and 3. This is discussed again later on in the book.

In any situation where an 'up hill' temperature lift is required, then a heat pump may provide a solution. There are many industrial applications for this technology, but few applicable to the home.

Refrigeration units emit great quantities of heat and this should be used, not wasted. However, this topic is beyond the scope of this book. The only comment worth making is that it is not always as beneficial as first envisaged. For example, a badly engineered heat-recovery system may increase the energy consumed by the system, thus minimizing any gains. Also, the heat available rarely matches the heat needed with respect to quantity or timing. For example, refrigeration emits most heat in summer when room heating requirements are low. Having said that, a well-designed recovery system could be a very beneficial addition to any medium to large refrigeration plant, and is becoming the norm in the modern food industry.

For the domestic fridge it is sadly unlikely that the recovery of the average 100W or so that comes from a domestic fridge/freezer could be a cost-effective proposition; in part because it already contributes to room heating in winter. Maybe the water-cooled heat-recovery fridge will become viable in ten years' time?

Choosing the Source

The Air Source vs Ground Source Debate

Everyone wants to know the answer to the simple question of which is best: air or ground source?

This seemingly easy question is rather hard to answer and, in reality, the situation in which it is used will dictate the appropriateness of either. We have therefore listed the cases for and against each type below.

The Case for Ground Source

The ground a metre or two below our feet stays at a relatively uniform temperature throughout the year, so in mid-winter is considerably warmer than the outside air. This means that it can maintain good efficiency, even on the coldest day of the year, and is therefore less likely to need alternative back-up heating.

Once installed, the system is non-intrusive, since the collectors are buried out of sight. The unit is housed within a building, so not exposed to the weather. It is therefore likely to be reliable and long-lasting. The system would be completely silent and discreet with respect to the neighbours.

The Case Against Ground Source

Such systems are more costly and potentially disruptive to install. There are no two ways about it: installing trenches will temporarily damage anything growing in the immediate area.

Table showing real-life COP figures for different types of property and heat pump. (Geothermal Centre Bochum, Germany, GZB.)

	Heat Pump Type	
Building Type	Ground Source	Air Source
Existing Build	3.3	2.6
New Build	3.8	3

Boreholes are less intrusive, but often an expensive option.

The Case for Air Source

Air-source systems are far easier, quicker and cheaper to install than a ground-source system. They can achieve very good efficiencies in spring and autumn, so could be viable to part-heat older buildings, but in well-insulated buildings they may mange the whole heating load satisfactorily (especially in warmer parts of the UK).

The Case Against Air Source

They will suffer reduced efficiency in mid-winter when air temperatures are low. This coincides with the building's greatest heat demand. A secondary back-up heating method is therefore more likely to be needed. If the back-up is electric heating, this could potentially put a high burden on the mains electricity grid during the coldest days when demand is already high. Units generally sit out in the elements, so may not be as long-lived as other heat pumps that are housed indoors.

In summary, a ground-source system should give a reasonably better annual performance if it is installed well, but it will cost considerably more to install. An air source may compete well in spring and autumn, but in the depth of winter it would have a reduced energy efficiency, which is usually accompanied by a reduced heat output.

The average real-life COP figures (SPF) shown above were produced by the Geothermal Centre Bochum, Germany (GZB).

The air source COP is 20 per cent lower than ground source for both existing and new buildings.

CHAPTER 6

UTILIZING THE HEAT

Also called the 'sink', or the 'load', this is where the heat is delivered and distributed to the rooms of the building, or where it is used to heat the domestic hot-water supply.

It is often thought that a room's comfort is simply dependent on the air temperature, but this is not the whole story. For comfort, the radiation of our surroundings plays an important role. This is because everything radiates heat at a rate dependent on its surface temperature. We radiate heat, as do the walls and items in the room around us. If we are in a room with a reasonable air temperature, but with cold walls, we sense little radiation and feel uncomfortable. However, if the walls or the floor were warm, we could be quite comfortable, even if the air was only 17°C. In this instance we would be receiving and absorbing a noticeable amount of radiation.

The issues of cold walls mainly relate to badly insulated buildings. As time passes, we are shifting towards greatly increased levels of insulation and the temperatures of everything within the room, including the walls, tend to even up. Given this trend, the methods of heating (the heat-emitters) get a bit easier. Unfortunately, we have a vast stock of old, badly insulated buildings and caution must be taken when applying heat-pump technology to these.

Traditionally we have heated houses using very small areas of red-hot coal or wood in a fireplace. Electric 'bar' fires are similar and only a very small area of hot element, at maybe 1,000°C, will give 1 or 2kW, which may be sufficient to heat a room. Heat pumps are at the other end of the spectrum and are only efficient at relatively low temperatures; so whatever the means by which the heat is transferred to the room, the heat-transfer surface will need to be

FUNDAMENTALS OF HEAT TRANSFER

Heat can transfer in three ways:

- **Conduction:** this is simply the principle of heat moving through any substance. Metals conduct heat well, unlike polystyrene.
- **Convection:** this is heat transfer due to the movement of a fluid or gas. As the medium warms, it expands and therefore becomes lighter; it rises up above colder parts of the medium. Hot air rises due to convection.
- **Radiation:** this transfer is due to rays of energy and is emitted from every warm object in the form of infra-red heat. The sun's energy is transmitted in this manner.

big. This will allow adequate heating with relatively low water temperatures. This is not a concept that heating engineers have needed to embrace until now. In essence, we want the heat to be taken away from the heat pump as efficiently as possible.

Whilst radiators are common and we are familiar with them, we can employ different technologies to heat our spaces. We'll class these technologies as 'emitters', as, by a variety of different methods, they 'emit' heat. We can classify these by the way they transfer heat around the building. Commonly, we 'move' heat around a building either in the form of 'hot water' or 'hot air'. We'll use this classification to help group them.

The heated water temperature is a guide to the likely COP of the system. The hotter the water, the lower the energy efficiency is likely to be.

Water as a Heat-Transfer Medium

Water is an ideal medium for transferring heat. It has a very high thermal capacity, meaning that you can transfer a lot of heat using a relatively small flow of water. For this reason, the 'wet' system, as it is commonly referred, has become the exclusive heat-transfer method for central heating systems and is likely to remain so.

Radiators

Panel radiators are by far the most common way of transferring heat into a room. They are relatively cheap, usually completely silent and not

Conversation between two heating engineers. (Andria Thwaites.)

too difficult to fit into any house. Hot water is pumped, as required, through pipes and the water flow can be controlled easily to maintain the required room temperature.

The name 'radiator' is a little misleading, since only around one-quarter of the energy is radiant. The majority of the heat exchange is actually due to air-convection currents. Most modern radiators have fins on the back that improve the convected heat output.

Boilers and radiators are old companions, and systems have evolved over the last thirty years of so. Whilst boilers have improved, radiators have remained simply a steel envelope with channels inside where the heated water can pass. Occasionally, a new product comes on to the market, which, for a variety of reasons, claims 'high efficiency'. However, the optimized radiator design may only give rise to modest improve-

THE DOMESTIC CIRCULATOR

Commonly know as the central-heating pump, these are made in their millions and most homes have one. They have not really changed much over the last forty years, and use between 50 and 100W of electrical input power for a typical home. The energy efficiency has increased slightly over the years due to better designs; however, there are still models on the market that are fairly inefficient.

There has recently been a shift in energy efficiency with the development of 'A' energy rated circulators. Instead of normal motors, these have highly efficient DC motors with special electronic control that not only saves power, but can also vary the speed of the pump, depending on the water flow requirements of the system.

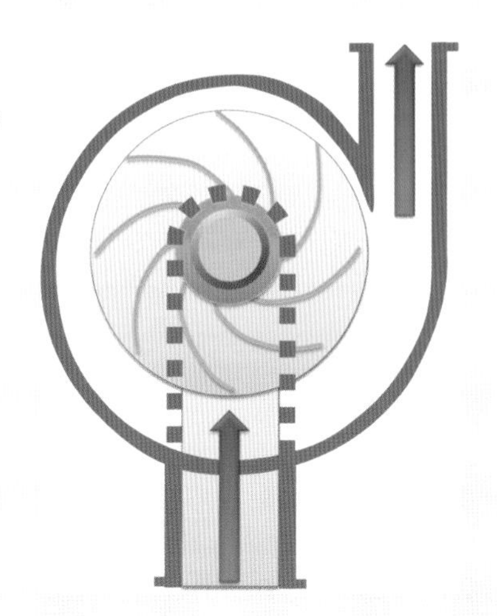

TOP PHOTOS: **A water circulator – commonly called a water pump.**

These 'A' rated pumps are excellent for use on the 'hot' side of a heat-pump system, and can either be set to one of three fixed speeds, or to automatically maintain a fixed pressure. It may also have an auto-adapt mode, but the advanced features are usually designed for conventional boiler systems. The simpler settings are usually best suited for a heat pump.

Some under-floor heating systems keep the pump running almost continuously, whereas the heat-pump unit may run typically for somewhere around 25 to 30 per cent of the year, since they automatically 'cycle' on and off.

We have illustrated the cost of running a pump over a five-year period, so you can make some assessments without getting your calculator out. As can be seen, the potential savings would sometimes cover the purchase cost of the pump in a relatively short period of time. On a new installation, 'A' rated pumps are usually worthwhile.

Type of Pump & Size of Installation	Power and Cost		Cost per 5 years		
	Input Power (Watts)	Cost per hour @ 10p/kWh	Running 100% of the time	Running 50% of the time	Running 30% of the time
Old Pump – Large House	90	0.9p	£400	£200	£120
Old Pump – Small House	45	0.45p	£200	£100	£60
'A' Rated Pump – Big House	20	0.2p	£88	£44	£26
'A' Rated Pump – Small House	10	0.1p	£44	£22	£13

LEFT: **Table showing example electricity costs to run a range of domestic circulator pumps.**

ments in energy efficiency for most situations. Whilst arguments about the importance (or otherwise) of quick-response and 'thermal mass' continue, it is not surprising that the simple, steel envelope, with fins, has remained a product of choice as they are easy and cheap to make.

As we have already established, heat pumps work best if the water being heated is as low in temperature as possible. The radiator, the connections and pipe work are important details to consider.

The temperature required for the heated water is dependent on the radiator size. In simple terms the bigger the radiator, the lower the temperature its surface will need to be for a given heat output. The general rule relating to heat-pump systems is – the bigger the radiators, the higher the COP. Indeed, to achieve comparable performance to an under-floor heating system, the radiators may need to span over half the wall perimeter.

The common radiator is made by spot-welding two steel sheets together in a special way so as to form an 'envelope' with channels for the water to pass. We took a thermal image of such a radiator, in use, so that the surface temperatures could be seen. These are represented as different colours.

The hot inlet comes from the bottom right-hand side and you can see how the hot (white colour) water rises by convection currents towards the top and travels across the top. This passes to the top left-side corner and is enticed down the far left channel. Water descends the vertical channels over the entire area and cools as heat is given off to the room, black being the coldest temperature. It is interesting to note in this case that the outlet at the bottom left is slightly warmer than 'black'. This is not caused by sludge in the bottom of the radiator (sludge problems are another matter), but is simply a characteristic of this configuration at certain flow rates. Is this an issue? No, not for conventional boiler systems, but with a heat pump we are looking to keep the flow temperature low so that the COP is high. The bottom of this radiator is fairly cool, so it is partially redundant. In a way, there is little point in fitting large radiators unless they are warm all over.

It is well known that bottom-inlet connections are not perfect for maximized efficiencies, but they are convenient and generally good enough. The old-school connections of – 'top inlet, bottom outlet, same end' (TBSE), can give a more even flow within the radiator, but are uncommon. As heat pumps become more common, it will be easier to obtain radiators that are opti-

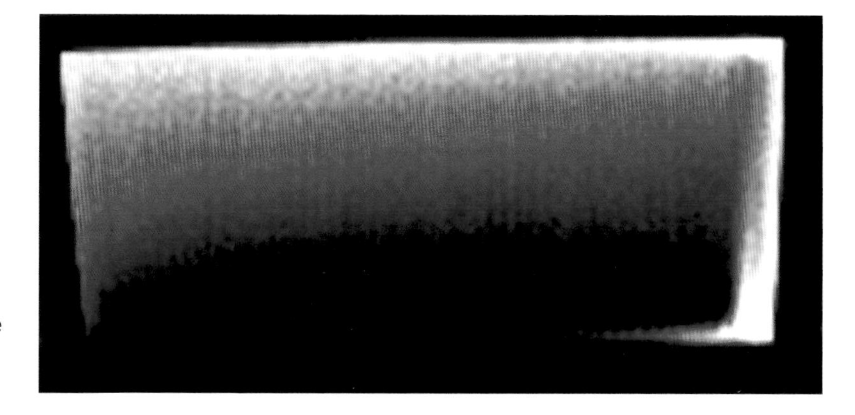

Thermal image of a standard panel radiator with normal bottom pipe connections. (JPW Construction.)

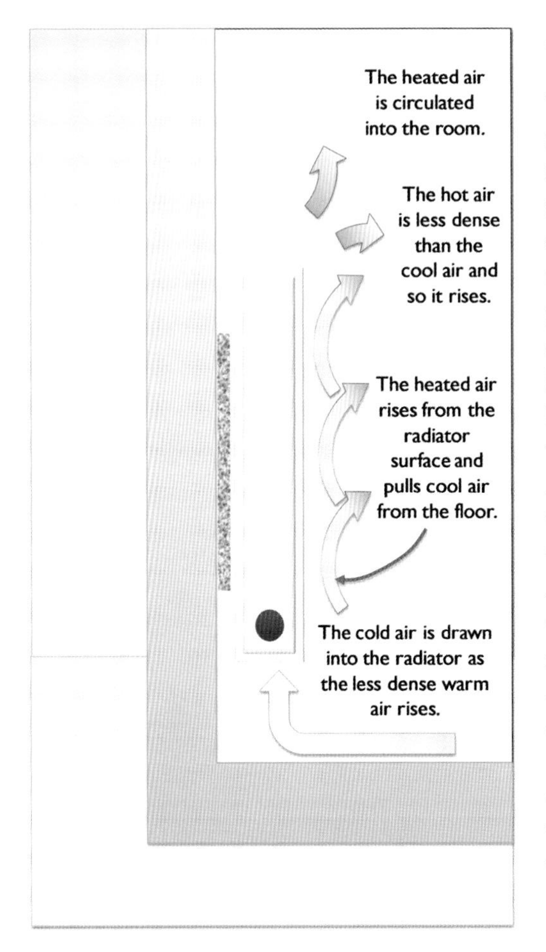

A panel convection radiator.

mized for operation at lower temperatures. The inner water channels will be improved so that simple connections can be used and more uniform water flows will help to minimize cold-spots at the bottom.

A rule of thumb states that the energy efficiency of a heat pump will increase by 2.5 to 3 per cent, if both the flow and return drop by 1°C. By ensuring that there are no dead-spots, we are likely to achieve the same heat output, with slightly lower water temperatures, so this is worthwhile.

Water Flow Rates

Temperature differences between flow and return (delta T, or dt), and water flow rates are interrelated. For a given heat pump (giving a fairly constant output), then the slower the water flow, the greater the temperature rise as the water passes through the heat pump. Heat pumps tend to prefer higher flow rates and there are several reasons for this. When operating at lower temperatures, we simply cannot have a large dt. For example, if a boiler flow were 80°C, then the return could be 60°C (the dt would be 20°C). If we now consider a heat pump with a flow temperature of only 40°C, then the return would have to be 20°C (given the same dt of 20). This could not happen, since it must be warmer than room temperature. This is one reason why dts in the order of 6K are common and are simply achieved by increasing the flow rate. (K is an abbreviation for Kelvin, and the symbol used to describe degrees temperature difference. It is convention to use K instead of °C in this instance.) However, there is another reason why heat pumps prefer a high flow-rate and this is due to the inner workings of the condensing refrigerant, which is generally at one temperature. A low flow temperature is more important with respect to the COP than a low return temperature, so high flows are preferred. This is not the case for a condensing boiler, where a low return temperature may be important.

It is important here to mention the heat pumps that use CO_2 refrigerant, which are new to the market. These do not have the same characteristics and can work well with lower flow rates. CO_2 heat pumps can be well matched to hot-water production, where large temperature gradients may be experienced.

It's also worth mentioning that thermostatic radiator valves (TRVs) reduce the flow as they control the temperature. They can make radiators operate akin to our infra-red photograph, as they start to close. This illustrates a problem that could result if too many radiators with TRVs start to close. This can be improved by turning down the water temperature setting on the heat pump and ensuring that most TRVs are set relatively high. This will tend to keep most TRVs open and make radiators operate with a more even surface temperature. It will, however, not matter if a few of the radiators, in bedrooms, for example, control by reducing the flow with a TRV (*see* next section about TRV control).

Given the need for adequate flow rates, it is important than the pump energy consumption is not increased; it follows that the distribution pipe work must not be overly restrictive. Whilst pipe sizes should be calculated methodically, this is not always carried out, since the practised heating engineer may know from experience what pipe size to use for most of the runs. Besides, boilers can be reasonably forgiving on this matter. If pipes are too small, a larger circulation pump may be needed. Your heating engineer will appreciate this and will ensure that the flow rate, as required by the heat pump, can be achieved, without the need for large pumps.

IMPORTANT

Traditionally, books on heating systems focus on design conditions that cope with the *coldest* winter conditions.

In this book we often refer to working conditions in average winter conditions, i.e. temperatures around 2 to 5°C. This is because we are mostly concerned with energy efficiency, and the vast majority of days are around these temperatures. To achieve the highest annual energy efficiencies, systems must be optimized to operate most efficiency around these temperatures.

If a heat pump is to cope with extremely cold weather, the emitter temperatures will need to be able to exceed the average temperatures stated. The energy efficiency during such times is less important since the duration of this type of weather is relatively short.

Sizing of Radiators

The heat output rating (kW) of a radiator is usually specified at the following conditions:

> Water flow 75°C; return 65°C (average surface temperature 70°C), in a room at 20°C.

This gives a mean temperature difference (radiator-to-room) of 50K (degrees).

If we want to use a heat pump, it will need to operate at a lower temperature and the correction factor chart shown (*see* page 54) can be useful. For example, if you wish to aim for a mean water temperature of 50°C, this would require a radiator that is about twice the standard size.

Figures are taken from CIBSE Domestic Central Heating Design Guide and assumes a room temperature of 20°C. This can be used to see how different temperatures affect the output.

A temperature of 50°C is actually higher than ideal for a heat pump, but we must bear in mind that the original radiator rating is derived from an intermittent-heating scenario, where heat from a boiler can be 'blasted' in for a few hours at a time. Our heat pump is likely to operate more continuously, so its temperature could naturally be lower. So, in practice, the average temperature of the radiator might be considerably

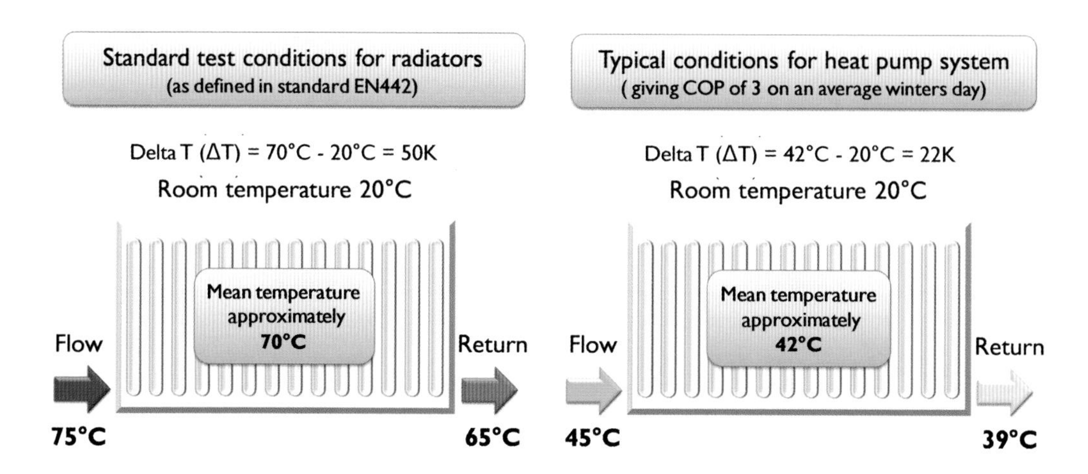

Comparison between standard test conditions and heat pump radiator under average conditions.

Mean Radiator Temperature	70°C	65°C	60°C	55°C	50°C	45°C	40°C
Delta T (ΔT) Radiator-Room °K=°C	50K	45K	40K	35K	30K	25K	20K
Reduction in heat output compared to ΔT @ 50°K	100%	87%	75%	63%	52%	41%	30%
Required area increase to give same output at reduced temperature	1	1.15	1.33	1.59	1.94	2.46	3.29

Table showing required area of radiator to give same heat output at reduced temperature.

lower than our suggested 50°C. This is good news, but the safest option is to go for large radiators if you want to achieve the lowest running costs.

As modern buildings tend to become better insulated, it may be possible to have radiators that are not significantly bigger than the ones that we see in standard boiler-heated houses.

The positioning of radiators with respect to windows can be contentious. Cold windows tend to create downward movements of air, and a radiator below it can tend to cancel this air movement. A radiator on an opposite wall would exacerbate the air-movement problem. However, this problem only really applies to old, badly insulated, single-glazed houses. As houses become better insulated, the radiator location becomes less critical. I tend to favour radiators away from windows, since one sees countless examples of inappropriate curtains that simply direct the radiator's heat towards the window space. If a radiator is on an internal wall, then at least there is no heat loss through the wall to the outside. A further point is the number of radiators per room. Often it is only one per room, but

> **TIP**
>
> To enable low running costs with a heat-pump system, the radiators need to be large. If the building is old and badly insulated, the radiators may need to be *very* large.

A thermostatic radiator valve.

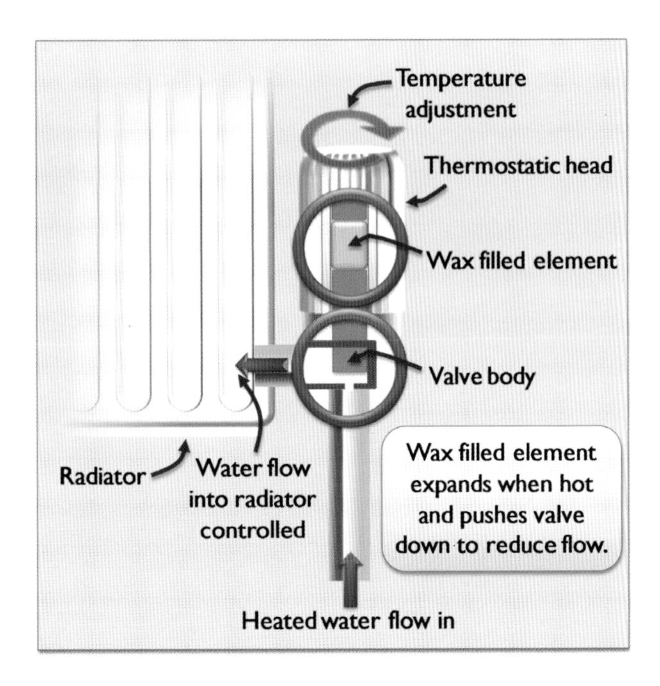

common-sized radiators are relatively cheap, so two radiators in one room might be a good plan.

Thermostatic Radiator Valves (TRVs)

One successful product that has improved the energy efficiency of many hundreds of thousands of heating systems is the thermostatic radiator valve, or TRV. Indeed, the current building regulations state that heated rooms must have a thermostatic control, one that responds to the actual temperature of the room. Oddly, the number of owners who understand its function properly are in a minority, so let's look at how they work.

We are very familiar with variable cooker hotplate knobs and volume controls on radios. In both cases, the setting relates to a distinct heat output or sound volume. Thermostatic controls are different, since the setting does not relate directly to the quantity of heat given off, but to a target room temperature (like a kitchen oven control). Once set, it will automatically open and close the valve for you, to achieve your setting.

The valve has a temperature-sensing element within it, such that its opening and closing is affected by the room temperature. The top of the valve can be adjusted from 1 (cold) to 5 (hot). Incidentally, it operates in the same direction as a water tap (which is the opposite to a radio's volume control), i.e. anticlockwise to increase, clockwise to reduce. The chart on page 56 shows the function of a typical valve.

As can be seen, the opening of the valve is dependent on both the setting and the room temperature.

Examples:

- If the room is cold, the valve is fully open, regardless of the setting position.
- If set to 3, the valve will remain fully open until the room becomes warm, then the valve will then start to close. It will close fully when the room is very warm.

	Room Temperature						
Setting	Cold	Cool	Medium	Warm	Very Warm	Hot	Very Hot
1	Fully Open	Half Open	Closed	Closed	Closed	Closed	Closed
2	Fully Open	Fully Open	Half Open	Closed	Closed	Closed	Closed
3	Fully Open	Fully Open	Fully Open	Half Open	Closed	Closed	Closed
4	Fully Open	Fully Open	Fully Open	Fully Open	Half Open	Closed	Closed
5	Fully Open	Fully Open	Fully Open	Fully Open	Fully Open	Half Open	Closed

Table showing control operation of TRV.

One of the confusions arises from feeling the radiator with your hand. It is quite normal for it to gently and slowly 'oscillate', e.g. it may go off for ten minutes, then as the room cools very slightly, it will open and very hot water may fill the radiator. Later the valve will close as the room warms.

If you are thinking of adjusting the valve *do not feel the radiator temperature*. This seems like very odd advice; however, there is sense to it, since you don't know if the radiator is about to automatically come on in response to room temperature, or is about to go off.

The fluctuating nature of TRVs can be misinterpreted as 'sticking'. Valves can occasionally stick, but it is quite normal for them to seem erratic. The best advice is to keep the control at a middle position and only adjust it by tiny amounts, then wait a few hours to see what temperature the room has stabilized to. You may be surprised to see how only turning it from 3 to 2½ will make a noticeable difference to the room (after some considerable time).

Heat Pumps and TRVs

TRVs were designed to be fitted to normal boiler central heating systems. The valves gradually restrict the flow as they attempt to regulate the room temperature. As the water flow through the boiler reduces due to valves closing, the boiler's internal sensor responds and turns it off, or reduces its flame level accordingly.

Unlike boilers, if heat pumps stop and start too frequently, or if the water flow reduces, they can suffer a loss of energy efficiency, so a system using TRVs must be designed to accommodate this.

If thermostatic radiator valves are fitted in too many rooms, then there is a danger that the water flow rate will, at times, be too restricted through the heat pump. Furthermore, since TRVs tend to jump between open and close whilst they attempt to maintain room temperature, it is likely that they will do this randomly. It would be better if there were some collaboration so that they all tend to operate together. It is therefore not uncommon to have a master thermostat in a main living room that directly controls the heat-pump unit. This room would not have a TRV.

Having raised a caution about TRVs, this does not mean that you should remove them if they are already fitted; however, you should think carefully about how they are used. In general, the best advice would be to keep several at a high setting, then reduce the water temperature setting on the heat pump until the rooms do not over heat. Use the TRVs in the bedrooms or kitchen, for example, to limit the heat as required. TRVs can be very useful in kitchens since they should respond accordingly if cooking activities are generating heat.

Internal Water Volume of Radiators

Panel radiators are heavy and can contain a lot of water; there is debate about the advantages and disadvantages of this. Arguably, the time it takes to heat the radiator up is undesirable and this heat could be wasted when the system stops, since the residual heat may not necessarily be required. However, for most of the time this argument is tenuous. Typically, the heat-up time for the radiator is in the region of only ten minutes and the residual heat is not necessarily wasted, but can remain useful to the house.

Heat pumps don't like stopping and starting too much, since it takes a minute or so for the system to settle down after starting, thus the COP takes a short while to 'establish'. It also potentially adds to wear and tear. To minimize the number of compressor starts, the water content of a system is often increased by use of a buffer cylinder. This simply adds a volume of water to the system. For applications where the heating is fairly continuous and there is no buffer cylinder, it can be a definite advantage if the radiators have a large water content (acting in effect, as a buffer).

RADIATOR DESIGN

It is interesting to note how opinions vary, some claiming that low water content and quick response is an advantage. Alternatively, a radiator could be chosen for high water content, giving the heat pump better run cycles. The debates continue as products evolve.

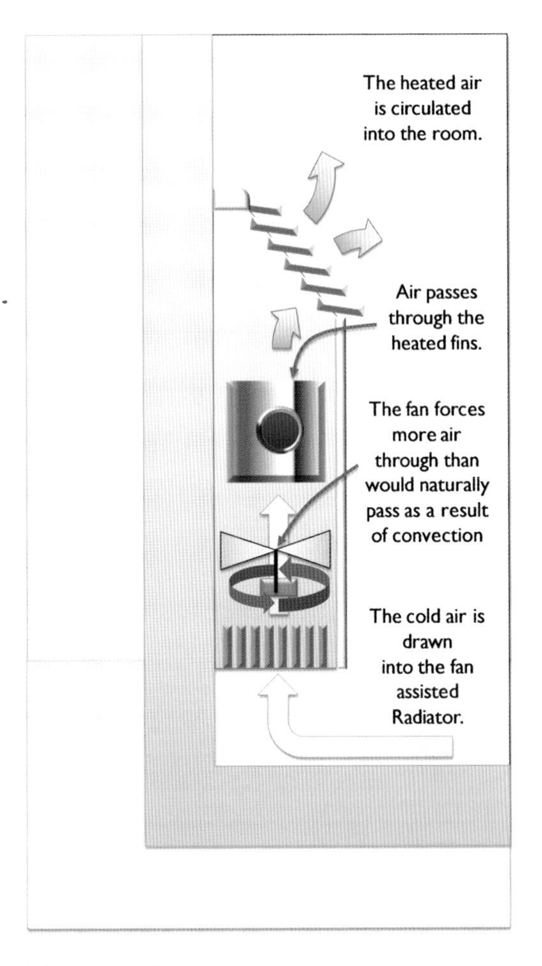

A fan convector.

Whilst the so-called 'high efficiency' radiators may have their advantages, old radiators with very high water content can, in many circumstances, work exceptionally well and could be chosen specifically for use with a heat pump.

Fan Convectors

Fan convectors are simply blown-air heaters that can be connected to any 'wet' central heating system. Oddly, they are sometimes called fan-assisted radiators, but some emit no radiation at all. In the past they have been noisy and debatably unsightly, but computer design and modern manufacture techniques can give us better fans, so these devices are now becoming much more acceptable. Electronic controls can also improve their operation. It is likely that such heaters will become more popular for use with heat pumps since they are far more compact than the large panel radiators that heat pumps call for; so they could be the answer for those who don't want too much of their walls taken up by radiators. Mixing panel radiators in some rooms and fan-assisted types in others, appropriately, may give you the best all-round results for quietness and performance.

Under-Floor Heating

Like the marriage of boilers and panel radiators, under-floor heating is considered the ideal partner for a heat pump. The obvious reason is that a room can be adequately heated with water that may be barely warm to touch, so the COP can be high. The actual required water temperature depends on several factors and many configurations are possible.

This type of heat emitter involves a large quantity of pipe embedded below the floor's surface. Warm water is simply pumped through the pipes, so that heat is transferred into the fabric of the floor. The heat conducts to the surface and is emitted to heat the room. Curiously, under-floor heating is often referred to as 'radiant' heating. However, it is actually a combination of radiation and convection of roughly equal proportions. But the unexpected radiation (how can something that is barely warm radiate?) plays a vital role in heat transfer and the occupant's comfort.

It should be noted that there are limits to the amount of heat that under-floor heating can emit. This is because the feet can become uncomfortable if the floor is notably warm. This can be an issue if full-heating a poorly insulated building.

Screed-type under-floor heating with close (100mm) pipe spacing designed for a heat pump.

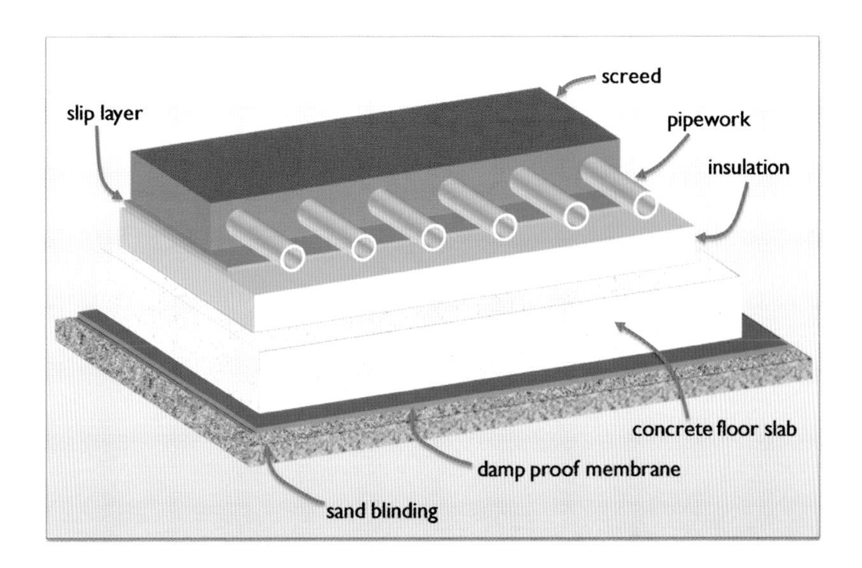

Under-floor heating with pipes in screed.

This method involves a cement-mix screed in which a matrix of pipes is cast. Insulation must be located below the screed and some sort of floor covering is used above. This can range from paint, tiles, timber and carpets.

The insulation below the screed is worth considering and it is not untypical to lose as much as 10 per cent of the heat down through the insulation into the ground. It is desirable, therefore, for this insulation to be thick. Usually polyurethane-type foam is chosen.

It is understandable that the more pipes that are buried in the screed, the lower the water temperature required; for example, one short pipe alone would need to get very hot to provide sufficient heat. The more pipe the better is the general rule for the sake of the heat-pump's energy efficiency. However, this notion can be an expensive option and gives diminishing returns, so a compromise must be sought.

When a large amount of pipe is used, then it cannot simply be added in one long length. This is because the pumping power would be too high, unless the pipe had an unmanageably large diameter. A practical compromise is to use multiple parallel circuits, as may be necessary in all rooms that are medium-sized and upwards. This detail will be calculated by your under-floor heating designer. Surprisingly, the power required to pump around a system with a large amount of pipe can be relatively small.

It is interesting to consider the natural self-regulating effect of high-efficiency under-floor heating systems. In well-insulated buildings, the floor's surface will not need to be significantly warmer than the room temperature. For example, a heated floor's surface could typically be only 22°C, in a room of nominally 19°C. If a neighbouring room were only 16°C, then the temperature difference (room to floor) would now be double, such that the heat transfer has also approximately doubled. Conversely, if a woodstove were alight, the room would warm a couple of degrees and the heat transfer from the floor would reduce significantly. Due to this self-regulating effect, a well-insulated house with several rooms will therefore tend towards an even temperature. Furthermore, if sunlight were to fall on the floor, the floor would rise in tem-

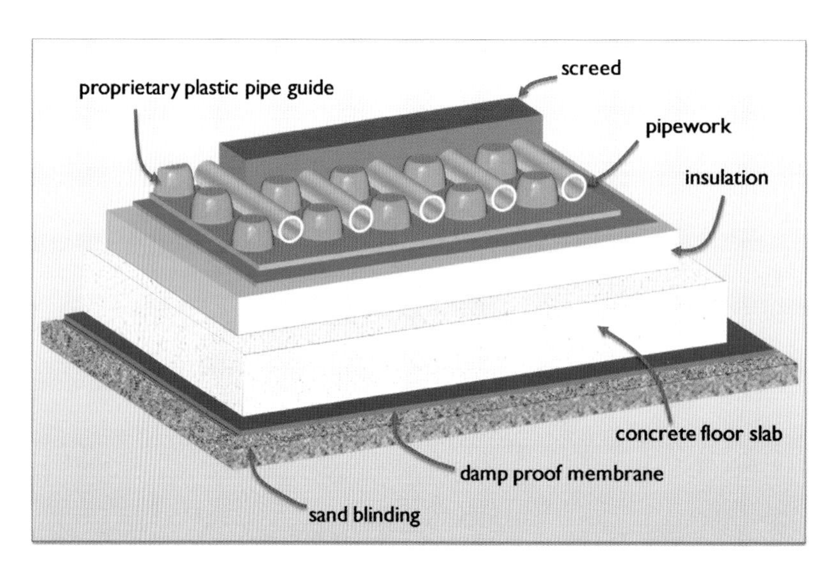

Under-floor heating run in proprietary plastic moulding.

perature and this would tend naturally to reduce the heat conducting up from the buried pipes.

Radiators are far hotter than the room temperature, so the temperature difference between the room and the radiator will vary by only a small proportion as the room temperature varies. The self-regulating effect is therefore negligible.

Of the many products available, plastic moulding is convenient and quick, but it should be noted that with some designs, the thermal conduction between pipe and screed may be compromised, since a significant amount of the pipe could be touching the insulation mouldings. Ideally a pipe would be cast in the middle of the screed and would not be in contact with any insulation, but this is hard to achieve. The old-school method of laying wire mesh on to the insulation, then attaching the pipes to this, is probably the best way of achieving the greatest screed contact to the entire surface of the pipes. This method also gives total flexibility relating to the spacing between successive pipes.

GOOD LOW-TEMPERATURE DESIGN

To minimize heat-pump running costs, it is important to obtain a good low-temperature design. This generally involves more pipe and costs more to install than standard systems.

Suspended Floors

Suspended floors are far more difficult to work with. The transfer of heat from the pipes to the floor surface is not as efficient as with the solid-floor method, so water temperatures need to be higher. A common method uses aluminium spreader plates to help transfer heat from the pipe to the underside of the wood floor covering. This system often requires water at 50°C or above, so efficiencies of a heat pump will be lower.

Another method uses a weak 'semi-dry' sand and cement mix to spread the heat from the pipes to the underside of the timber. Generally,

Aluminium spreader plate for suspended floors.

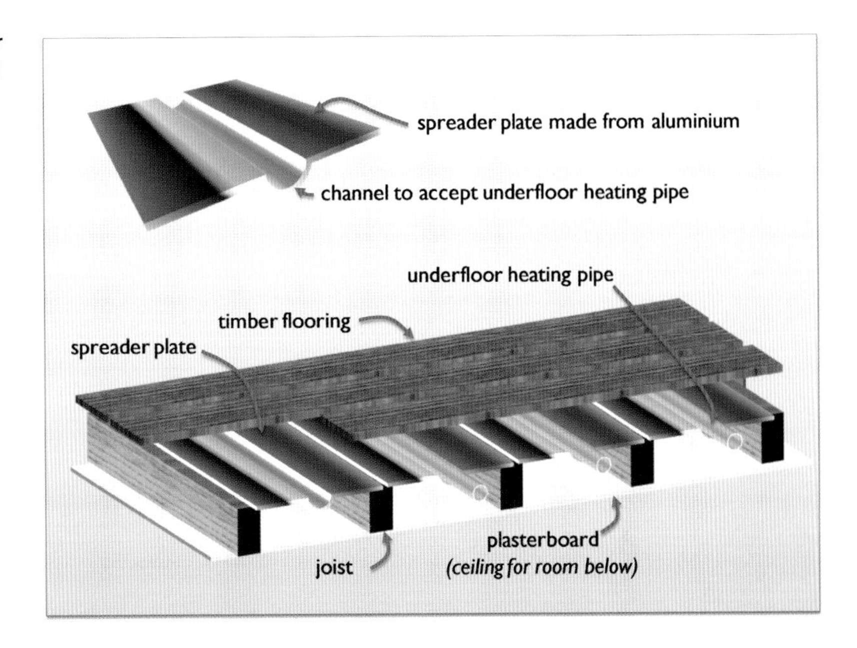

this has similar temperature requirements to the aluminium plates.

Manifolds

When the under-floor heating industry was being established in the UK, conventional boilers were the predominant heat source. These systems are typically designed to operate at around 50°C, but the boiler water could be considerably hotter than this, so a mixing or blending valve is used to limit the temperature within the floor pipes.

Heat pumps do not need mixing valves, since the water that the heat pump 'sees' should be as low as possible and this temperature should not be 'diluted' by a mixing valve. Mixing valves can also impose a pressure drop, which could

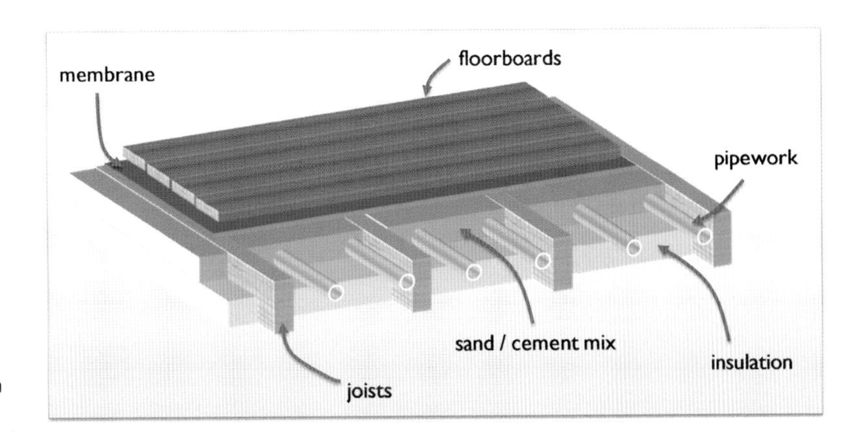

Dry mix 'biscuit' method for suspended wooden floors.

Typical boiler design manifold with mixing valve.

Heat pump design manifold with no mixing valve.

increase the power required for pumping. The same issues relating to flow rates and temperature drops apply, as covered in the previous section on radiators.

Floor Coverings

The floor covering is a very important aspect relating to thermal performance of the floor. The thermal conductivity of the materials between the warm pipes and the floor surface is important, since any thermal resistance means that the water pipes will need to be hotter to achieve the same floor temperature and room heat-output. The increased water temperature reduces the COP of the heat pump.

The best surfaces are bare or painted concrete. Flagstones or tiles are potentially as good and should ideally be laid with the fewest air voids as possible.

Solid-floor finishes have often been synonymous with cold feet, since in the past, solid, tiled floors have mostly been un-insulated and unheated. However, experience some nice under-floor heating and this perception is quickly dispelled. The gentle thermal emission from below can be very comfortable. For those who really need something soft, a few rugs in strategic areas may not hinder the heat transfer significantly.

Timber or carpets are popular floor coverings and are perfectly acceptable with under-floor heating. However, they will impose some energy-efficiency penalty when a heat pump is used. In the examples opposite, we have suggested that such coverings may, on average, necessitate a 5°C increase in water temperatures. This could drop the COP from 3.6 to 3.2 in winter. To minimize these effects, it is important to minimize any air gaps between the pipes and the floor surface; this includes any carpet underlay, of which a high thermal conductivity type must be chosen.

In some cases, a house would have solid floors on the ground floor, requiring a nominal 35°C and aluminium plates upstairs, requiring say 45°C. These temperatures can only be achieved by using a mixer valve to blend-down the temperature of the ground-floor water. However,

How floor covering affects COP.

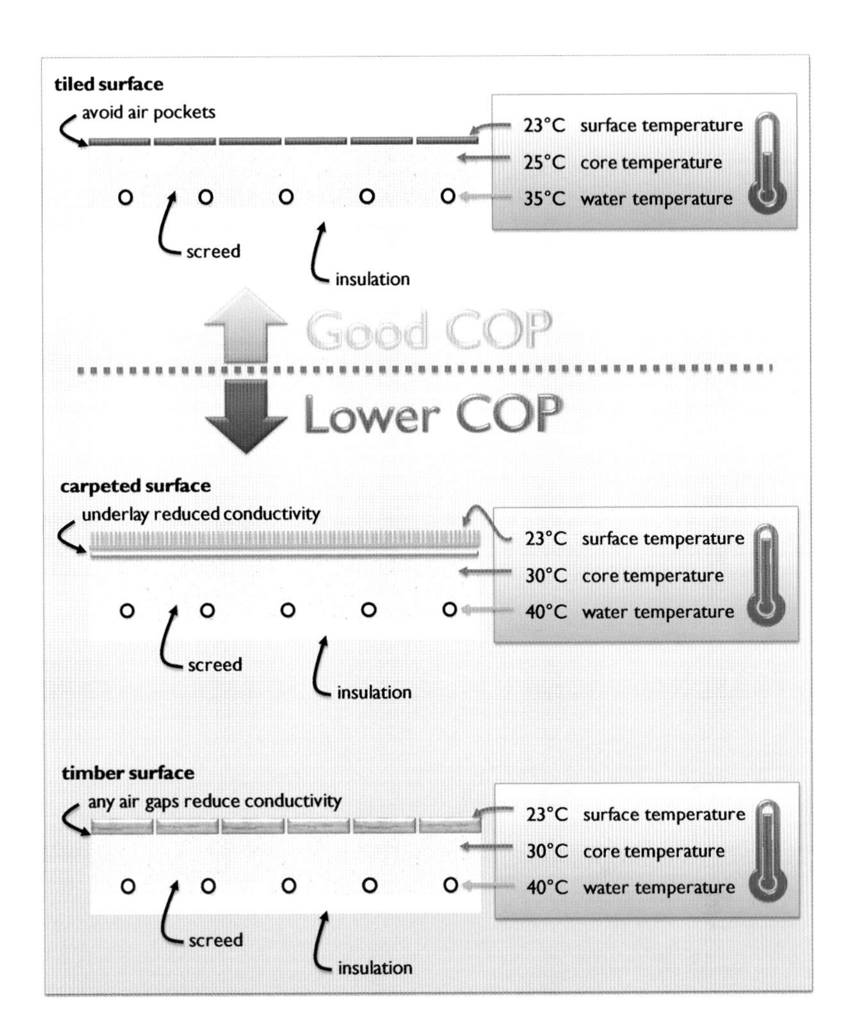

this is not an ideal set-up, since all heat is produced at 45°C (at reduced COP). This situation may be improved by using time functions to run the whole system at 35°C (better COP), then set the time function to elevate the system for a limited number of hours per day, when upstairs heat is most needed. Many people, however, like cooler bedrooms, so the constant lower setting may suffice. It is also worth considering insulation levels, since it might justify the cost of extra insulation for any rooms with 'compromised' emitter circuits. This also applies to radiators that may be fitted to an upstairs office or study, for example – even a radiator at 35°C may provide adequate heat, if the room's insulation is good enough.

CHOICE OF FLOOR COVERING

Tiled floors are far better heat emitters and will give lower running costs than timber of carpeted floors.

above: Wall-heating capillary mat is fixed to the wall and covered with a special plaster. (Clina Heiz- und Kühlelemente GmbH.)

Wall Heating

Floors might be the best option, but sometimes the disruption of digging up a good floor is not welcome. In such cases it may be possible to emit the heat from a wall. Systems are available, involving a matrix of very small pipes. These are literally plastered on to a wall using special products. As you can see from the specification, below the heat emitted is very high for a very low water temperature. Such systems could give excellent results. There are several systems on the market with greatly varying performances and differing costs.

The picture with the red pipes opposite shows a simple method using 12mm pipe in an upstairs room of a very well-insulated timber-frame house. Whilst less effective than the capillary mat system, it proved to be very effective in this application.

THE IMPORTANCE OF THERMAL INSULATION

If fitting wall-heating to external walls, they must be well-insulated, otherwise heat is wasted through the walls. This also applies to floor or ceiling heating.

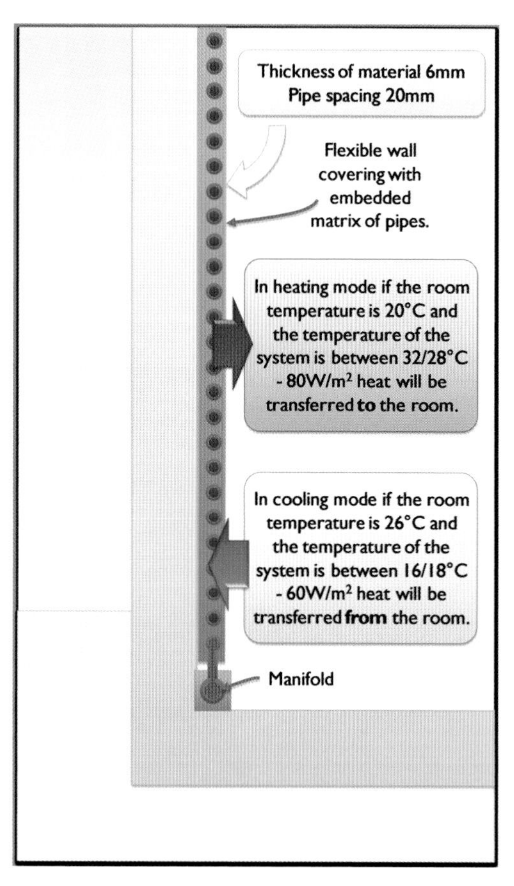

Diagram of wall-heating capillary mat system.

Wall heating in low-energy house.

Ceiling Heating

Ceiling heating is another option and since there are no objects in the way, the full ceiling area can emit heat. However, experience in domestic situations with such heating is limited. There is some evidence that people prefer warmer feet than heads, so this heating may not be the best solution. Again, a lot depends on the required level of heat. In a well-insulated building with low heat demand, this system might work well.

Ceiling systems are more likely to be chosen if the heat pump is reversible or uses passive cooling. The ceiling is the best surface for cooling and this is done by reducing its temperature to only a few degrees below the room. Dew-point sensors within the room controller are used to monitor humidity levels and ensure that no condensation can form, by limiting how cold the water can be.

The Buffer-Tank Debate

A buffer tank (or buffer cylinder) provides an added volume of water to the heating system. It is curious how manufacturers do not universally agree on the necessity of this device. Many systems work perfectly well without one, but some manufacturers insist on its use.

Any heat pump will require an adequate flow of water through it, so that the heat is taken from it efficiently. Consider a scenario where a heat pump is fitted to emitter circuits that periodically turn themselves off, for example, radiators with TEVs or under-floor heating with zone valves. There is a risk that the water flow in such systems will become restricted and hence compromise the heat pump's performance.

The obvious solution would be to fit a bypass valve that can automatically open to allow water to bypass the emitter circuits. Boiler systems are often fitted with such a device. However, heat pumps are far from happy with this solution, since the water would rise in temperature rapidly when the valve opens and the heat pump would stop. Unlike boilers, heat pumps do not operate efficiently when they 'cycle' for short periods. This is where buffer cylinders are needed and can ensure that compressor run-times are not too brief. The cylinder can be fitted in-line with the bypass valve such that there is always a body of water that acts as a load for the heat pump.

The diagrams below and opposite show possible in-line configurations. In either case, if the heating-circuit flow reduces too much, then the flow can travel around the bypass valve and the buffer cylinder. The volume of water 'buffers' the rapid rise in water temperature. The first configuration is with the buffer cylinder positioned in the flow after the heat pump. This is mostly used with air-source systems, since they can periodically produce a slug of cool water whilst the defrost mechanism operates (reverse cycle defrost). This may last for only a minute and causes no detriment, so is a minor point, but it may confuse the owner. The buffer cylinder tends to absorb the cool slug.

Other heat pumps tend to have the buffer in the return line. This has some advantages and allows a faster response of heat direct to the emitter circuits.

For either option, there is sometimes a need to keep a circulation pump running continuously. This is necessary so that the sensor gets a meaningful temperature reading from flowing water.

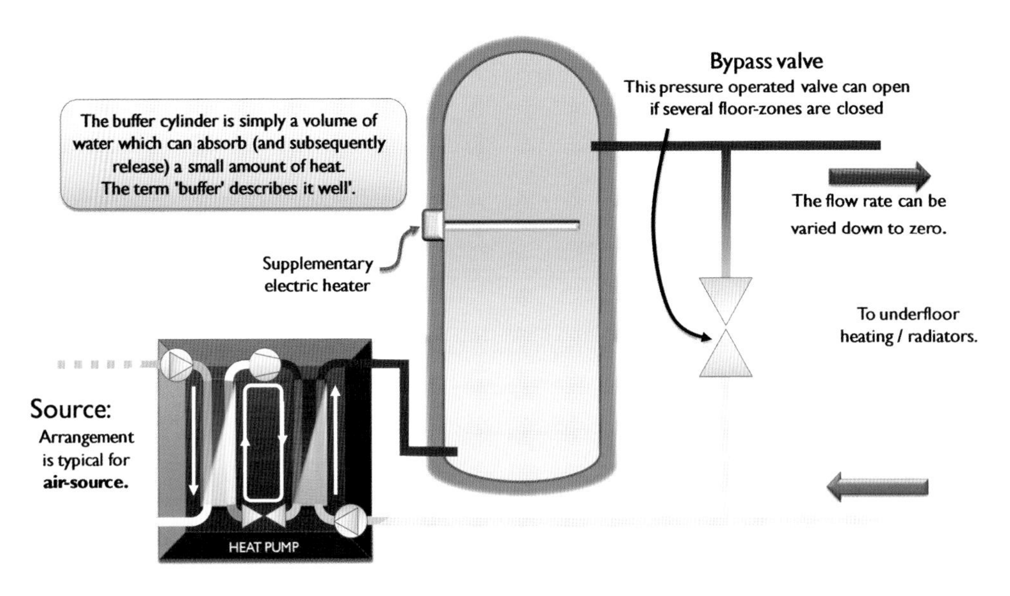

Air-source heat pump with buffer in flow pipe.

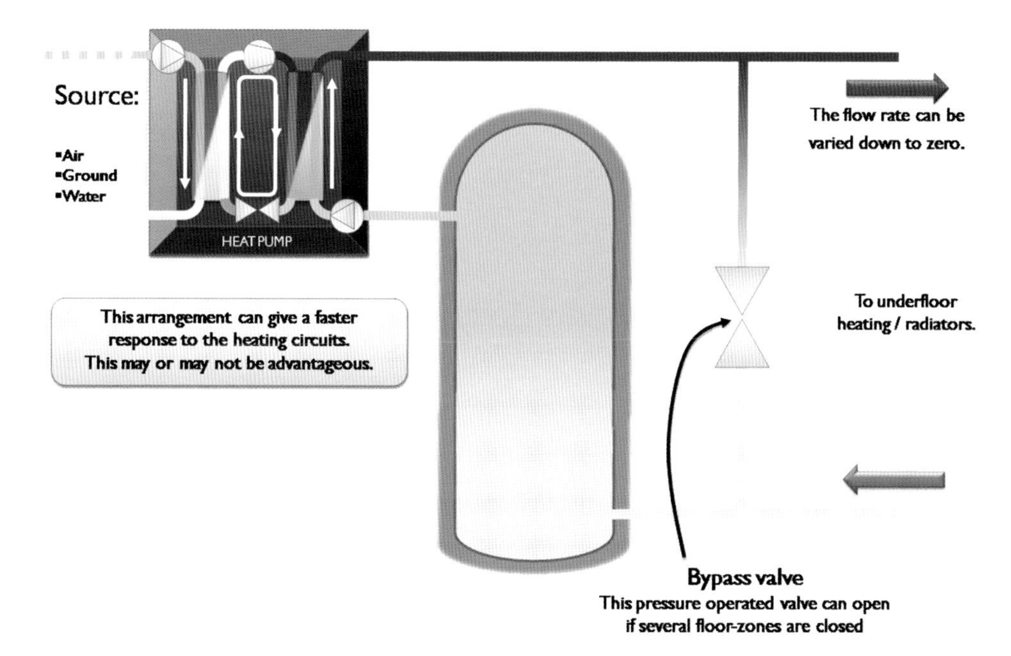

Water-source heat pump with buffer in return pipe.

The alternative arrangement shown on page 68 has the buffer cylinder in parallel. This is inherently simple – the heat pump simply heats the buffer, then the heating circuit can draw off this heat, as and when required. The parallel arrangement requires two circulators in the system; however, the cylinder is also a convenient place for a water-temperature sensor, so with this arrangement, circulators can easily rest when not required.

The non-buffer arrangement could not be simpler: the heat pump merely circulates directly to the emitter circuits, but in this case the water flow around the system must be adequate at all times that the system is operating. This can be achieved if sufficient under-floor zones or radiators are open all the time. Unlike a boiler system, a single bathroom radiator would not be sufficient and the usual arrangement is to have a main living area open all the time. A few extremity rooms, like bedrooms and kitchens, may have zoning and could turn off without detriment.

From the manufacturer's point of view, the buffer tank eliminates potential problems in the case of a system being fitted to unknown emitter circuits, so it is a safer strategy. It also creates a convenient division between the heat-pump installer and the heat-emitter installers. However, buffer cylinders are costly and also take valuable space. It should not be too difficult to ensure that the emitter circuits have adequate flow and capacity, and effectively act as a 'buffer'.

Variable speed inverter-type systems can adjust their heat output, so these units are less likely to need a buffer cylinder. As time passes, no doubt the buffer will tend to be designed-out. That said, we are not taking sides on this debate. It is a matter of what is appropriate for the manufactured equipment supplied.

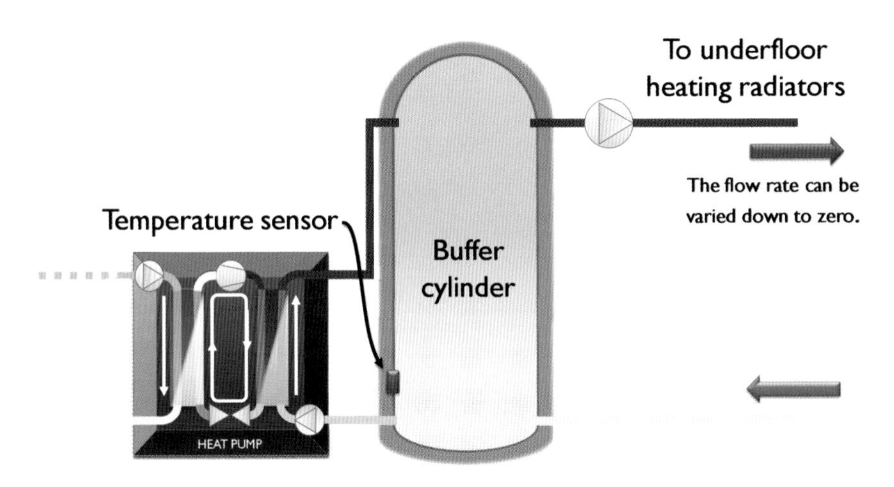

Buffer cylinder parallel arrangement.

Some buffer cylinders are combined with the hot-water cylinder. This is a space-saving feature but often compromises the energy efficiency of the room heating function, since the heat pump may always operate at a relatively high temperature. For most applications it is better to keep the two separate. Sophisticated internal design could, however, solve these problems, but such cylinders would be relatively expensive.

Air as a Heat-Transfer Medium

Room air can be heated directly by blowing air over a finned heat-exchanger. Standard air-conditioning units function like this and it is common to have a 'console' in each room that can either blow (re-circulate) hot or cold air around the room.

Such consoles are relatively quiet and are usually located at a relatively high level, which is an ideal position for cooling-mode and are rarely in the way; having said that, such units are not the most desirable items to have in our living-rooms.

Central ducted systems are somewhat rare in the UK. These systems have grilles or registers fitted in walls or ceilings, and air is ducted to the appropriate place in the building.

Any blown-air system will cause air movement within the room. This can cause draughts, which may prove to be slightly uncomfortable. However, when cooling a room in summer, air movement can be welcome, so it is not surprising that ducted air systems are popular in areas of the world where cooling is the predominant need. Any discomfort during the fleeting winter is short-lived.

The required volume of airflow diminishes as the heat requirements of the house reduce. Thus, in a very low-energy house, the airflow can

Air-conditioning wall console.

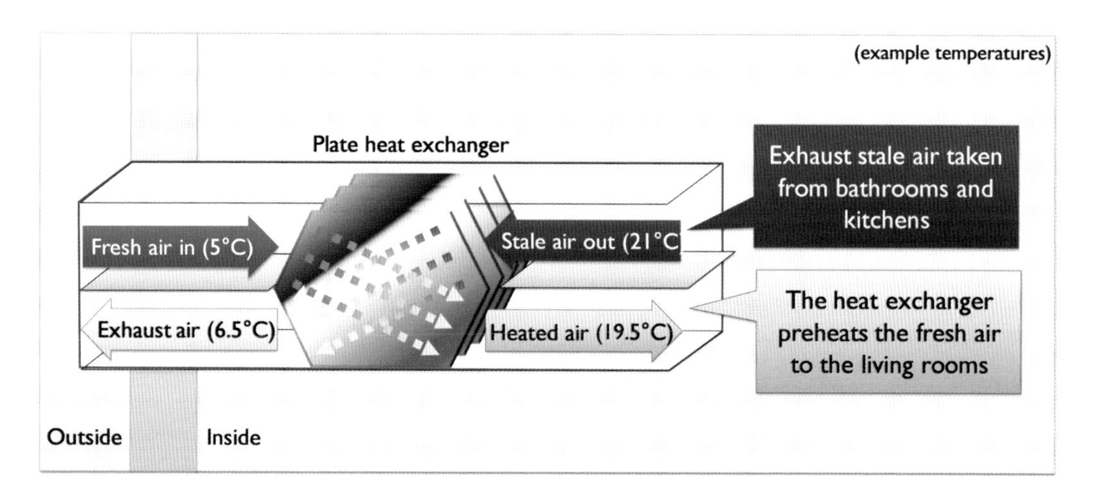

Diagram of passive heat-recovery ventilation (HRV).

be very low, so that any worries about excessive air movement are negated. Duct diameters can be smaller too, so as houses become better insulated, air-blown heating may become more attractive.

Air systems usually have dust filters, since dust is present in the air and equipment would become clogged without one.

Heat-Recovery Ventilation (HVR)

This is in some way similar to a central ducted heating system; however, this product is fitted to satisfy ventilation air-change requirements alone. Air changes in the region of half the room volume per hour (0.5 ACH) are typical and result in relatively small ducting sizes and gentle airflows.

A passive system can be used that does not involve a heat pump. A good system can recover as much as 90 per cent of the heat that would otherwise be lost – it simply uses two small fans and a multi-plate heat-exchanger.

Since the ventilation loss is a significant proportion of a well-insulated building's heat requirements, such a unit could be economically

HRV unit claiming 90 per cent efficiency. The plastic heat-exchanger is partly withdrawn.

viable, since it might mean that a slightly smaller main heat pump could be installed for the room heating load in this case.

Heat-Recovery Ventilation with Heat Pump

Whilst recovering as much as 90 per cent of the heat that is otherwise wasted, such HRV systems still impose a small net loss of energy on the building, so it is possible to add a small heat pump to extract the remaining energy from the exhaust air and feed it into the building. Such systems have existed for many years and provide a net input of heat. This is obviously not achieved without an energy input for the compressor. It should be noted that energy efficiency can vary considerably from model to model, and most systems that include a heat pump use a relatively low-efficiency, passive heat-exchanger.

AIR LEAKAGE

One consideration for any such heat-recovery ventilation system is the air leakage around the windows, doors and walls of buildings. Most of our housing stock will actually have sufficient ventilation simply due to the cracks and gaps in the structure of the building. On windy days, ventilation can be excessive! Even if houses are sealed very carefully, they might still be getting a considerable proportion of the required ventilation by natural means. If a heat-recovery ventilation unit is fitted, one must ensure that the building is very airtight since, otherwise, it will simply ventilate excessively and therefore not reduce energy losses as promised.

The Compact Unit

'PassivHaus' is an international standard used for very low-energy houses. The first house in Darmstadt, Germany, was tested from 1991 and proved to use around one-tenth the energy for room heating compared to a standard house. This is very impressive and was accomplished by the use of exceptionally high levels of insulation,

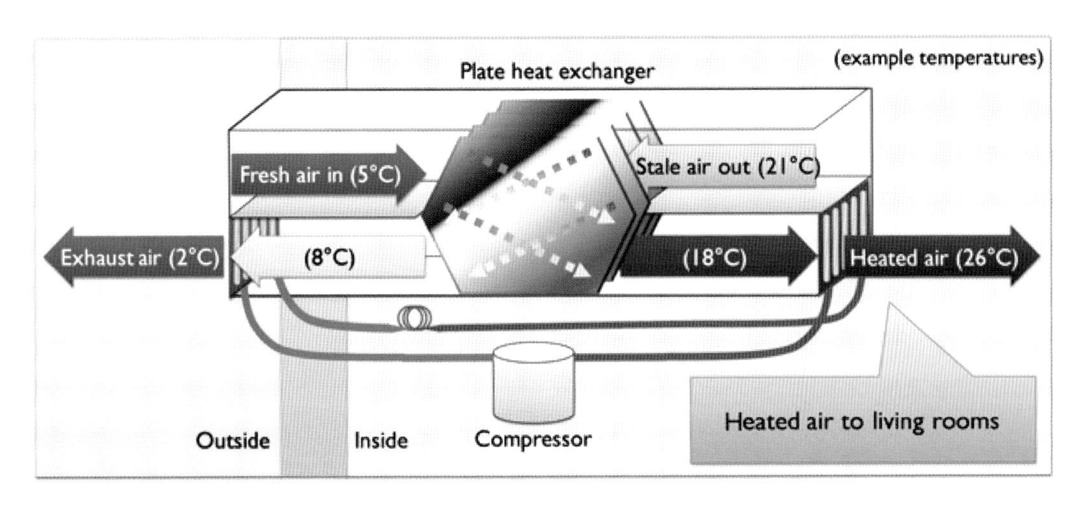

Diagram showing a simple heat-recovery unit, including a heat pump.

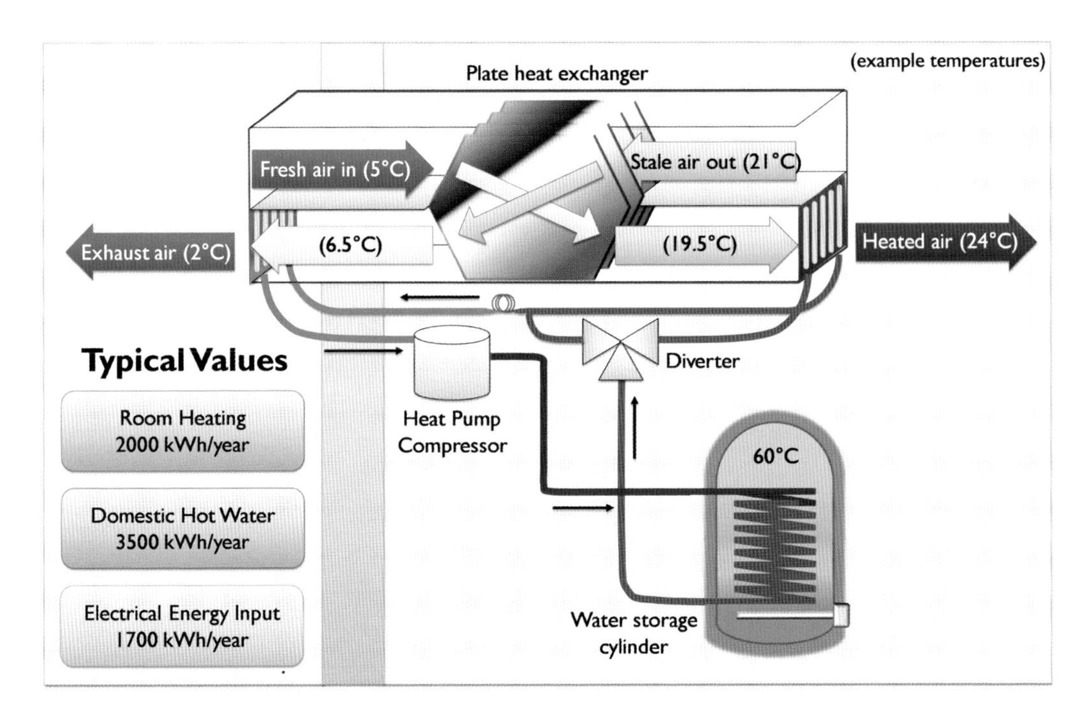

Diagram of a compact unit for PassivHaus.

good air-tightness and efficient heat-recovery ventilation. Such passive houses require so little heat that any gas boiler would be far too large. One option would be to allow the boiler to heat a buffer cylinder, then to draw off heat slowly, as required. That said, boilers may not be the ideal solution and electricity could be a more practical method; but electricity is not a 'clean' form of energy, so any means of reducing its use is welcome.

Very low-energy houses usually have both passive solar heating and solar thermal hot-water heating. This can contribute greatly to the annual energy needs, but there are times when the solar radiation available is simply not enough to satisfy demand.

Houses also require ventilation, but the natural ventilation rate is normally very hit and miss, and depends greatly on how windy it is. As we make houses more thermally sealed, then the air-change rate is reduced. This leads to bad quality indoor air; some sort of controlled mechanical fan ventilation is required.

Recovering heat from ventilation air was central to the PassivHaus strategy. This was accomplished by simply passing the exhaust air close to the incoming fresh air using a suitable passive, plate heat-exchanger. The power used by small fans (one inlet, one exhaust) to accomplish this can be in the order of only 50W.

Passive heat-recovery can recover as much as 90 per cent of the otherwise wasted ventilation heat. Being less that 100 per cent, there is a small net loss of energy. It was realized that there was still energy left in the exhaust air after the passive heat-exchanger, so, it was a logical step to utilize a small air–air heat pump that could extract some of this heat and provide the shortfall in heat, plus a bit more. This could be accomplished for a relatively small input of electricity for the compressor.

Following on from this, there is also a hot-water demand that cannot always be met by solar. It therefore made sense to incorporate a hot-water cylinder into the system, such that water could be heated at times when the room heating was satisfied. Having two places for the heat to go (rooms and hot water), it was possible to pre-heat one whilst heating the other and vice versa, if necessary. It was also possible to control the system so as to direct the heat appropriately, as required at any one time. The 'compact unit' is a convenient package that can satisfy the energy requirements for low-energy houses, even in mid-winter. It only applies to exceptionally well-insulated houses, since the heat available in ventilation is a relatively large proportion of the total heat demand.

Although system designs can be very different, the typical COP achieved by a good compact unit is in the region of 3. This does not sound highly impressive. However, we must be careful of these figures. The passive, plate heat-exchanger can, at times, recover a very high quantity of heat for only 50W. Ironically, if the passive heat-exchanger is small and inefficient, then the heat pump's COP can look better, but the overall efficiency of the unit is worse. It is therefore very important to look at real house test data rather than the efficiencies of a specific piece of the equipment.

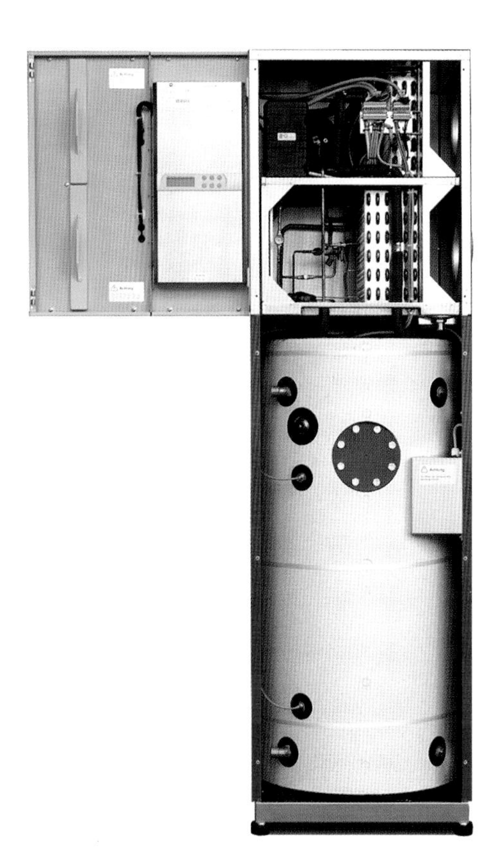

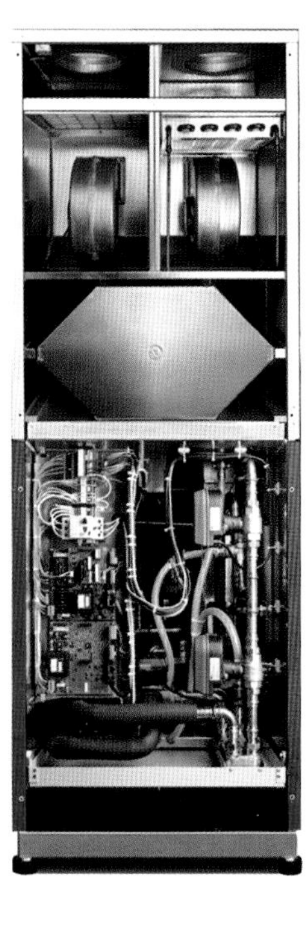

Cutaway showing the inner workings of two Drexel and Weiss compact units. (Drexel and Weiss GmbH.)

The left-hand model (*see* page 72) shows the water cylinder with heat-pump unit above, and the passive heat-recovery unit is within the blue section (top-left). The right-hand model shows the squashed hexagon-shaped, high-efficiency, part-parallel, plate heat-exchanger in the middle. Above are fans for air in and air out. This one actually combines a ground-source heat-pump below to provide a net heat input, which is designed to work in combination with a standard solar hot-water system. This particular unit can be used with PassivHaus or houses that are well-insulated, but not super-insulated, so need extra heat input.

It is probably worth a word of caution here, since the variation in quality and efficiency of equipment can vary considerably. Better manufacturers would have a good track record and available field data from installed systems. Such systems will be not be cheap, but should last a very long time, so are an investment for the future.

Domestic Hot-Water (DHW)

Hot water is universally piped to every bath, shower and sink. It is a comfort that we take for granted and is usually referred to as domestic hot-water, or the abbreviation DHW. In the past, the amount of energy that a household would expend on this commodity was only in the order of one-fifth that of the total heating usage. With the trend towards greater insulation of buildings, the space-heating demand has dropped considerably, whilst hot-water demand has remained static, or if anything, has increased. The energy used for hot water is now the biggest proportion of the total for some very low-energy houses. This means that instead of hot water being seen as a by-product of the main heating and requiring secondary attention, it is now becoming the component that needs the biggest consideration.

The use of hot-water cylinders to store heated water is a method we are familiar with. However, combi-boilers can instantly heat water, such that water is only heated as it is required. This method had proved popular and is now very common and has the advantages of space-saving and no standing heat losses of a hot-water storage cylinder. The energy losses for both types, instant combi-boiler, or conventional storage in a cylinder, are not clear-cut, so both types remain prominent in the market place.

Solar heating systems always need a storage cylinder and do not easily integrate with instant gas heaters. So the current popularity for solar water heating is no doubt shifting the market back towards the conventional boiler and hot-water storage cylinder.

Heat pumps also require cylinders, since it would be impractical to make a heat pump that could respond quickly enough to the sporadic nature of hot-tap use. All in all, the hot-water cylinder is unlikely to disappear.

Configuration for Heating and Hot Water

Most heat-pump models currently available have the facility to heat a hot-water cylinder as well as room heating. The normal configuration would be for it to 'divert' from one function to the other. For example, it may heat under-floor at 35°C then divert for a period and operate at an elevated temperature of up to 60°C for the hot water, then return to 35°C, as required. This arrangement ensures that hot-water heating does not compromise the energy efficiency of room heating.

Some heat pumps have the cylinder built in and can, in some cases, be cleverly optimized to achieve higher performances with high water temperatures.

The upper temperature limit of different heat

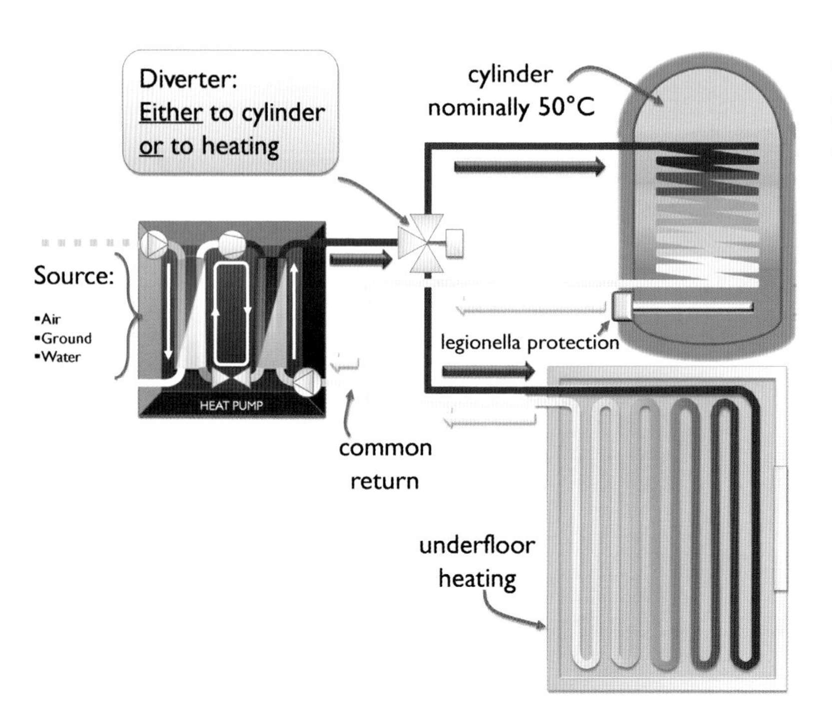

Diagram showing typical pipe configuration for heating and hot-water modes.

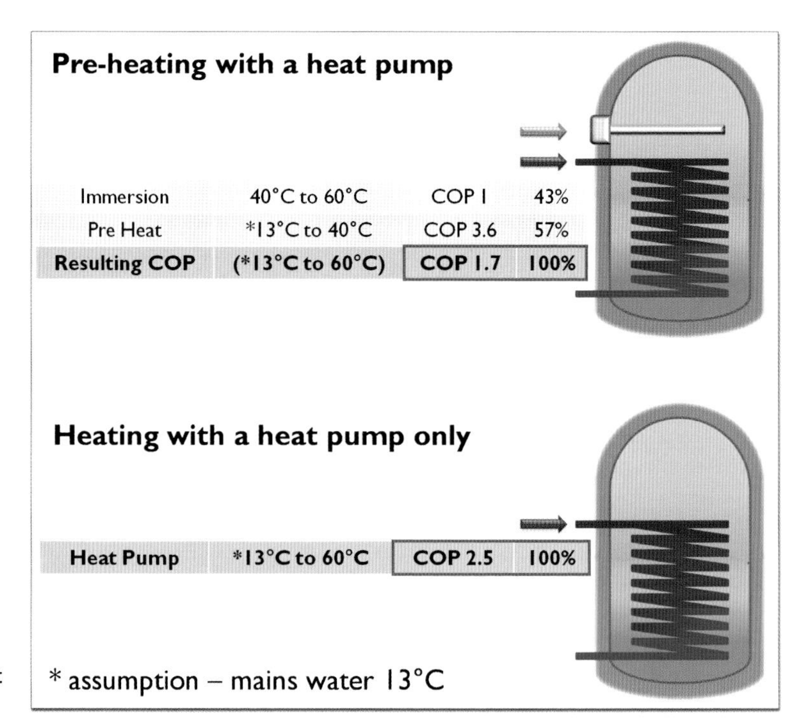

Comparing pre-heat arrangement with heat pump only.

pump models varies and is mostly affected by the type of refrigerant used. Some achieve only 50°C, others 65°C.

It is not easy for manufacturers to optimize their heat pumps to operate efficiently over a very wide range of temperatures and this is why some manufacturers offer a 'high' temperature range and a 'medium' temperature range.

The illustration opposite shows a system operating all the way to 60°C (assuming it can achieve this) and compares it to a pre-heat arrangement that is topped-up by an immersion heater. The immersion with its COP of 1, knocks back the net COP more than you might first expect. This demonstrates how it is always best to use the heat pump in favour of the immersion heater.

The Calorex Powergen system, as shown in our case studies, was specifically designed to achieve temperatures of 65°C, thus eliminating the need for any electric top-up heating. It has a track record of good results.

Cylinder Types

Conventional Cylinder

This is the cylinder arrangement that we are most familiar with. A coiled heat-exchanger transfers heat to the cylinder from the primary water of the heat pump. The size of the coil is very important when a heat pump is used, since, for the sake of energy efficiency (COP), the coil needs to be significantly bigger than an equivalent boiler-fed system. Ideally the coil would be around three times the size of one for a comparable boiler system – 3m^2 of surface area not being uncommon for a typical domestic heat-pump. The diagram on page 76 indicates the difference between a cylinder designed to be heated by a boiler and one to be heated with a heat pump.

Note: A heat pump works just as well with either a finned or plain coil – it just needs to be big enough.

Some cylinders are in the form of a tank inside

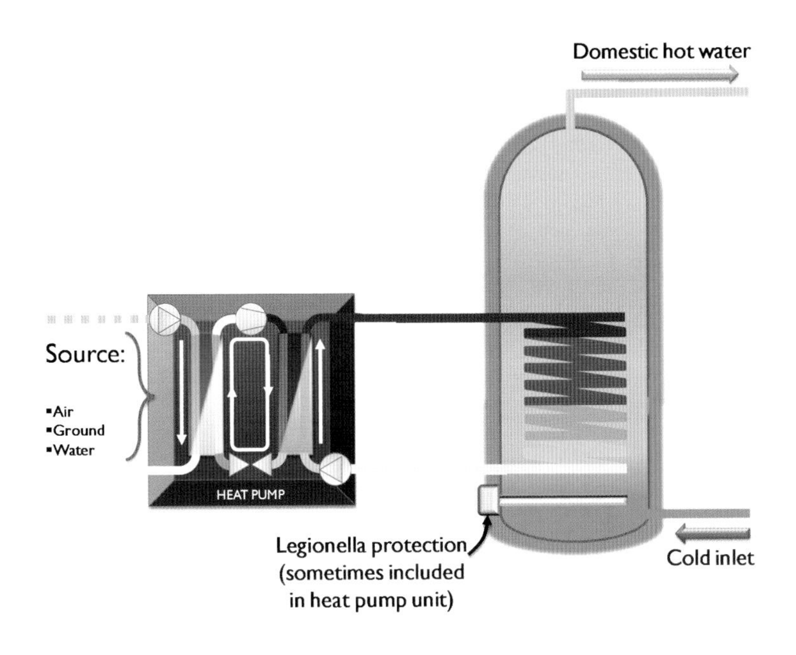

Conventional cylinder with heat-exchanger coil.

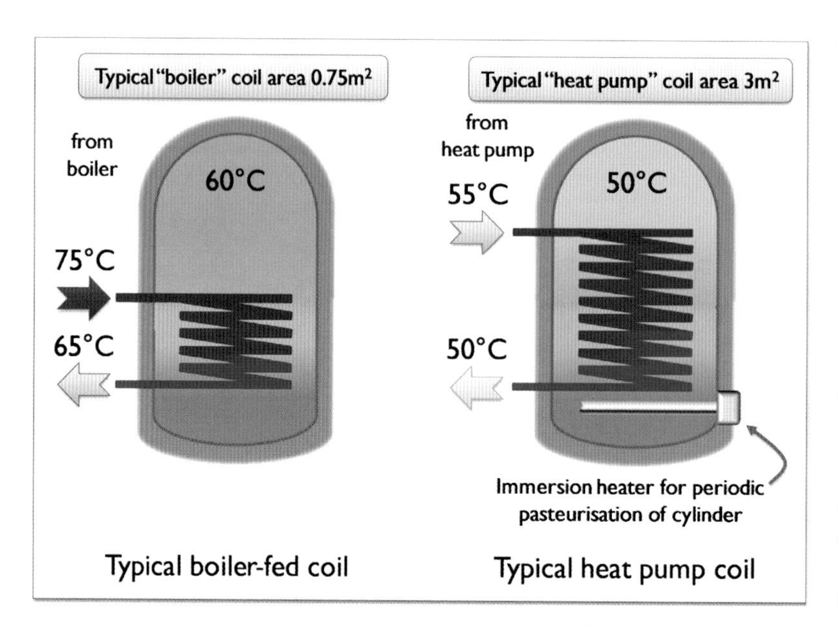

TOP: Diagram of boiler-fed vs heat pump-fed cylinder coils.

BELOW: The larger coil on the left is bigger, and 'finned' to enhance the heat exchange. On the right is a standard boiler coil. (Newark Copper Cylinders Ltd.)

a tank. These are made of stainless steel. The inner is the hot-water store and the outer is the equivalent to the coil.

Whilst manufacturers of one type often seem to disapprove of the other type, we find that either method gives equally good results.

As hot water is drawn off from the top of the cylinder, cold water enters at the bottom. A natural principle called 'stratification' keeps the cold at the bottom and the hot at the top. This is helpful, since the hot water can remain at a useful temperature, even if the bottom half is full of cold water.

Thermal Store

This term is usually used to describe a system where a cylinder of water is heated directly from the heat pump. The heat is transferred to the tap water by passing mains pressure water through a coil in the cylinder.

Advantages:

- Water is instantly heated from cold so *Legionella* risk (*see* page 78) is minimized or eliminated.
- Hot distribution pipes are at mains pressure, so small-bore distribution pipes can be used; this saves heat and water.

Disadvantages:

- Water temperature is flow-dependent: high flow causes a drop in temperature.

Heat pump configured to provide DHW with 'thermal store'.

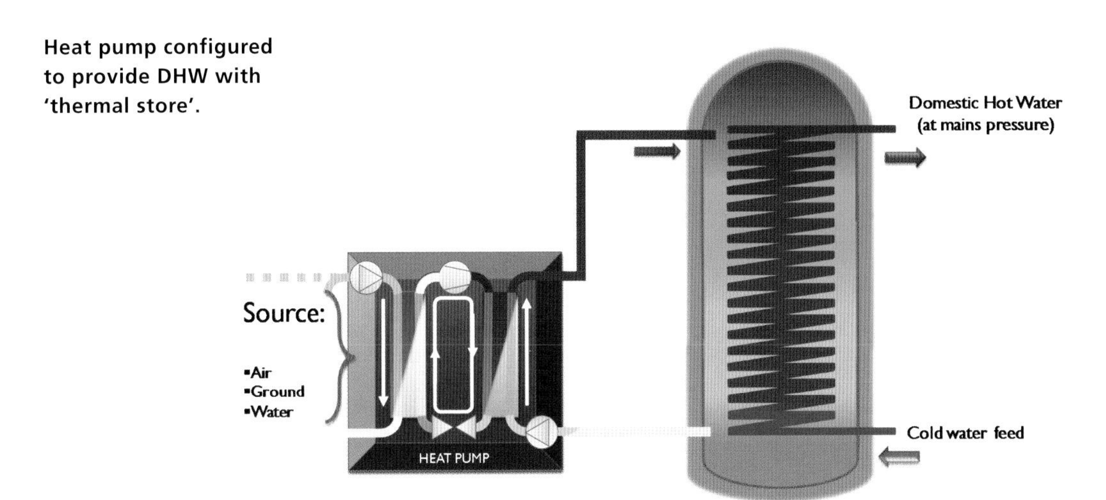

- Heat is taken from all levels within the cylinder as the cold water passes the heat-exchanger coil. This reduces stratification, so the compressor can switch on more frequently.

Thermal store cylinders can also be used as a combined buffer cylinder. This can compromise the efficiency of room heating unless it is designed well. This could, however, be a neat solution if optimized carefully.

We hesitate to draw conclusions with respect to the choice between conventional and thermal store. The conventional cylinder can at first sight promise better energy efficiency and a reduced risk of a bath running cold at the end. However, the thermal store can offer many advantages. It is a system that could be developed and may prove to be the winner in the future.

Clearly, the topic of hot-water heating is one that will evolve over time. Our current methods usually cause the heat pump to operate only towards its upper (less efficient) limit, but there is plenty of scope for optimization, if there was a need. In the near future we will no doubt see systems like CO_2-refrigerant heat-pumps with optimized cylinders that promise considerable savings when heating water from cold up to hot.

The possibility of 'batch heating' from cold is just one example of a method that could be employed at only the cost of an increased cylinder size and a few standard components. This could significantly improve the water-heating COP; however, the controllers of many heat

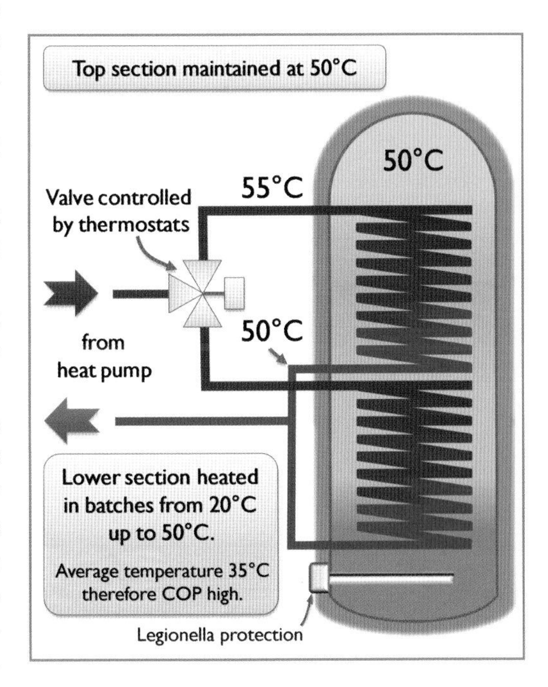

Diagram of batch heating cylinder.

pumps cannot cater for any deviation from their standard configurations.

Legionella

Legionella is a type of bacteria that can breed in warm water and is transmitted though the air. The most well-known outbreaks of serious illnesses were caused by air-borne transmission from very large air-conditioning water cooling-towers.

Solar heating cylinders are one area for concern, since they could remain tepid for long periods in the winter. Heat-pump cylinders may also favour lower temperatures, since they are less efficient at high temperatures and storage temperatures of 45°C might be chosen for sake of energy efficiency. At such temperatures, there is potential for the cylinders to serve as a breeding ground for *Legionella* bacteria, which can cause infections classed as legionellosis, resulting in either legionnaire's disease or Pontiac fever. It should be noted that only a small percentage of the population are susceptible to infection by *Legionella*, but if infected, the consequences can be extremely serious.

Legionella bacteria could be present in the domestic water supply in small quantities. However, if water lays dormant, the bacteria have the chance to rapidly multiply and spread. The table below shows the characteristics of Legionella bacteria over a range of temperatures.

If a cylinder were kept no lower than 50°C, there should be no multiplication, but any contamination would not be killed off. For this reason, cylinders should be periodically heated to 60°C (or to current regulations). Some heat pumps can achieve a cylinder temperature of 60°C, but many cannot reach such temperatures and an electric element is generally used to top-up to the required temperature. The required frequency of sterilization is debatable and some controllers offer settings for this action once weekly, others do it daily. It is unfortunate that the energy demand for this regular, direct, electric heating can be significant, so this issue must be addressed sensibly.

Distributing the Hot Water to the Taps

The detail of getting the hot water to the taps should not be overlooked, since potentially a lot of water and heat can be wasted. We have all experienced taps that take a considerable time before running hot. This is not only a waste of water, but also a loss of heat, since the pipe-run is always left hot after the tap has been turned off. Considerable savings can be made if the pipe runs are optimized.

The chart illustrated opposite comes from the AECB Water Standard. It shows how much water is contained in pipe runs. If a pipe is too small, then the flow rate will be low. If it is too big, it will potentially be a waste of water

Temperature	Legionellae Survival Characteristic
70 to 80 °C	Disinfection range – Legionellae die completely.
At 66 °C	Legionellae die within 2 minutes of exposure to temperature.
At 60 °C	Legionellae die within 32 minutes of exposure to temperature.
At 55 °C	Legionellae die within 5 to 6 hours of exposure to temperature.
50 to 55 °C	Legionellae can survive but do not multiply in this range of temperature.
20 to 50 °C	Legionellae can multiply and grow within this range of temperature.
35 to 46 °C	Ideal growth range for Legionellae.
Below 20 °C	Legionellae can survive but are dormant below this temperature.

Characteristics of *Legionella* bacteria.

Water pipe outside diameter (mm)	10	10	12	15	15	22	22
Material	Plastic	Copper	Copper	Plastic	Copper	Plastic	Copper
Wall Thickness (mm)	1.7	0.6	0.6	1.7	0.7	2.2	0.9
Litres per metre	0.03	0.06	0.09	0.11	0.15	0.24	0.32
Metres per litre	33.3	16.7	11.1	9.1	6.7	4.2	3.1

Pipe sizes and water volumes. Figures taken from AECB water standard.

and heat. This is sometimes referred to as a dead-leg loss.

It is interesting to note the difference in the internal bore size of plastic and copper, due to the wall thickness. This has a very large effect on the flow resistance, so it is a mistake to think that 15mm copper acts anything like 15mm plastic.

To find out how much water is contained in your distribution pipes, it might be worth doing an experiment. First thing in the morning, before any water has been used, place a bowl in a sink and turn on the hot tap until it runs hot. The volume in the sink is the same volume of hot that remains in the pipes after hot-tap use. It might be possible to reduce this by modifying the pipe runs.

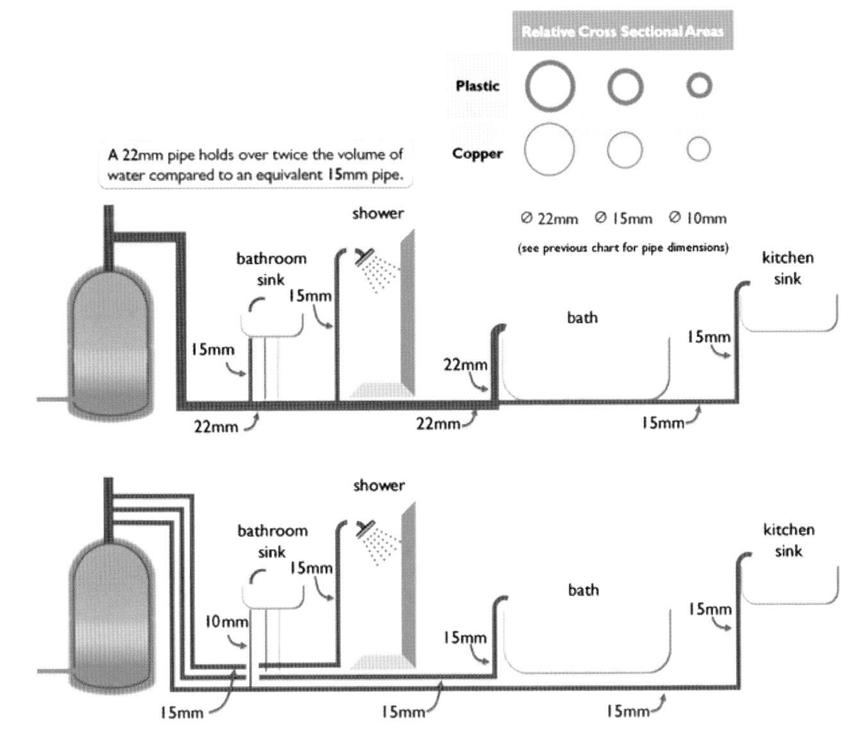

Improving pipe-runs to minimize water and heat losses.

The traditional method of piping taps is to start with a large diameter and to reduce-down as you branch off to each tap. Typically, the run to the bath is large and this may extend on to other taps. Waste occurs when, for example, a kitchen sink uses the same big pipe run as the bath. Kitchen sinks can be used very frequently, so it could be beneficial to run a separate smaller pipe directly from the cylinder to this sink. A multi-outlet manifold could be fitted at the cylinder so that several separate supply pipes run directly to sinks. A compromise between the two examples may be the most viable solution and it may not be too radical to use a pipe of only 10mm diameter.

Secondary Pumped Return

This is used to overcome the delay that would occur if the taps are a long distance from the cylinder. The secondary pumped return loop is common in hotels and can result in taps running hot immediately. Considerable heat can, however, be lost when this system is used, so it should be considered carefully. The pipe runs should be insulated very well and, if they are, then the required circulation flow can be tiny and the return pipe can be very small in diameter. Pumped systems are often fitted with a time clock, such that the pump can be off at times when draw-off is unlikely; thus heat loss is minimized.

The circulation can dilute stratification, i.e. it can mix hot from the top with cold from the bottom. This is a disadvantage and the position of the return pipe from the loop should be chosen carefully. Electronic controls could be used here to minimize losses.

Solar DHW and Heat Pumps

If a heat pump and solar feed into the same cylinder, it is important to let the solar heat the bottom section of the tank. Solar is 'free' heat, so always needs a dedicated volume of water to heat.

Exhaust Air Heat and Hot-Water Heating

To maintain a healthy air quality, dwellings

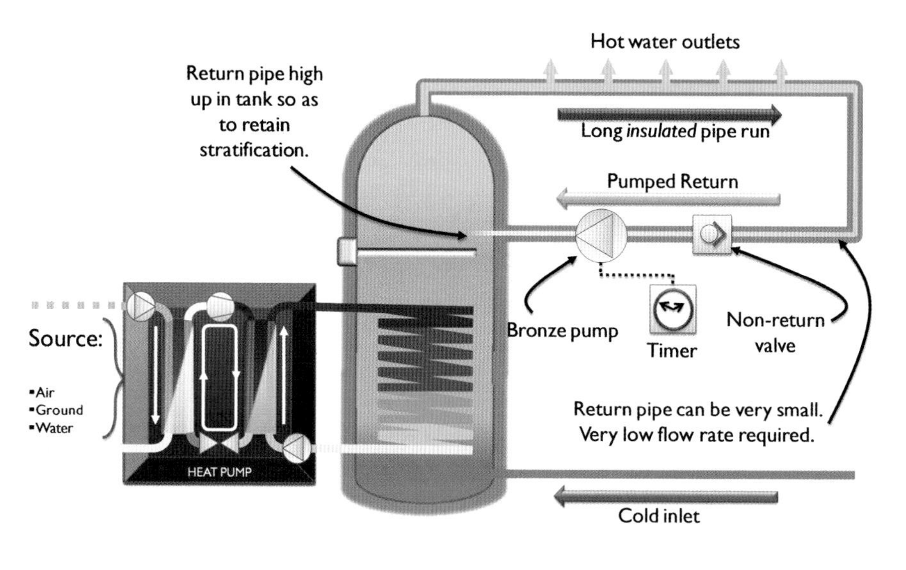

A diagram of a secondary pumped return loop.

require an exchange of air, so warm, stale air must be removed. It is interesting to note that the energy available in ventilation air is a little in excess of the energy required for our normal hot-water needs, so potentially this should be a good match. Indeed, heating water cylinders using exhaust air heat recovery is a tried and tested method for blocks of flats. However, the match is not perfect, since ventilation is required constantly, but cylinders often need to be heated in a shorter time. Once the cylinder is hot, the recoverable heat from the air is superfluous and as a consequence would be wasted (unless diverted for room heating, for example).

If the heat pump is sized to match the exhaust energy, the recovery time (the time needed to reheat the cylinder) is exceptionally slow. To reduce and improve the recovery time, it is tempting to extract more heat from the exhaust air. This could lead to a risk of ventilating at unnecessarily high rates simply to achieve adequate water heating. This is in effect robbing Peter to pay Paul and could result in an increased load on the house's heating system. That said, any exhaust-air heat-pump (used carefully) should be significantly better than an electric immersion heater.

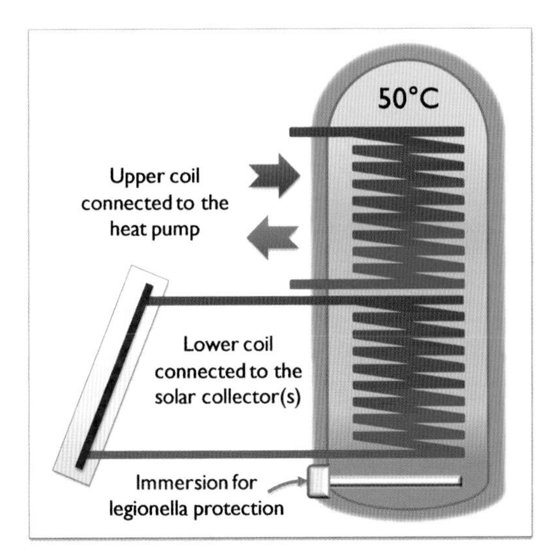

Combining a heat pump with solar thermal.

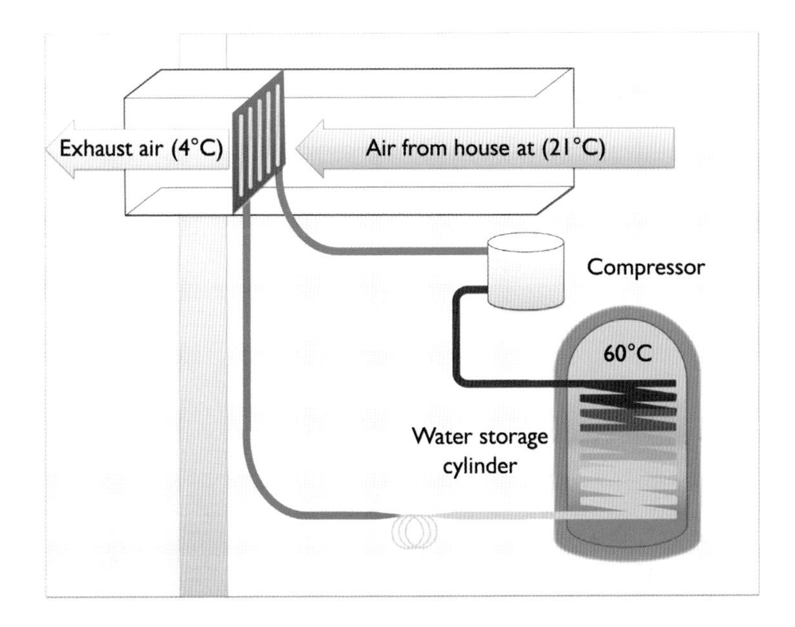

Exhaust-air heat-pump heating hot water.

Swimming Pools

A swimming pool requires a great deal of heat to keep it warm. Since it is likely to be warmer than the air above it, there is a considerable heat loss due to evaporation. This is the biggest heat loss, so it is highly recommended to use a removable cover. For larger pools, these can be retractable and automatic. Its primary purpose is to stop evaporation, so it does not necessarily need to be thick. However, the most practical product actually looks a bit like heavy-duty bubble-wrap and has the advantage of ensuring that the cover floats well, so that the upper surface can remain dry.

To give a very approximate heat-demand figure for a pool heated in summer, it might need around 150W/m^2 of surface area if a cover is used, but this could range from between 400 and 800W/m^2 if the pool had no cover.

A Duratech 19 air-source pool heater.

Most pools are operated with a timed routine for pool covering. A private pool may be covered all the time that it is not in use, which could be very considerable; this will contribute greatly to saving energy. However, community pools will probably be uncovered for a substantial number of hours per day, so the size of heat pump will need to be chosen accordingly. As the need to save energy becomes ingrained, the idea of not covering a heated pool overnight becomes unthinkable.

Equally as unthinkable in our modern age is the unheated pool, so pool heating of some form is the norm. Over the summer, there is an abundance of solar heat; however, our climate is somewhat unreliable and the large thermal capacity of a swimming pool means that it will take many days to heat it up using solar panels. For example, a sunny day might be preceded by many gloomy days, so the pool may be cold, then if we get a few successive days of sunshine followed by cloud, the pool may only just be getting warm from the solar panels when more overcast weather comes. A heat pump can, however, deliver heat more constantly, i.e. at night, or when it's overcast. In the summer, the air temperature is relatively high and, on occasions, it could even be a few degrees warmer than the pool. Air-to-water heat pumps are therefore the favourite choice for pool heating and there are many to choose from.

The water temperature of an outdoor pool is generally kept in the region of 23–30°C over the summer. This is a very agreeable temperature for heat pumps to operate at and high energy-efficiencies can be achieved. It is no surprise that the swimming-pool heat-pump industry was the first 'heating' application for heat pumps that really took off in the UK.

The unit shown opposite has an integral heat-exchanger that is resistant to the corrosive nature of swimming-pool water. This is potentially far more energy efficient than using a standard heat-pump with an extra (intermediate) heat-exchanger to deal with the corrosion issue. This is because the extra heat-exchanger introduces a temperature drop, causing the heat pump to operate with a lower COP. There is also an energy loss due to the extra circulation pump that would be needed. It's important to know exactly how energy efficient any proposed system would be, since there could be significant variations from type to type.

If you only heat your pool in the summer months, (from June to early September) then you should not have issues of ice build-up in the air heat-exchanger, so a model without a defrost mechanism could be chosen. If the pool is used for an extended season, not only will the heat pump need to be bigger, but it would need a proper defrost method to melt possible ice-build-up. Both defrost and non-defrost models are available.

A ground-source heat-pump would only be viable for pool heating if the pool were used in winter too, ground source being much more expensive to install and less energy-efficient than an air source that is running mid-summer.

If a ground-source system is already fitted to a house as a heating system, it may make sense to also use it to heat your swimming pool in summer. But it is very important to ensure that your ground collector is big enough to cope with a large summer load, since the average ground-source installation relies on a significant rest period during the summer for the ground to recover its temperature. If an extra load were put on to an existing ground source, it may be important to limit its use by monitoring the source temperature to ensure that its temperature does not drop too low. Some controllers would allow you to monitor the temperature and possibly to adjust the lower limit for the ground loop.

Indoor Pools

One would expect the greatest heat-load to be heating the pool water. However, the air above the pool actually poses a greater challenge than the water below. Water at around 28°C (typical pool temperature) will evaporate. This can be minimized by keeping the air above it (the pool hall) very slightly warmer – maybe 29°C. This does not stop evaporation, it just reduces it, and so unless something is done with the air, it is still likely to become quite humid and steamy. Such moist air is very bad for the fabric of the building, since it is bound to condense at some place within the building's structure. In the 1970s this might have been solved by simply ventilating; however, heating the fresh incoming air back up to 29°C is very energy-intensive. For energy- and money-saving reasons, some form of 'passive heat recovery' has been commonly used for many years.

Another option is to re-circulate and dehumidify the air with a self-contained heat-pump unit. Such units function by cooling the air as it enters, thus condensing-out water, then putting that heat back into the air before it returns to the pool room, with a slightly reduced humidity.

This option is not free to run, but it does contribute to the heating of the building. This heat may or may not be useful depending on the time of year. To make such systems more cost-effective and energy efficient, variations and refinements have been developed that put heat back into the pool water when it is required. Units such as these are a vital part of any indoor swimming pool. Adding passive heat recovery ventilation can be very cost-effective.

Cooling

In the British climate, the period when buildings may overheat is relatively short. None the less, overheat they may. The excess heat is often due to sunlight falling on to anything inside the room, thus warming up the room. It may also come from activities within the room that generate heat. These two issues could be minimized dramatically if dealt with at source. Clever shading of the sun will help a great deal and low-energy appliances may also help to reduce heat build-up. It is worth considering the benefits of 'weighty' buildings here, since few older buildings ever need cooling.

There are many days when the sun is strong and when buildings can overheat. However, the air outside might be cool enough, so that simply opening windows and doors will render the house at a comfortable temperature. Fan-driven extractor systems might be a better automatic method of keeping cool.

There may also be other methods that could help to a greater or lesser extent. These could include 'evaporative cooling', where the evaporation of water causes cooling of incoming air from outside. These only work to a point and rely on the incoming air being relatively dry. Ceiling fans are another option that can be very effective and are very cheap to operate. Simply keeping the windows closed when it is hotter outside than in, is an easy habit that could also help.

Whilst these methods might help, there are certain periods of the year when no help can be gained from the outside air, since it might be uncomfortably hot. At such times, some form of direct cooling, or 'air-conditioning' (as it has come to be known), might be the only option.

Air-conditioning units are simply air-to-air heat pumps and these blow (recirculate) cooled air inside the building and reject heat in the form of hot air to outside. If the outside is, for example, 30°C, the finned air-condenser from where the heat is rejected may be at quite a high temperature. On the hottest day, many air-conditioners are bordering their upper working limits. At this limit, the energy efficiency is not particularly good. However, if we have a ground-source trench or borehole, it is likely to be considerably colder than the air and is an ideal heat-sink, where the heat can literally be 'dumped'. This results in an energy-efficienct cooling system.

If we recall our original equation for the COP of a heat pump, it states:

Heat output = Heat extracted from the ground + Electrical power input.

In reverse mode (cooling) we have the following:

Cooling load (kW) + Electrical power input = Heat to ground.

If we put typical figures to the above equations, we see that the heating COP is not the same as the cooling COP. Whilst we assume in this book that COP relates to heating, we must differentiate between COP(heating) and COP(cooling):

Heating COP = Cooling COP + 1.

The energy efficiency ratio (EER) is a term more commonly used in place of the term COP(cooling) to describe the energy efficiency of refrigeration and air-conditioning equipment.

Passive Cooling

The passive method of cooling is much cheaper to operate, since it functions by circulating the ground liquid directly around under-floor heating or fan-coils without the heat-pump compressor running. This system may operate satisfactorily until mid-summer, when the temperature of the ground source may rise to a point where it is no longer cold enough to be of use. Too many very hot days in summer might render it useless. Since the energy used to circulate the liquid may be only 5 per cent that of the compressor power, this option should be used, if possible, and is sometimes called 'free cooling'. It may, however, have a limited effect if the trenches are shallow or the ground is relatively dry. Boreholes are usually a better proposition for passive cooling.

It is possible to use passive cooling up to the point when the 'cold' has been exhausted. At this point the compressor can start and the system can become 'active'. Thus you get the best of both worlds by having as much free cooling as possible, but also cooling via the heat pump if needed.

It is worth mentioning that there may also be a demand for hot water when a heat pump is operating in cooling mode. At such times the system could be configured to heat your hot water, whilst simultaneously cooling your rooms – an elegant arrangement.

Regenerating Ground Collectors

Any of the above cooling applications using a ground-source system will be outputting heat into the ground and consequently re-charging the ground with heat. It may therefore be possible to fit a smaller collector than would otherwise be needed with a heat-only system.

Some caution must be taken over this strategy for domestic situations since the amount of energy dumped into the ground may be a small proportion of the total heating taken in winter. Any heat dumped into the ground may only speed-up its recovery from the previous winter and it may not translate into a warmer trench come January and February.

In commercial situations, the heating and cooling loads may be more equal, since incidental gains can be considerably higher. Offices might have far more solar gain and far more internal heat generated from office equipment and server rooms, for example. In such cases the 'ins' and 'outs' may be a good match and a borehole array may be acting as a giant buffer store. This may be important in urban locations where ground space is limited and borehole arrays could be more compact.

Any form of passive cooling should be of benefit, since any heat input to the ground is a good thing and passive cooling is almost free to operate. It should be remembered that active heat-pump cooling is not free and it may be a mistake to think that the use of this system in summer is having a significant benefit with respect to total annual running costs. It is usually better to minimize both the cooling or heating demand of the building by good housekeeping methods before switching on a heat pump.

Whilst on the topic of regeneration, it may be possible to improve a situation where an undersized ground collector has been installed. Small collectors get colder and colder as winter passes and the COP diminishes in the process. However, there is still a significant amount of solar radiation in winter. A winter month's energy could be almost a fifth that of a summer month's energy. A simple un-glazed solar collector could be configured to circulate the brine (which might be around 0°C) around the borehole or trench. This is unlikely to be a cost-effective option for an installer, but a possible way for a practical individual to improve a system's COP or alleviate problems caused by an under-performing ground-collector. For back-of-envelope calculations, the sun can deliver almost 1kW/m^2 on bright, sunny days, even in winter. However, such times are very infrequent and the total heat delivered by this manner may be relatively small.

CHAPTER 7

HEATING HOUSES

In this section we explore things from a different viewpoint. We look at the heat demand of the building, see how heat pumps can fulfil this need and then consider the implication of different design options.

When we are not involved in strenuous activities, we humans tend to be most comfortable in surroundings with temperatures of around 19–21°C, and this is what we have come to expect from our living environment.

It is important to note that the room's air temperature is not the only factor to consider, since radiant heat also contributes to comfort. This radiation comes not only from the walls, the floor, the ceiling, but also every object in the room. We don't feel comfortable when surrounded by cold walls since they radiate little back to us. In effect, they absorb the radiation that we emit. If, however, the walls or the floor are warm, we can feel quite comfortable even if the air is relatively cool. Indeed, this can be a very healthy environment, with the added bonus that ventilation heat losses due to air changes are reduced if the internal air temperature is lower.

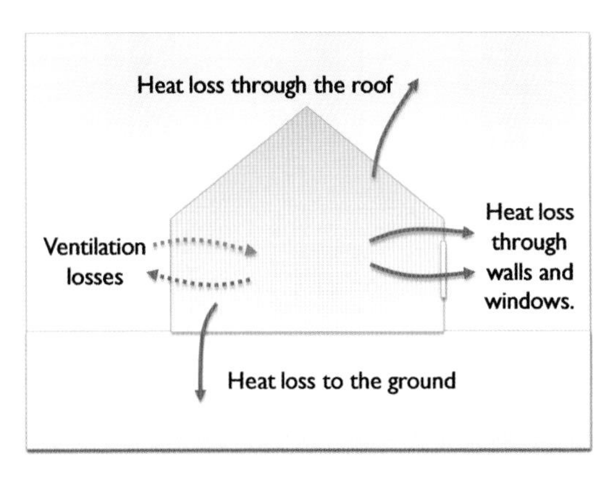

Home heat energy losses.

The issue of radiation has implications for intermittent heating. If time clocks are used and rooms are heated-up from cold, then the walls will lag behind the air temperature. To achieve comparable comfort, the air temperature will inevitably need to be warmer to compensate, since the wall surfaces may take a long time to warm fully. This is confirmed by the claim that under-floor heated rooms can achieve 'comfort' with air temperatures some 2°C lower than conventionally heated rooms.

In order to design a heating system to achieve comfortable indoor conditions, we need to consider how much heat might be needed.

The heat that we put into a building is constantly escaping through the fabric of the structure. It also escapes due to the necessary ventilation air changes (hot out and cold in), without which our houses would become stuffy and unhealthy.

Assessing Heat Requirements

The UK Government's Standard Assessment

Procedure (SAP) is a methodology for calculating the energy performance of buildings. It is used to demonstrate compliance with building regulations for dwellings. This is a comprehensive means of estimating not only the heat demand of the building on the coldest days, but also the expected annual energy demand by using localized weather data in the form of degree-days. Degree-days are a relatively simple method of indexing the heat demand at any location. To make the necessary calculations, an outside (summer) temperature is chosen where no heat should be needed. This varies from house to house. For example, the room's natural internal temperature might be a few degrees above the outside temperature due to incident gains from appliances, occupants and the sun. A typical baseline temperature is 15.5°C, and no heating should be needed at this outside temperature.

The degree-day figure is based on this baseline temperature. For example:

If the outside temperature were on average 10°C for 24h and the baseline temperature is 15.5°C, the degree-day figure total would be:

$$(15.5 - 10) \times 1 \text{ day} = 5.5.$$

On a mid-winter's day with an average temperature of zero, the degree-day figure for that day would be:

$$(15.5 - 0) \times 1 \text{ day} = 15.5.$$

Typical figures for the whole year for the UK can range from 1,500 to 2,200, depending on location. These figures are published for each geographical area year on year. Given a design heat loss for the building and a degree-day figure, one can estimate how much total energy should be needed over the year.

SAP is more concerned with energy consumption of a building than as a tool for assessing the heat demand of a building in mid-winter. There are many different methods that heating engineers use for estimating the heat demand of a building. This can be carried out longhand by simple maths related to the 'U' values of every element of the building. To make it easy, many online calculator programs are available where one can enter the sizes of walls, ceilings and windows, etc. and enter the materials that they are made of. The expected ventilation rate will also be included. The calculated result estimates how many kilowatts of heat should be needed to keep the house warm on the coldest days.

It is worth noting that the usual heat-loss design temperature is many degrees higher than the minimum air temperature experienced. For example, the minimum temperature might be –10°C (apart from extremes), whilst the average minimum temperature over 24h will usually be several degrees warmer and would be a more representative figure to work with. A typical design temperature might be –3°C.

Maths aside, there are also rules of thumb that are used to estimate heat demand. A heat value per square metre of living space can give a reasonable assessment of likely requirements for a comfortable internal living temperature. For reasonably well-insulated buildings built to current building regulations, the heat demand may be in the order of $50 W/m^2$. Old buildings could require as much as twice this and a super-insulated PassivHaus could call for only $10 W/m^2$ floor area.

The shape of the building should be considered when using such estimates. For example, a long, thin house will have more outside walls than a square house and will therefore require more heat. Likewise, a house has fewer ceilings and floors losing heat than a bungalow.

Sizing Heating Systems

Apart from the old kitchen range that might be

kept burning continuously, we have traditionally heated buildings only when we need them warm. Boiler systems are often operated on a time clock, since there may seem little point in heating a building when you are not at home. Thus any boiler must be big and powerful enough so as to heat a room or building in a fairly short period of time, for example it might switch on at 6am ready for us waking maybe one or two hours later. There is always the contingency of running extra time to cope in the depth of winter. The actual size of boiler obviously needs to be considerably bigger than our estimates of steady-state heat needs.

If the heating were enabled continuously, day and night, we would expect to use considerably more fuel. However, we actually need to inject less total heat than one would think to achieve comparable comfort. As previously mentioned, the temperature of the room's internal fabric is important. But a further factor favours continuous heating with heat pumps. With continuous heating, the emitter temperature can be considerably lower, this improves the COP of the heat pump significantly. If a radiator is on all the time, is very surprising how 'tepid' it may be and still maintain a warm room.

Even if a constant-heating strategy is adopted, it remains true that the heat loss of a building relates to its average temperature, so dropping the temperature at night just a degree or two may save some energy. This may or may not be deemed worth the complexity, but if the function is already fitted to your controller, it could be used. The type of building obviously plays a part here and buildings that retain their heat are more likely to favour a more continuous heating regime.

Sizing Heat Pumps

There are further reasons why the continuous-heating strategy may be favoured for heat-pump installations, namely:

- It is too expensive to install a heat-pump system that is big enough for quick heat-up. Not only would the heat pump need to be big, but the radiators and other parts of the system would need to be larger to some degree.
- It is better to run a little heat pump with longer run-periods. There is no 'strain' implied here, to the contrary, a smaller heat pump is likely to encounter less strain than a large one. One of the reasons for this is that the radiators or under-floor heating are likely to be at a lower temperature, hence the energy efficiency will be higher.
- The number of compressor stops and starts will tend be less with a smaller heat pump, especially during spring and autumn. This not only reduces wear and tear, but improves the energy efficiency.
- All in all, large heat pumps that run less frequently are rarely viable (unless off-peak electricity is used).

If we design for continuous heating, we need more accurately to match the maximum heat demand of the building to the heat-pump size, so that it may run all day and all night on the coldest days. Since manufacturers offer heat pumps in only specific sizes (e.g. 5kW, 7kW, 9kW, 11kW), the choice of size may involve some aspect of logical compromise, rather than it being based on accurate heat-loss calculations. Borderline selection sizing is not uncommon.

Taking the sizing issue a step further, if we look at the outside air temperatures over the average winter, the number of hours at 'minimum' temperature is few. So we could consider fitting a relatively small heat-pump and boosting the output with an alternative 'less economical' heating method, given that the cost of this could be a small fraction of the total yearly heating bill.

This method of operation was developed in Sweden where it was found practical and economical to fit a heat pump as small as two-thirds the expected maximum heat demand (kW) of a building. In their case, direct electricity being the favourite 'top up', in part due to the abundance of hydropower electricity.

The graph below helps us to see how small the winter 'peak demand' can be. The curve shows a Midlands UK city's yearly outside temperatures in a line, arranged (sorted) with the coldest to the left. We notice that the number of hours below zero Celsius, for example, only account for a small proportion of the heating season's heat. (The area under the graph represents the quantity of heat required.)

As can be seen, the number of hours that the temperatures dropped below zero was only about 500 hours (6 per cent of the year). We have also added an example heat demand (kW) that falls-off to zero at 15°C outside. It may, therefore, be acceptable to use a top-up electric heater or boiler to boost (add to) the heat pump's output, thus making up for the shortfall represented by the area of the small blue triangle as compared to the area of the triangle above the 15.5°C line.

Supplementary Heating with Heat Pumps

Where a heat-pump system is designed also to operate with a secondary heat source, it is often referred to as bivalent. This secondary heating is only made to operate if the heat pump cannot supply adequate heat (in terms of kW output), or if it cannot achieve a high enough temperature.

This type of heat source can have a host of names depending on the manufacturer and includes 'supplementary', 'secondary', 'additional', 'auxiliary', 'top-up', 'back-up'. In this book, we tend to use mostly descriptive terms for the specific context.

This supplementary heater generally comes in two forms:

- An electric heater, which is often integral to the heat-pump unit.
- A gas or oil boiler.

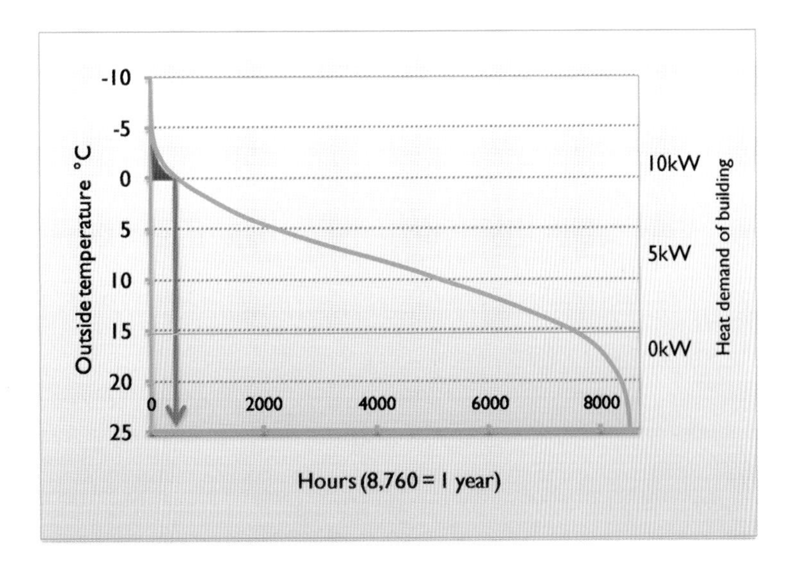

Number of hours below specific temperatures, ranked in order.

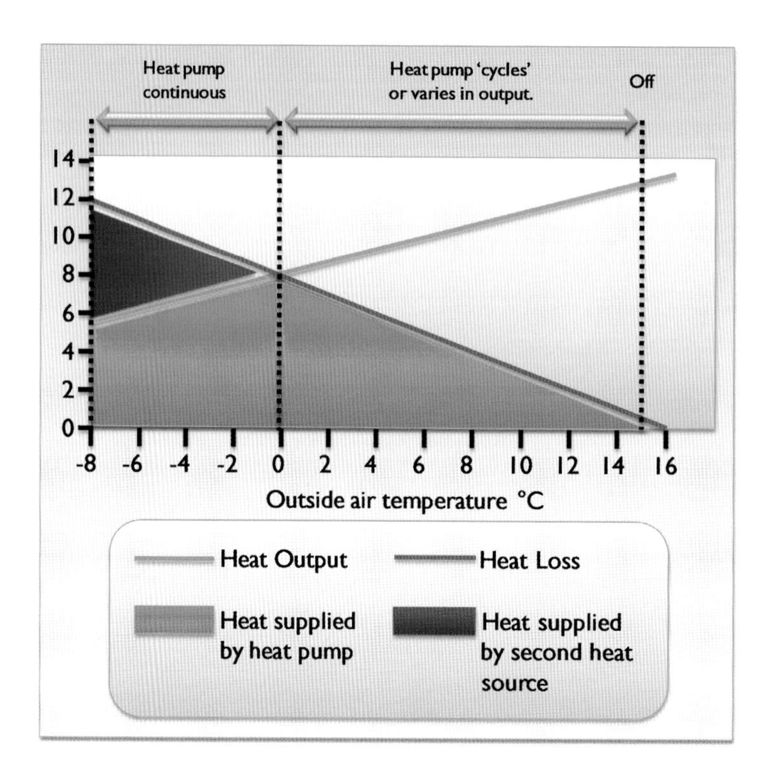

Graph showing heat pump operating with back-up heat source.

The 'undersized' heat pump can cope with the full heating load down to a certain point, where its heat output equals the theoretical heat demand for the house. Any weather colder than this is likely to require support from the secondary heat source.

The graph above shows the outside temperature on the horizontal scale. The maximum heat demand of the building coincides with the coldest outside temperature and the heat demand drops off to zero when it is around 16°C outside (where incidental gains within the house satisfy the heat demand). The relationship roughly follows a straight line.

The heat output, as shown on the graph, is typical of an air-source heat-pump and follows a slope inclined at an opposing angle; the potential heat output is at its minimum when the outside temperature is lowest. The slope of a ground source would be almost flat, since the ground is a more stable temperature, hence the output is more constant.

At any temperature warmer than the crossover point (or bivalent point), the heat pump periodically switches off, as appropriate. Anywhere below this point, it is likely to run continuously and require support from another heat source.

An electrical heater is by far the easiest, simplest and most straightforward method of supplementary heating. The heating element itself is just like a normal immersion-heater element, as fitted to most domestic hot-water cylinders. In the case of the heat pump, it is usually fitted inside the heat pump on the water outlet side of the unit, or it can be fitted into a buffer cylinder, if there is one.

Internal electric back-up heaters can easily be incorporated into heat-pump units, and for this reason many manufacturers fit them whether they are used or not. They may also perform the important role of *legionella* protection of the hot-water cylinder.

Since the period of heating shortfall is relatively small, the net contribution provided by this secondary heating will also be small. It is found in practice that a heat pump sized at 75 per cent of the buildings coldest-day heat demand, it can provide about 95 per cent of the energy. However, if an integral electric heater provides the shortfall, it may be more representative to show it in relation to the actual reduction in COP as shown by the chart below.

The 5 per cent provided by the electric heater is produced expensively, so this translates to an overall loss of 12.5 per cent in this example and the COP would reduce from 3.5 to 3.1. This may be acceptable compromise, but it's a matter of keeping an eye on statistics.

One can see the advantages of fitting a small heat-pump alongside a back-up heater, but this strategy is not universally agreed. In countries like the UK and Germany, many advocate a heat pump large enough to provide all heat requirements, with no back-up heating. This may depend on the country's energy costs, or methods of electricity production.

If the back-up heating comes from a boiler, the heated water may be 'blended' into the heat-pump's flow water using a modulating mixing valve or it may be injected into a buffer cylinder. There are many configurations and options for the integration of a boiler and each manufacturer has its own methods.

A back-up method using a boiler may be a worthwhile arrangement in an older property where the boiler and emitters are already installed and in good condition. The heat pump, which may be considerably smaller than the installed boiler, can take the heating load for much of the year, but the boiler would be available to supplement when the heat pump is inadequate. If old radiators are used, it might be necessary for the boiler to take full load, since the heat pump's upper temperature limit may be exceeded when full-heat is required to the rooms.

Such arrangements might suit an air-source system. The heat pump can offer a valuable contribution during intermediate weather conditions, whilst allowing the boiler to take the lion's share of the load in mid-winter when the air source's efficiency would be at its lowest.

				Energy input compared to total heat output
Example 1	Heat Pump	100%	COP 3.5	28.5%
Example 2	Heat Pump	95%	COP 3.5	27%
	Electric Heater	5%	COP 1	5%
	Total	100%	COP 3.1	32%

Reduction in energy efficiency is about 12.5%

Effect of electric heater on heat-pump efficiency.

Whilst the boiler-assisted bivalent method is far more common in Germany than it is in the UK, one would think that the boiler back-up would be a viable option for many installations in existing buildings.

Bivalent Control Strategies

The normal control strategy monitors the outside temperature. If this is below a certain temperature (0°C in our previous graph), then the secondary heater is ready for duty, if required. The next stage of the control strategy can have many forms but, in general, the heated water temperature is monitored to see if it is near its set-point (setting). If significantly lower, it is likely that the heat pump needs assistance and some form of time delay is started. Unless the temperature rises appreciably during the delay period, the heater will switch on and add heat to the system, but will only do so for as long as it takes to achieve the water set-point. In the mean time, the heat pump keeps running.

Switching Off the Heat Pump During Low Ambient Conditions

Unlike a ground-source system, an air-source heat-pump will have a low efficiency when the air temperature is at its lowest. In cases where such a heat pump is operating alongside a gas boiler, it may be advantageous to divert all the load over to the boiler, since the boiler may be cheaper to run or deemed to use less CO_2 during such times. It is usually possible to set a cut-off temperature limit where the heat pump stops and the boiler takes over.

The Maximum Temperature Limit of a Heat Pump

Any heat pump will have a maximum water temperature limit. This can range from 50°C up to 65°C, depending on the model. If the heating system requires a temperature in excess of this, it would be necessary for the heat pump to stop running and allow the electric heater or boiler to take full heating load.

Note: Some heat pumps claim high temperature capabilities, but sometimes this already involves the automatic use of an internal electric heater.

Typical examples of bivalent operation include:

- Electric back-up fitted internally to heat pump. Heater assists when heat pump cannot maintain required temperature. Heater elevates temperature of hot-water cylinder for *Legionella* protection.
- Oil boiler back-up in an old building. The boiler assists the heat pump below say 2°C outside. If the radiators need to be above 55°C, (due to weather compensation control) the heat pump stops and the boiler takes full load.
- Gas boiler back-up with air source. The gas boiler assists the heat pump in ambient temperatures below zero. The heat pump stops at –5°C where it is thought the boiler is more beneficial.

The above three examples illustrate parallel, alternative and part-parallel operation, respectively.

Wood as a Back-Up Fuel

As we have mentioned, a relatively small heat-pump is often fitted. This may be sized very close to the design heat-loss of the building. This can be a little risky since, if the building needs to be heated from cold in winter for some reason, it could take some considerable time. It is some comfort to the occupant (and the installer) to know that there is some form of back-up. Wood-heating could fill this need very nicely. This type

> **JARGON BUSTER**
>
> **Monovalent:** Heat pump heats the building alone, without help.
> **Bivalent:** Heat pump operates with support from an alternative heater.
> **Dual-mode:** Control function for a heat pump with alternative heating device.
> **Bivalent parallel:** Heat pump continues to operate alongside secondary heater.
> **Bivalent – alternative:** Heat pump stops and alternative heater takes full heating load.
> **Part-parallel:** Heat pump can operate along with secondary heater to a certain limit, then it stops and the secondary heater takes over.
> **Mono-energetic:** This is a bivalent system where the secondary heater is electric. Therefore there is only one energy source: electricity.
> **Bivalent point or dual-mode point:** Outside temperature below which the back-up may be required. This setting is a parameter configured into the controller.

of back-up is not considered bivalent since there is no control communication between the two heating devices. It could, however, be a viable combination in more rural areas and could promise a low environmental impact since wood is a relatively low-carbon fuel. It may have the following advantages:

- The heat pump is automatic and can provide energy-efficient background heating in mid-winter.
- Heat pump could supply full heating in spring and autumn, efficiently.
- The occupant has the choice to light a fire if they choose, thus potentially saving electricity.
- The stove may be lit less frequently than wood-only heating.
- Rapid heat-up could be achieved, if necessary.
- Contingency for extreme winters.

Given that air-source heat-pumps give a lower COP in mid-winter, it could be possible to provide some background heat with the air-source, but to rely significantly on wood-burning in the middle of winter, therefore using the air source predominantly when its efficiency is high. This option is not everyone's preferred solution since it requires a significant amount of work, but for those who already use wood, a relatively small heat pump could be a worthwhile addition.

An efficient woodstove.

CHAPTER 8

ENERGY EFFICIENCY OF HEAT-PUMP SYSTEMS

We have looked at the various types of heat pump and how they function, considered house heating and possible need for a back-up. It is time to revisit the important issue of their energy efficiency and what affects it. As we have already established, a heat pump is a device that effectively transfers heat 'up hill' against the natural direction of flow that we are familiar with, i.e. it transfers heat from cold to hot. We have also looked at the basic principle that the greater the difference in temperature rise, the lower the energy efficiency will be.

In a real-life situation, there are many other things that affect the actual effectiveness of a heating system and the final energy bills. Let us first look at a theoretical 'ideal' heat pump and then reconcile this with real life.

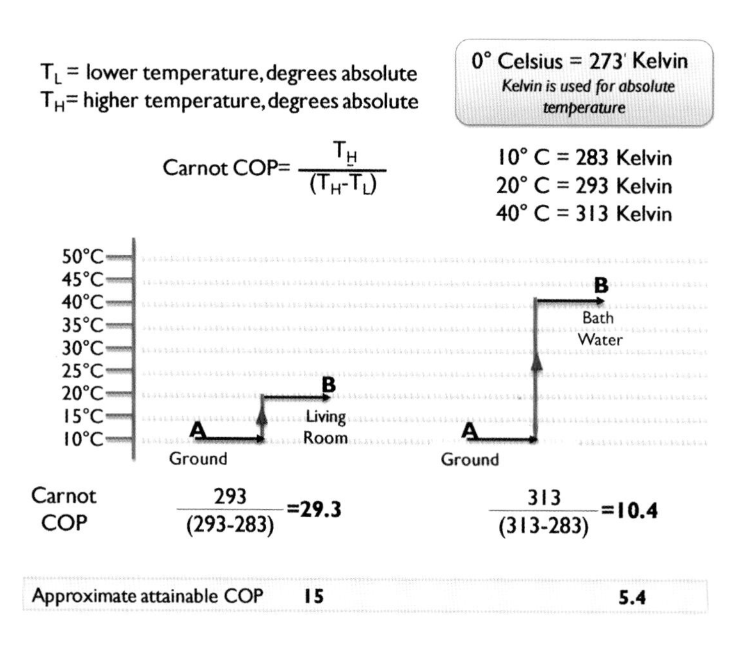

Two examples of theoretical thermal efficiency.

Carnot Efficiency

Sadi Carnot, the French physicist, gave his name to a formula that calculates the energy efficiency (COP) of an ideal heat-pump. Sadly, thermodynamic processes are far from perfect and the second law of thermodynamics tells us that. Even the most efficient car engine is barely 30 per cent efficient due to the constraints of thermodynamics.

The actual attainable COP of a normal heat-pump unit could be a little over one-half of the theoretical ideal, and this is expressed by the 'Carnot efficiency' (50–55 per cent).

The illustration on page 94 shows two examples of processes that could be useful to us.

Heat can only flow from hot to cold. It cannot naturally flow 'upwards' (as shown by the vertical red arrow). We are showing the energy flow from point 'A' to point 'B' by means of a heat pump.

The first theoretical example is taking heat from the ground at 10°C and transferring it into a room at 20°C. The difference in temperature is small and the theoretical COP could be about 29. Given a non-perfect compressor and other losses, we could achieve a COP of approximately 15.

The second example shows a theoretical perfect heat-pump heating bath water. The COP here is over 10 and, with a Carnot efficiency of 52 per cent, we might manage a COP of 5.4.

Real-Life Efficiencies

This is all very well, but it assumes no temperature drops to make the heat actually flow in and out of the heat pump. In the real world, we will

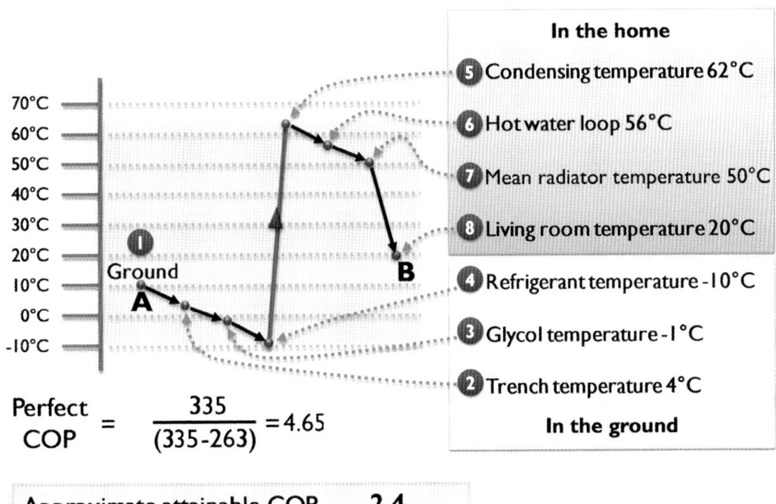

Real-life heat-transfer processes involve temperature drops.

need means of transferring the heat to its place of use and this will require temperature differences, otherwise nothing will flow.

If we now look at the process of getting from point 'A' (*see* the diagram on page 95), into the heat-pump's internals, then out again to heat the room at point 'B', we find that there are a lot of necessary steps along the way that incur a temperature difference (temperature drop).

Now we have a real-life example of a not particularly efficient heat-pump with the same small lift from 'A' to 'B' as in example 1. As we can see, to get a flow of heat we incur several 'drops' in temperature along the chain of heat-transfer stages – the refrigerant needs to be at –10°C to be able to extract a certain quantity of heat from the ground and the hot refrigerant needs to be over 60°C for there to be an adequate heat flow into the room. It can be seen that the radiator-to-room causes the biggest temperature difference.

If we now look at the Carnot COP, we see that it is about six times worse than our example 1 above, simply due to the many steps in the heat-transfer process. Is it therefore possible to minimize the temperature drops?

The example below is still taking heat from the ground into a room, as example 1, but does so with much closer temperature differences and, in this case, uses under-floor heating. It has larger heat-exchangers and a much bigger ground collector.

Now we have a COP of 4.1, which is a considerable and worthwhile improvement on the COP of 2.3 of the previous example. This was achieved by improvements to the heat transfer at several points in the system. If money were no object, we could achieve even more, but we need to arrive at a workable compromise that is cost-effective.

Finally, let us consider our example 2, where we were heating bath water to 40°C.

If, as shown on page 97, we put in some realistic temperature drops, we see that the heat

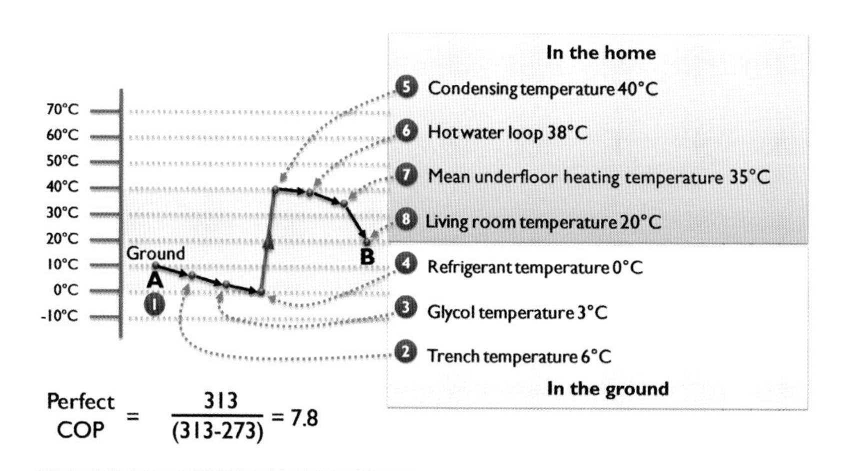

Improving the COP through good system design.

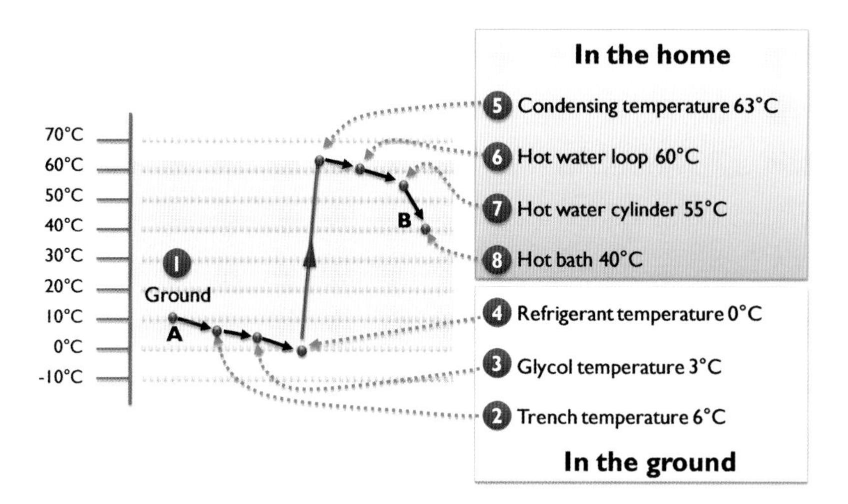

Heating bath water.

transfer at the 'hot' end of the system is quite small. This is to be expected since the heat transfer from refrigerant to water is inherently efficient. If we also consider the need to store the hot bath-water before use, this would incur another refrigerant temperature rise, since we need to store it considerably higher than bath temperature. This again causes another unavoidable drop in COP.

We have not calculated the Carnot COP in this case, since we can see that the COP is related to the height of the red line and that we need to minimize the temperature drops as much as we can at every point.

The energy efficiency of the inner workings of the heat pump is one thing, but a complete system involves other components to collect and distribute the heat. These obviously have an effect on the *overall* energy use, which is what counts in the end.

Pumps and Fans and Ancillary Components

An air-source system will need a fan to draw air over the finned evaporator. Typically such fans can require power inputs of between 4 and 8 per cent of the compressor input, so their input is relatively small. This detail is optimized by the manufacturer and therefore requires no further thought.

Water- and ground-source systems require a circulation pump to circulate and enable the liquid to flow. The flow depends on the diameter or total cross-sectional area of all internal waterways. The required energy to pump the liquid will therefore depend on the 'constriction' of the complete liquid circuit, so power demand could vary considerably. The pump power should be in the order of 5 per cent of the compressor input power, so again, this input is relatively small, but this is an aspect where small savings may be possible.

On the 'hot' side of the system, there will be at least one conventional domestic circulation pump (circulator). The power demand could vary greatly, but it is generally between 2 and 4 per cent of the total input.

There can be several pumps on a system and some of these could sometimes run almost continuously. This is sometimes necessary to keep a pipe thermostat-sensor reading a meaningful temperature (if the flow stops, they only record the surrounding air temperature). However, constantly running pumps can be a waste of energy.

How Does the Water Flow Rate Affect the Efficiency?

As the warmed water circulates, it transfers heat from the heat pump to the emitter circuits. If the water flow rate is high, there will be a small temperature rise as it passes through the heat pump (since there is a greater volume to heat). Conversely, if the water flow rate is reduced, there will be a large temperature rise between the heat pump inlet and outlet. In this case, it may at first appear that the heat output has increased, but actually the heat output is likely to be about the same.

In such cases where the flow rate is low, there is a greater temperature drop from inlet to outlet of the emitter, and the return temperature back to the heat pump is cooler. We know that the heat output to the room relates to the average temperature of the emitter surface. To compensate for the 'cooler' parts of the heat emitters, the inlet temperature may need to rise several degrees. This usually causes the heat pump to operate less efficiently.

For the standard heat pump, no net gain has been achieved by slowing the flow; to the contrary, there is likely to be a net loss. This is due to the nature of the refrigerant condensing inside the heat pump, which takes place at a fairly constant temperature.

However, 'Transcritical' heat pumps using CO_2 refrigerant have different characteristics. These are new to the market and currently uncommon. They require a large temperature gradient along the hot CO_2 heat exchanger, therefore a lower flow rate is needed. The same is true in boilers where there is an enormous temperature gradient between the flame and the flue outlet.

Another factor to consider relating to this topic is the energy required for circulating the water. This should not be excessive, as could be the case if high water flow rates are trying to be achieved. Thus a compromise should be sought between high flow rates and excessive pumping power.

Flow Rates and Pressure Drops

Water will travel down a pipe or around a circuit if it is pushed, i.e. if it is pumped. Energy is required to make it move, so it important to minimize this so that energy is not wasted. One might aim to use no more than 5 per cent of the total input power to circulate the liquid around a ground loop.

The issue of the flow of water in a pipe circuit is exactly analogous to the flow of electricity in wires:

- Electrical current travels down a wire due to a voltage or potential difference.
- The current depends on the resistance of the cable (as quoted in Ohms).
- Water travels down a pipe due to the pressure difference from one end to the other.
- The actual flow rate depends on the pipe's resistance.

This is understood with precision by all electricians, but the situation with pipes and flow rates is always a bit less clear. Why should this be? Electricians can quickly, easily and accurately measure the voltage, current and resistance at any point they choose, while plumbers have no such luxury. Rarely do they have any pressure

$$\text{Volts} = \text{Current} \times \text{Resistance}$$

or rearranged as

$$\text{Current} = \frac{\text{Volts}}{\text{Resistance}}$$

Ohms Law.

tapping points, to measure the pressure difference (voltage) and they have no means of measuring the flow-rate (current).

Imagine if electricians could not measure the voltage-drop, the resistance or the current. They would install wiring and only trust that the cables were the right size. Well it would not really be that bad, they would have to do what plumbers do: use look-up charts to calculate the pipe size and trust that the pressure drops are correct. Ultimately, the flow is known by checking temperature differences once the system is operating and this is very rarely a problem.

Pipe Diameters and Lengths

Having considered that the flow in a pipe depends on two things:

- the pressure down the length the pipe (ultimately produced by the circulating pump) and
- the diameter or restriction of the pipe,

we can consider how to minimize the energy needed to circulate it.

If we increase the pipe-size diameter, then we need less pressure to circulate it, hence the pump consumes less energy. This can be an expensive strategy, so a compromise is found between energy expended in pumping and the cost of pipe and fittings.

Remember: the bore-size of plastic pipe is considerably smaller than copper pipe.

The Bottleneck Principle Does Not Apply

We are all familiar with traffic-flow bottlenecks and how this can affect journey times. Water-pipe networks are different and the motion of water depends on the sum of the pressure drops down every section of pipe. This is dependent on the pipe diameter and, ultimately, its length. Every electrician knows this since you cannot base a long-distance cable size on the cable size of the appliance used at the end of it. It is the length of cable, or pipe that must be considered.

The Devil is in the Detail

There are many hundreds of thousands of heat pumps operating very efficiently around the world. There are, however, a small number that are not.

Heat pumps are a little more sensitive to their operating conditions than most other heating technologies and there is a multitude of aspects that relate to a complete house-heating system. It is therefore important that all of these aspects are matched well at design stage. It should be stressed that this caution should not worry you unduly, but it should warn project planners and installers not to take the optimistic attitude – 'it will probably be OK'.

Efficient car – inefficient car. (Andria Thwaites.)

To illustrate this I would like you to consider a car. There are various issues that could influence the speed and fuel efficiency. For example:

- The payload.
- Tyre pressures.
- The wind resistance.
- Size and fettle of the engine.
- The temperament of the driver.

Consider just the first two. A car with either a high payload or a car with soft tyres may cause only a modest reduction in fuel efficiency. However, if we have a car that is both filled to capacity and that also has soft tyres, then the resulting losses compound, since the tyres are squashed more due to the weight; thus the tyre pressure is more critical when the car is loaded.

One could think of other combinations of the above list that would also compound and reduce the fuel efficiency dramatically.

Let's put these into a table so you can see positive and negative situations.

Your car may cope with one or two 'potentially bad' circumstances, but if you have too many you are asking for trouble.

Potentially Good and Potentially Bad Heat-Pump Applications

Heat-pump systems can be similar. Let's make another list, but this time it's not for a car, but for a house with a heat pump.

- Insulation level of the house.
- Operating temperatures of radiator or under-floor heating.
- Size of heat pump and use of electric top-up (if any).
- Temperature requirements of the occupier.
- Size/efficiency of ground collector.
- Efficiency of heat-pump unit itself.
- Poorly configured hydraulics (pipes and pumps).
- Settings of the controller.

Again, issues can compound. For example, consider a heat pump fitted to a house whose owner likes the rooms nice and hot, and the heat pump is fitted with an electric back-up heater to make up any shortfall of the heat pump's output. The extra heat-demand caused by the required high room-temperatures will result in higher radiator

Potentially Good	Potentially Bad
The Payload	
Few occupants	Carrying a heavy load
Tyre Pressures	
Correct pressure	Too soft
Wind Resistance	
Streamlined and aerodynamic	Loaded roof-rack
The Engine	
Well tuned, well sized	Too powerful
Driver Behaviour	
Gentle acceleration, moderate speed	Heavy on the throttle and brakes

Good vs bad fuel efficiency.

or under-floor heating temperatures being required. These higher temperatures will reduce the COP of the heat pump. Furthermore, the top-up heater will automatically be used far more than it would if the householder were more frugal. Additionally, other parts of the system, including the source, are likely to be 'stretched' beyond their ideal performance. Thus the energy efficiency and running cost can get progressively worse if too many things are 'not ideal'.

Heat-pump efficiency is influenced greatly by its working conditions, so it is important to make sure that you don't have too many factors working against you. The chart below gives an indication of what is potentially good and what could potentially be bad. One, or maybe two, on the right-hand column might be perfectly acceptable, but if you want the best out of your heat-pump system, it is preferable to keep to the left column as much as possible.

There are many parts to a complete heating system and given the need to minimize temperature drops within the system, it is important to ensure that all aspects are well designed. In general, manufacturers have already worked out the needs of a system, so following their guidelines should result in an energy-efficient system. That said, sometimes issues arise when linking parts of the system that come from different suppliers.

At this point we have covered many of the finer details and are better placed to look at the important aspect of the control systems that we cover in the next chapter. For those simply looking to install a system, you should be interested in the information in Chapter 11.

Potentially Good	Potentially Bad
Insulation Level of the House	
Well insulated	Poorly insulated
Type of Emitter	
Underfloor heating or very large radiators	Normal sized radiators
Size of Heat Pump and Use (if any) of Electric Top-up	
Well sized heat pump	Small heat pump with electric top up
Heat demand of the occupier	
Minimum for comfort	Luxuriously warm
Size / efficiency of ground collector	
Large ground collector in wet ground	Small ground collector in dry ground
Fuel the heat pump displaces	
Electricity, oil or LPG	Mains natural gas

Good vs bad heat pump.

CHAPTER 9

THE CONTROL SYSTEM

One very important aspect to any heat pump is the control system. Given that the whole system will have many interrelated components, the functioning of these must be switched on or off automatically when needed, according to a control strategy. An electronic controller is fundamental to most heat-pump units. This controller is also the interface where the user can communicate with the system, interrogate the functions and program their particular requirements. Many have attractive digital LCD displays and can seem quite complicated until you spend a little time reading the instructions. Increasingly, they attempt to be simple so that you can adjust things without too much bewilderment and grief.

Some heat pumps, however, have very simple controls. Whilst possibly missing out on certain refinements of functions, simple controls can have their advantages. It is possibly better to set a simple controller correctly that a sophisticated one incorrectly. Not all users have the aptitude or inclination to think through any required settings, so the area of user-control will no doubt be an important subject for future development.

The temperature levels that we like to live in are in many ways what we grow used to. A temperature of 21°C is the norm and is generally accepted for older people. Some people tend to live in temperatures of up to 24°C and dress very lightly. Others tend to happily economize in temperatures below 20°C and dress accordingly. The

HEATING SYSTEM SETTINGS

Heating systems generally have two temperature settings:

- The room thermostat.
- The setting of the water circulating around the radiators.

The Energy Saving Trust advises that turning the room thermostat down by 1°C can save up to 8 per cent on fuel use. Your house will not be quite so hot, but significant energy can be saved.

Further to this, heat pumps and condensing boilers are sensitive to the second setting – the heated water passing through them. For every four degrees reduction in this temperature, about 10 per cent can be saved on heat-pump running costs (for the same delivered heat). It may be possible to reduce the setting and still achieve the same room temperature, hence reducing input, for the same total heat output.

To put it another way, if you can manage to reduce the water temperature that your heat pump 'sees', but still maintain the same room comfort, you can save on heat-pump running costs.

TOP: **Simple controls.**

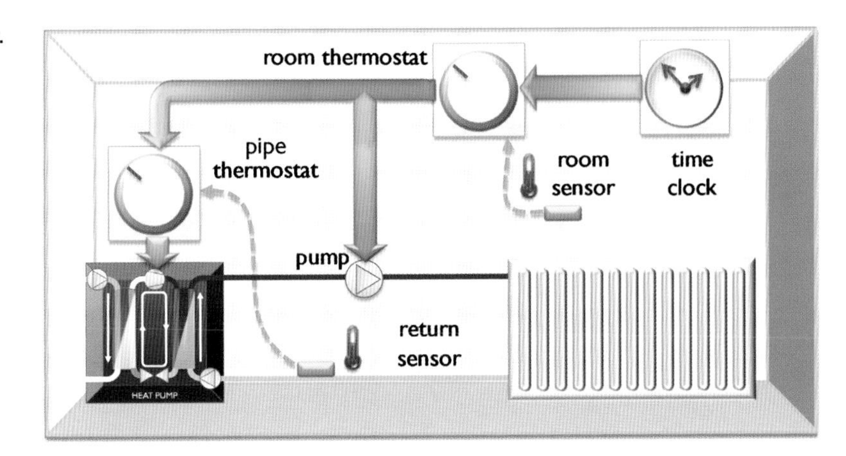

BELOW: **A simple control knob.**

shift towards lower temperatures might involve a few slightly uncomfortable days while you become accustomed to it, but nearly everybody gets 'acclimatized' in the end. From then on, you are saving energy and money for ever. And on a more ethical note, although one can live in whatever temperature one wishes, it is worth the thought that over-indulgent heating (expense aside) may not be environmentally responsible.

Simple Controls

The main function of a controller is ultimately to regulate the heat delivered to the building and to do so whilst achieving the best energy efficiency. In its simplest form, it could involve simply a room thermostat to switch the circulation pump and a thermostat on the heat pump to control the compressor to regulate the water temperature that the heat pump produces.

Note: on the diagram on the right, COP figures have been superimposed on to the scale as examples that roughly relate to the temperatures on the dial.

If a simple thermostat is used on the heat pump, it will need to be set at a temperature that is high enough to give adequate room heat for the emitter system that is used. As we know, the heat pump should heat water at the lowest possible temperature so that the energy efficiency is kept high, but not everyone would have the inclination to make regular adjustments. For this reason, an automatic method of reducing the setting was developed. It is referred to as 'weather compensation'. This is covered over the next few pages.

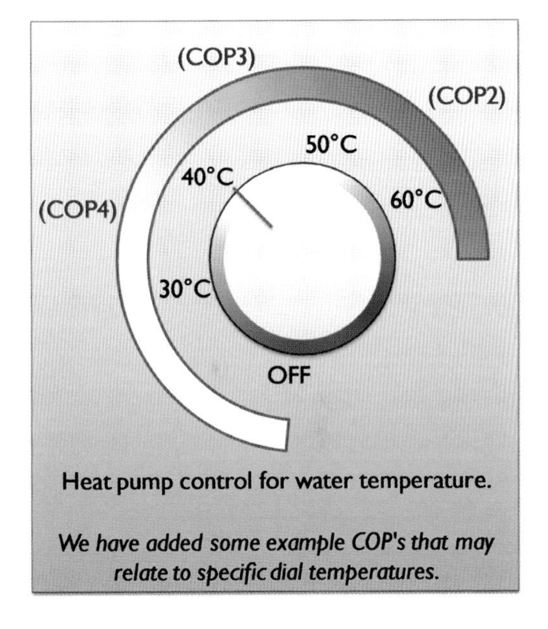

Heat pump control for water temperature.

We have added some example COP's that may relate to specific dial temperatures.

Integrated Controllers

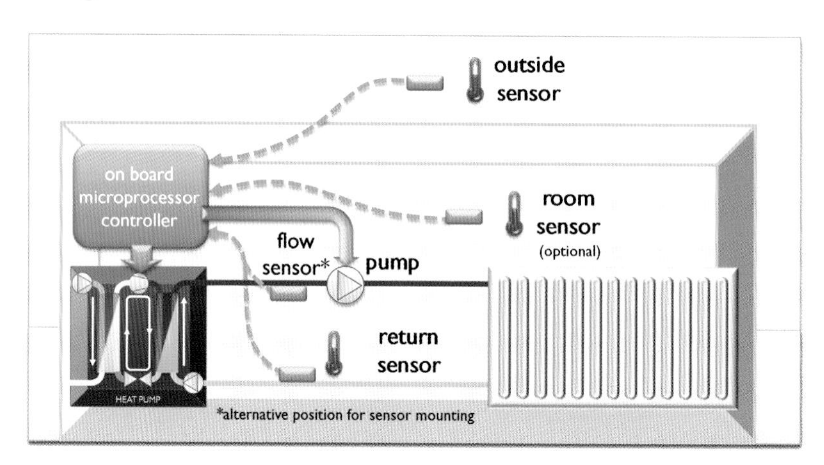

A microprocessor controller integral to the heat pump.

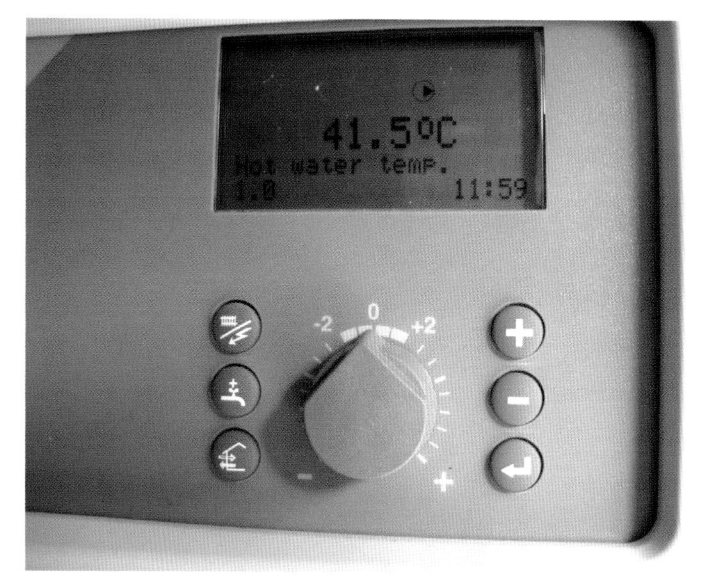

Typical electronic controllers as fitted to most heat-pump units:

MIDDLE LEFT: Worcester Bosch.

MIDDLE RIGHT: Dimplex, showing heating return set-point.

BOTTOM: Nibe, showing hot water cylinder temperature.

Heat-pump controllers usually have the following facilities:

- Heat-output control.
- Time and setback (e.g. lower night-time temperature) functions.
- System information (hours run, compressor starts, various temperatures).
- Control of top-up or back-up auxiliary heater (bivalent control).

Note: Most controllers, like many devices, are now capable of automatically adjusting 'clocks-forward' around 25 March and 'clocks-back' around the 25 October.

Your commissioning engineer may have

GETTING THE BEST FROM YOUR CONTROLLER

Your user instructions will tell you how to set up your system and these should be read very carefully.

There are one or two tips that might be of interest to those of you keen to minimize your energy use:

- The importance of reducing the settings to the lowest possible temperature cannot be emphasized enough. If the heated water reduces by only 2°C, you are likely to save about 5 per cent on compressor running costs. This is over and above any energy savings due to slightly cooler rooms.
- Periodically reduce your heating curve (weather compensation) a little bit. If you don't feel colder over the following days, then leave it at the lower setting (remember: this should auto-adapt as the weather changes).
- If you have a simple fixed-setting thermostat, adjust it month by month to suit the weather and to suit your needs (don't forget to turn it down in spring!).
- If you are able to program 'off' periods for the hot water, then try to arrange the 'off' time to happen before the end of a period of potential use. This can tend to make the bottom section of the cylinder cold. When the 'on' happens, the system starts heating the cold water and does so at a higher energy efficiency. Whilst promising a modest saving, you run the risk of running out of hot water during an 'off' period. This may, or may not, be a priority for you.
- Even if you have chosen to heat your house continuously, it can be worth programming a set-back of just 1 or 2°C, such that your unit is encouraged to rest for maybe two periods over 24 hours. This encourages some longer run-times, which is beneficial.
- Reducing TRV settings might compromise the heat-pump's energy efficiency.
- Ensure that any top-up heater is not working more than you would like it to. There are usually means to limit this. Read your user instructions.
- Browse your user instructions to see what specific information you have.

Note: The total annual cost of any electric top-up heater may be small, even though it's expensive for several days of the year. Keeping the heated water temperature as low as possible is key to low running costs.

access to a whole list of further parameters, which may include: summer cut-off temperature, anti-cycling delay, pump cycle, hysteresis (differential), bivalent point, temperature limits and so on. Don't worry if that sounds daunting, you can remain blissfully ignorant of such issues if you wish. However, you should always get a copy of these parameters when your system is commissioned. This could be invaluable information for future engineers visiting your site and needing to re-program your controller.

Weather Compensation

This control method automatically varies the heated water temperature dependent on an outside air-temperature sensor. This is the recommended way of control and is particularly suited to ground- or water-source systems in average to well-insulated and lightweight houses. It can potentially save a significant amount of energy, so it is a function included with almost all controllers.

The graph opposite illustrates a simple example of weather compensation control.

The horizontal axis shows outside temperature, the vertical shows the heated water temperature of the heat pump. One of the example heating-curves, A, B or C, must be selected in the controller.

If, for example, curve B is chosen, then the return water temperature would be 35°C when it is zero outside. This may be sufficiently warm for under-floor heating (the flow could be 41°C, *see* box below). As the outside temperature gets colder, the water gets warmer, thus giving more heat to the room. Conversely, the settings will automatically reduce the water temperature as the outside conditions gets warmer. This control maintains the minimum possible temperature for the given outside conditions, thus the maximum energy-efficiency is achieved for the given heat demand.

In a house with radiators, then curve C would probably be needed. This will give higher temperatures resulting in lower energy-efficiencies, as expected with radiators.

Please note that in real life, the curves would offer a finer adjustment. Most controllers would also allow maximum and minimum limits to be programmed in.

The figure opposite shows an alternative weather-compensation control. Here, two points

THE DIGITAL TEMPERATURE DISPLAY

It is very important to know if the reading refers to the flow temperature or return temperature.

At concept stage, we often consider the flow temperature, but the controlling sensor is commonly on the return pipe. This may typically be 6°C colder than the flow. It is sometimes necessary to add or subtract around 6°C when making comparisons.

Variable speed inverter drive systems, control using a sensor on the flow pipe. With these systems, things are a little more straightforward. For example:

- Standard ground-source with flow of 40°C and return of 34°C – display shows 34°C.
- Japanese-style inverter-drive air-source with flow of 40°C and return of 34°C – display shows 40°C.

Both examples are operating at the same temperatures.

Graph illustrating weather compensation control.

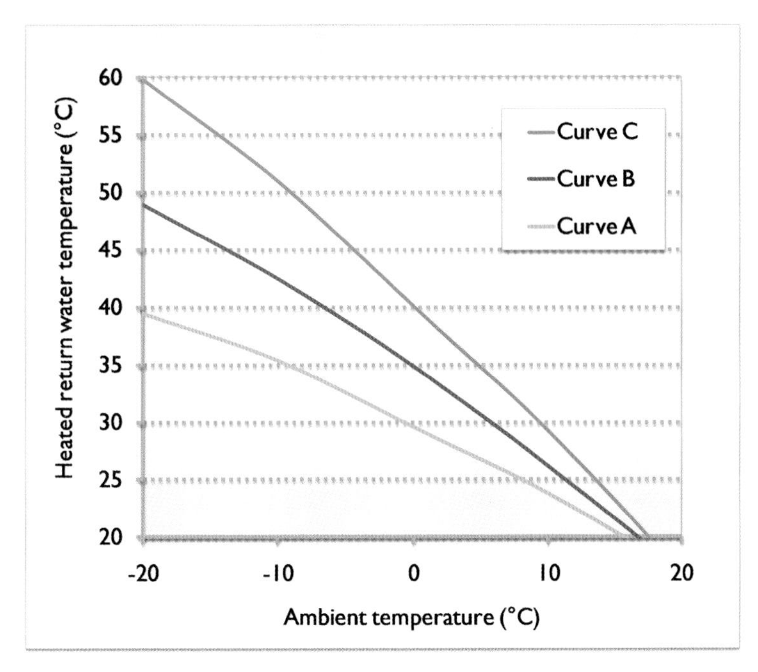

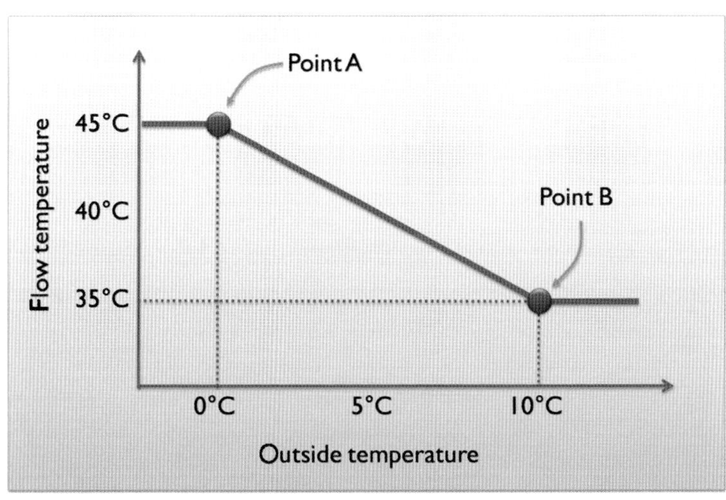

An alternative method of weather compensation control.

are programmed in for specific outside temperatures. In the example given, the flow temperature will be at 45°C for any outside temperature below 0°C and will be at 35°C at anything above 10°C, with a sliding scale in-between. The four temperature values can be changed in any direction required. One advantage to this control is that it easily allows a maximum or minimum limit:

- In an old, stone building where the thermal mass of the walls require a radiator temperature that is never below a certain temperature.

- Where the occupier wishes to 'cap' the maximum temperature, thus limiting the maximum COP.

This control can be a little more tedious to set and possibly a little more perplexing than the options A, B and C on page 107.

Weather Compensation Pros and Cons

Advantages:

- Helps to reduce the working temperature to the lowest required at any time.
- Potentially increases COP by a considerable amount and is recommended.

Disadvantages:

- In old, solid-walled buildings and exceptionally well-insulated buildings, the outside temperature is not necessarily the best indicator of actual heat requirements at any one time.
- Outside air-sensors may not represent heat needs, since it ignores direct solar gain.
- For air-source systems, the increased setting may increase the run time during colder nights, this could encourage it to run when the COP is lower.

All in all, weather compensation in some form will usually save a reasonable amount of energy. At best it can save a great deal. It must, however, be set up correctly. This is usually best achieved by trial and error.

Air-Source Weather Compensation Anomaly

Weather compensation automatically increases the water temperature in the heating system when the outside temperature drops. On a cold, frosty night, this control will make the heat pump operate at a high temperature and therefore at a lower COP; however, the middle of the day could be relatively warm. If the building being heated were solid stone, then some advantage could be taken by running the unit in the day, thus storing some heat generated at a high COP. Indeed, air source and heavyweight buildings could be a good match. Weather compensation variations over a 24-hour period will, however, be disadvantageous in this respect. A better scheme may be for the controller to take the average temperature over 24 hours and adjust its curve setting on a 24-hour basis. This would have a worthwhile effect of slowly adjusting the control as the seasons change. For the current systems on the market, it is advisable to use some degree of night setback. As time goes on, controllers will no doubt become more intelligent in such matters and it is only a matter of time before the weather forecast data are fed directly into the heat-pump controller.

Other Settings

All controllers have 'system information'. This should include a record of the total hours that the heat-pump compressor and the auxiliary heater have clocked-up. This is worth keeping an eye on. Note down the hours, and the date and time.

Some heat pumps allow you to switch off the electric heater. However, care should be taken to ensure that any *Legionella* protection is still satisfied.

Worcester Bosch have a nice facility where you can fit either a time clock or manual switch to their 'external input'. This can be configured to inhibit the electric heater at times when you don't want it. Most heat pumps allow you to limit or minimize the amount that an electric heater is used, but it is rarely simple to configure.

One little detail that is worth bearing in mind – by limiting compressor use by, for example, too many degrees of night setback, there is the possibility of increasing the electric back-up use. This is because the system could see a temperature short-fall immediately after the set-back period (when it comes back on). It might call upon the electric heater as a boost at this time. Compressor running is always preferable to the electric back-up heater.

Smart Metering

The supply utility companies are keen to smooth-out peaks and troughs in electricity demand. This has led to some European countries trialling systems where they can switch off non-urgent loads like heat pumps. No doubt this is a topic that we will need to embrace in the future and it is maybe something that we need to be ready for.

Electrical Supply

The electric motor that drives a heat pump is hermetically sealed into the compressor. When a compressor starts, it draws a very high current for a fraction of a second. Ideally, such motors would be three-phase, which is best suited to motor starting. Unfortunately, the domestic electricity supply in the UK is exclusively single-phase. Sweden and Germany to name but two, are countries where three-phase domestic supply is common; interestingly, these countries were early adopters of heat-pump technology. Now that the heat-pump market is well-established in countries like the UK and France, where single-phase supplies dominate, more and more single-phase products are available. There should no longer be a lack of suitable single-phase products for even the largest of homes.

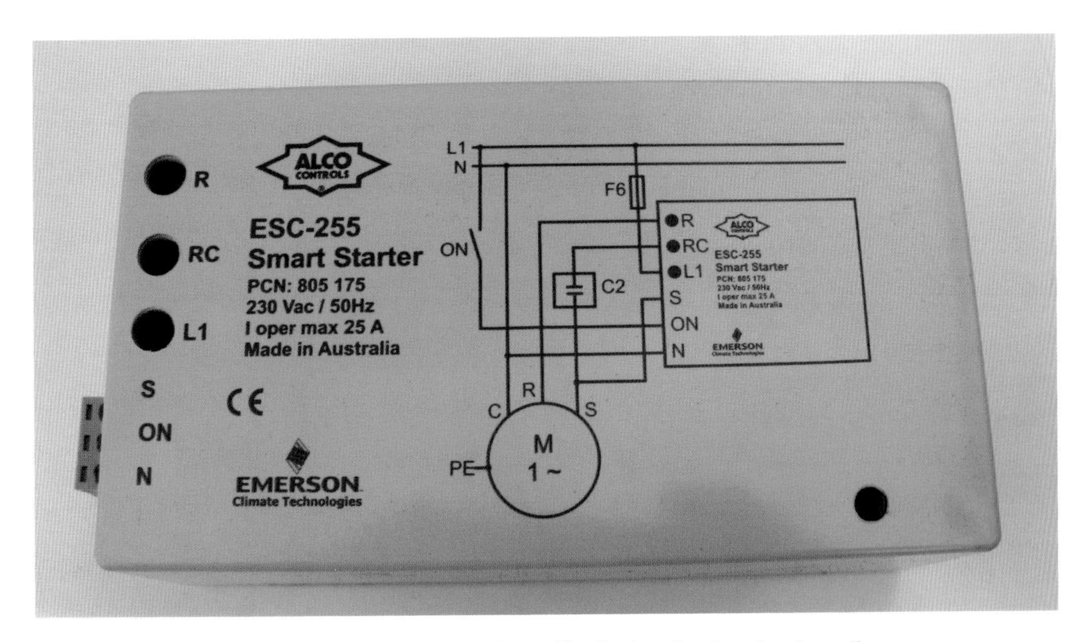

An example is the 'soft start' that is designed specifically for the Copeland scroll compressor.

That said, the starting surge could potentially be a problem and it is a requirement of the electrical supply utility for permission to be sought before connecting a heat pump. This requirement is enforced since there is a risk of interference causing lights to dim every time the heat pump starts.

Soft-start devices are available that can reduce this potential problem and are usually fitted by the manufacturers. The best types are dedicated to a specific compressor.

Locating a Heat-Pump Unit

The working mechanism of a heat pump is essentially the same as that of a fridge. The compressor at the back of a fridge has no sound-attenuation measures, deemed unnecessary for an item in a kitchen. Heat pumps have more powerful compressors that give out more noise; however, they are usually lagged with a jacket and the unit casing is usually lined with sound-absorbent material. That said, heat pumps do emit a noise that can tend to be carried through slight vibrations in the building. Noise is very subjective. What is an irritant to some is of no bother to others. Whilst sound levels vary model to model, it is generally accepted that one would not install a heat-pump unit below or adjacent to a bedroom or living-room, and care should be given to the base that the unit is placed on. Pipe runs can transmit noise, so sound-deadening hose connections are often used.

It is not always possible to fit a heat pump inside a small house. This Kensa heat-pump (below) is located outside. This one is in Cornwall, so may not need an insulated shed.

Air-source heat-pumps must be carefully located, since noise could potentially irritate neighbours. For that reason, they will require planning permission. That said, the latest models are very quiet.

This Kensa heat-pump is located outside. (Kensa Engineering.)

It would seem advantageous to locate an air-source unit in a warm, sunny location. This might be the case, but given that the unit may process up to 1m^3 of air every second, the solar heat that may have built up over hours can quickly be exhausted. The advantage may therefore only be slight.

The buffer cylinder (if one is fitted) is always better located inside the building, this avoids unuseful heat losses in winter. The hot-water cylinder location is more important. If pipe runs from heat pump to cylinder and from cylinder to taps are too long, then energy will be wasted to a certain extent. Ideally, these pipe runs should be relatively short.

Servicing

One of the selling points of a heat pump is that it requires very little maintenance, but any piece of mechanical equipment will need servicing from time to time. Boilers require an annual service and suffer from a build up of residue from the combustion of gas in air. Given that typically 1,000m^3 of gas per year are burnt, then this should be no surprise.

Heat pumps are like fridges, the inner workings can keep going with no attention whatsoever. The refrigeration components and their connecting pipework were evacuated during manufacture and filled with an exact weight of refrigerant. This fluid tirelessly travels around the heat pump in clinically clean conditions; the refrigeration circuit is therefore inherently reliable and requires little or no servicing. Water and brine circuits may, however, need an occasional check. Both the source and emitter circuit will have pressure gauges and these should not drop below a certain level. Very occasionally a top-up may be required and any loss in pressure should be investigated and the problem should be resolved. It is prudent to know the strength of glycol concentration in the source pipes, since serious problems could result if the degree of frost protection is insufficient. This concentration should not change over time unless, for example, the glycol (brine) circuit has been inadvertently topped up with water.

It is only the open-source system that may need regular maintenance for cleaning and filter changing of the source water. Ducted air systems also have filters and it is not unheard of for owners to be unaware that certain filters exist.

One advantage to the advanced digital controllers, as now fitted to most heat pumps, is that they can usually tell you lots of useful information about your system. They also have good system protection and good fault analysis.

You should find the following:

- Flow and/or return temperature.
- Source temperature.
- Hot-water temperature.
- Total compressor-run hours (from first switch-on).
- Total second heat-source hours (if fitted).
- Number of compressor starts (from first switch-on).

Some systems give more, some give less. However, this information can be very useful if you want to ensure that your heat pump is working at its optimum efficiency.

If you are interested in monitoring your system, it is often worth getting your electrician to fit an electric meter on to your heat-pump's supply. Reconditioned meters are very cheap and would take the guesswork out of what proportion of your electricity is used by the heat pump.

With built-in controllers you should be able to rest assured that, in the unlikely event of something going wrong, the system will simply shutdown and flash to alert you to attend to something, or call an engineer.

Having implied that heat pumps need little attention, like any mechanical device, things can fail. The list shows some examples of potential faults. Each heat pump will have its own list of faults and suggestions for a remedy.

Item	What could happen	Likely cause	What would result	Remedy
Pressure of glycol loop	Loss of pressure	Leak near heat pump	Unit could stop when pressure zero	Mend leak, pressurise with antifreeze
Pressure of heating loop	Loss of pressure	Leak somewhere	Unit could stop.	Mend leak, pressurise
Water filter (if fitted)	Blockage	Dirt from installation. Possible bacterial growth.	Drop in efficiency/ unit could stop	Clean. Add inhibitor.
Glycol concentration	Too weak	System incorrectly topped up with water	Ice in system, unit could stop	Mend leak, pressurise with correct amount of antifreeze
Air-source heat exchanger	Blocked with leaves or dust	To be expected over time	Drop in efficiency.	Clean (very carefully!!)
Settings	Setting may not be at optimum	Inadvertently changed. Incorrectly commissioned	Less efficient operation/ higher running cost	Set controller and thermostats correctly
Refrigeration circuit	Rare issue within refrigeration circuit	Leak (very unlikely), component failure	Reduced efficiency	Thorough service by engineer.
Low refrigerant pressure	Unit would stop	Brine circuit not flowing, or too cold. Outside fan not working. Possible refrigerant leak	System shut-down	Ensure glycol circuit is circulating. Check fan.
High refrigerant pressure	Unit would stop	Heating water not circulating	System shut-down	Ensure heating water is flowing

Possible fault conditions.

CHAPTER 10

ENVIRONMENTAL ISSUES

Heat pumps have for a long time been presented as an environmental method of heating. They are classed as a low-carbon technology and are often considered as a 'renewable' form of energy. Amongst environmentalists, their credentials have not always been viewed positively; indeed, in Denmark during the 1980s they were considered undesirable by many, since their adoption would increase electricity demand and this could shift the country towards nuclear power. Whereas their neighbours in Sweden embraced the technology due to their plentiful hydro-electricity, which was far better utilized powering heat pumps than the normal electric fire.

Unfortunately, we live in a commercial climate that likes to gloss-up the case for its particular product. This is far from a new phenomenon in our society. You don't have to look far to find an advert claiming 'free energy' from a heat pump. This is sort of true, but only the same way that 'buy one, get one free' operates in a supermarket because you have to pay before you get your free offer. The hype also stimulates sceptics, so that personal opinions about it can vary from 'it's brilliant' to 'it's a scam'.

In reality, the application it is used in dictates how good it is, and the relative benefits of heat pumps can be assessed by considering and comparing them with various other heating methods.

Judging the net worth of heat pumps has always seemed an intangible topic. For the immediate future, one might weigh up the immediate environmental impact with respect to CO_2 emissions. But in the long-term, and if we are to get our act together, we must inevitably find alternatives to fossil fuels and develop low-carbon methods of power generation. Electricity is bound to be the energy source of the future. We therefore need to develop and improve heat-pump technology so that it is ready to take its place as one of the many methods to help satisfy our energy-hungry ways of life.

Opinions of the long-term future can vary greatly, but for now, carbon dioxide seems to be the most important environmental factor to consider, and heat pumps are almost invariably driven by electricity, which can potentially be 'dirty' to produce. This must be considered if a balanced view is to be achieved.

Electricity

The 'Sankey' diagram is a very useful way of illustrating energy flows. The width of the thick lines relates to the quantity of energy.

The simple Sankey diagram overleaf shows both the power station and a heat pump. As can be seen, in this simple example, only one-third of the primary fuel is converted to electricity and two-thirds of the energy is lost up the cooling tower. A heat pump, however (with a COP of 3), uses electricity to capture ambient energy. This

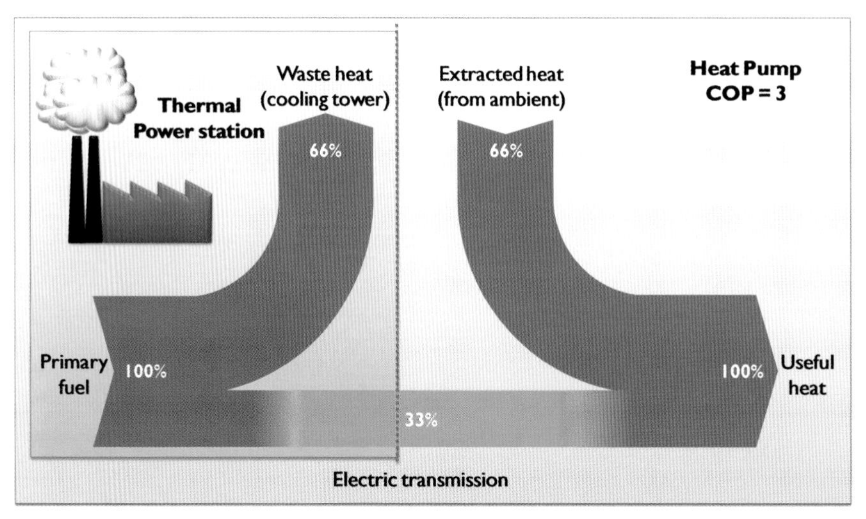

A Sankey diagram showing a traditional 'inefficient' thermal power station coupled to a heat pump.

can give a useful heat output that is only equal to the primary calorific value of the power station's fuel.

The values used in this example are, in many ways, not very impressive, since using simpler technology, we may be able to burn the primary fuel directly (in a household boiler) at an efficiency of up to 90 per cent, so the heat-pump example is only slightly better than burning the fuel directly in your home.

Obviously the efficiencies of both the power station and the heat pump can vary, so let us look at a best-case scenario (opposite). This illustrates advanced combined-cycle electricity generation and a heat pump with a COP of 4. Furthermore, some of the heat from the power station is recovered directly for district heating. The total useful heat in this example is over twice that of the calorific value of the primary fuel.

Unfortunately, not much of our electricity comes from such high-efficiency power stations, but, in reality, comes from a multiple of sources. It is, therefore, important to evaluate the country's 'mix' of inputs, since these combined give a value of carbon dioxide emitted.

The value for carbon dioxide produced by electricity generation varies over 24 hours and also over the seasons. The real-time 'carbon mix' can be viewed on the internet at http://www.realtimecarbon.org/. It is interesting to note that the carbon intensity is lower at night. This is in part due to the fact that the nuclear base load (which cannot easily be turned down) becomes the bigger proportion of the total.

The current average value is somewhere around 0.5kg CO_2/kWh. An official UK figure of 0.43kg CO_2/kWh was produced by the government and this reflected expected future downward trends. However, in 2010 it was re-evaluated and the current figure is 0.517. This figure as used in the government's standard assessment procedure (SAP) for energy rating of dwellings.

All predictions suggest that the CO_2 emissions caused by electricity generation will decline considerably in the future, so it may be more rational to assume a lower figure, as it will no doubt be considerably 'cleaner' in years to come. Any equipment installed today should be running well into the future.

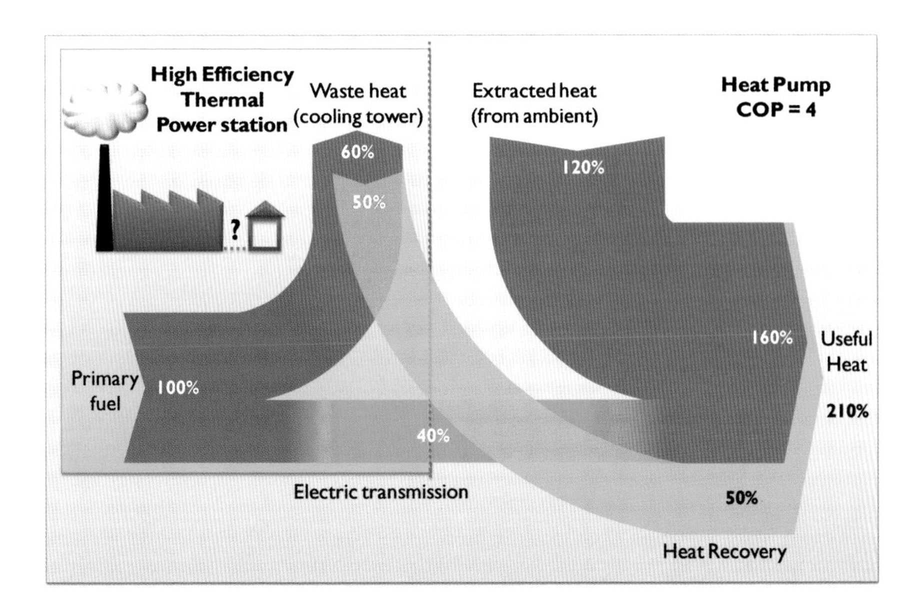

A Sankey diagram showing efficient fossil fuel generators with heat recovery, coupled to heat pumps.

The topic of 'green' tariffs can be bewildering. The notion of 'bestowing' your electricity payment to a 'clean' provider is questionable and results in others having to buy a greater percentage of 'dirty' electricity. On the other hand, if you purchase electricity from a venture that only supports renewables, then you could argue that such ventures would not happen without your money. It seems reasonable to think that 'green' tariffs are good and clearly some are better than others.

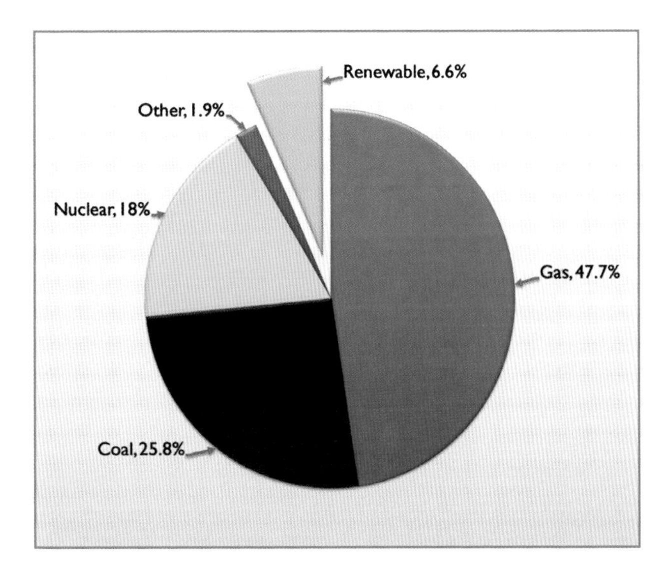

The UK grid mix (Ecotricity).

As time passes, we know that fossil fuels will become scarcer and the percentage of electricity provided by renewable generation methods will increase. It is likely that electricity will be the dominant energy of the future, at which point heat pumps will come into their own, since a heat pump with a COP as low as 2 could still be advantageous.

Off-Peak Electricity

As already discussed, the carbon intensity varies over the 24-hour period and tends to be lowest between around midnight and 4am.

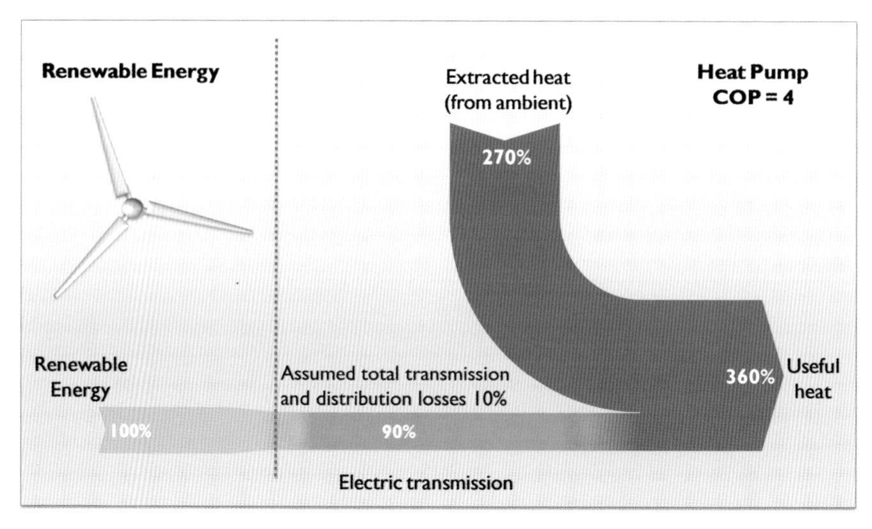

A Sankey diagram showing renewable generation powering a heat pump with no carbon emissions.

Maintaining sufficient capacity to meet the nation's need is a challenge for those managing the grid, so any levelling-off of the peaks and troughs is welcome. For this reason, cheaper night-time tariffs were introduced to encourage night use and possibly to reduce the use of peak-time electric heaters. The Economy 7 tariff gives a seven-hour period at night at reduced rate and this is typically used in heavy storage heaters that accumulate heat in bricks during the night and emit this heat during the day.

One of the disadvantages of this system is that the storage is rather crude and, inevitably, more heat is given out at night than is needed. Furthermore, the storage bricks run out of heat by the evening, so in reality, your house follows a 24-hour temperature profile that does not exactly match your needs. This can result in an overly warm breakfast time, if the house is to be warm enough for the evening. Obviously, the type of house is an important factor here.

There are systems that store heat more effectively, and types using large water tanks have been around for many years. Heat can be drawn from these, as and when needed.

If a heat pump is to use off-peak electricity, it would need to be large enough to provide a whole day's heat in only 7 hours so it would need to be significantly bigger and hence more costly to install.

Furthermore, if heat is to be stored, it would need to be at a considerably higher temperature than normal, therefore reducing the efficiency (COP). If stored in a water tank, the tank would need to be very big, so it would at first seem an impractical proposition to use off-peak electricity with a heat pump.

However, rather than using only the off-peak period, it would be possible to simply shift as much running-time as possible to the night period. Remember, for much of the year, the heat requirements are only a fraction of the winter peak.

Part-peak/off-peak use can often stack-up on cost-saving grounds, since off-peak electricity is significantly cheaper (be mindful that peak units may be more expensive than normal flat-rate tariffs).

The 7-hour tariff is not best suited to heat pumps; however, there are other periods of the day that could be considered 'low-peak'. For this reason, some 10-hour tariffs are available that are split into three times: night, mid-afternoon and mid-evening. Whilst this 'off-peak' rate may not be as favourable as the night-only tariffs, these tariffs may be more compatible with a heat-pump system.

Operating these tariffs can require a higher level of control sophistication and possibly some user adaptability, so it is not always plain-sailing. One has to be aware of what is coming on when. Also, judgements may be needed relating to the necessity of operating during more expensive 'peak times'. Such issues may be seen as an opportunity to some, or a hassle to others.

Unlike electric storage heating, the off-peak heat-pump is storing some heat in the fabric of the building. Solid, stone walls and under-floor heating have much greater storage capacity, whereas rooms with internal insulation have little 'mass' to hold the heat (buffer cylinders store only a very small amount of heat). It is interesting to think that all the little bits of heat being stored in millions of houses during off-peak times could mitigate the need for a power station or two.

The off-peak issue will no doubt be tackled with increased sophistication in the future with smart metering. There are various methods that could be adopted; for example, increasing the tariff as the national load increases, or automatically dropping-off loads (like fridges and heat pumps) that would not mind a brief 'enforced' rest at peak times. These sophisticated methods make economic sense to the supply companies, since this can reduce the maximum demand on the national grid.

Comparing CO_2 Figures with Other Fuels

Fuels can be rated by the CO_2 emissions emitted whilst in use. The graph below shows values for

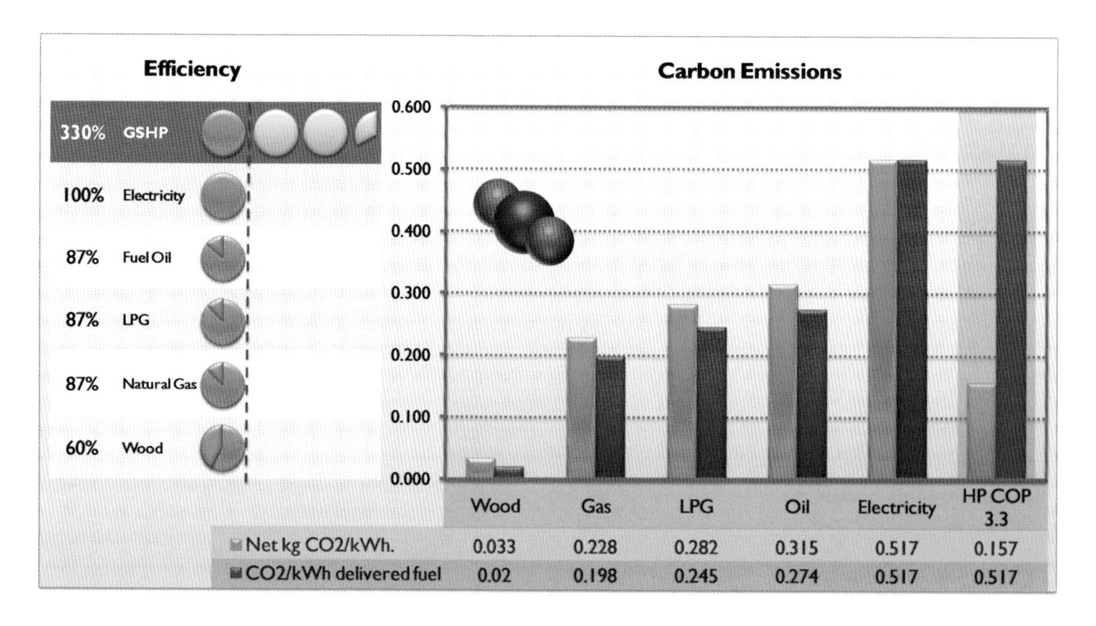

Pollution of various fuels.

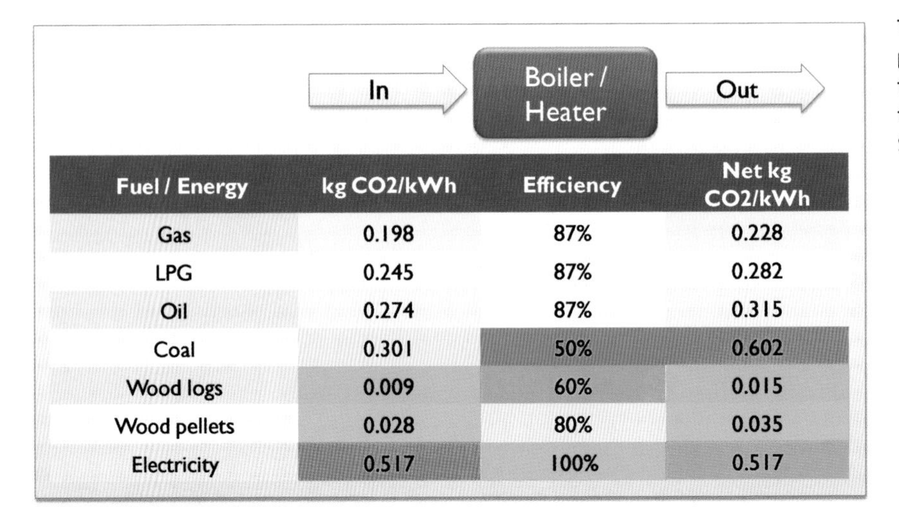

In	Boiler / Heater	Out	
Fuel / Energy	kg CO2/kWh	Efficiency	Net kg CO2/kWh
Gas	0.198	87%	0.228
LPG	0.245	87%	0.282
Oil	0.274	87%	0.315
Coal	0.301	50%	0.602
Wood logs	0.009	60%	0.015
Wood pellets	0.028	80%	0.035
Electricity	0.517	100%	0.517

Table of pollution of fuels taken from BRE – SAP2009.

the delivered fuel and also the net value as it's used. The difference between the figures relates to the efficiency of the appliance.

Electric heaters are 100 per cent efficient at point of use, since all electricity ends up as useful heat. Modern boilers are rated at about 90 per cent efficient (SEDBUK database). However, according to a Carbon Trust study, the value could be 4 to 5 per cent less when in actual use. (A similar reduction could be expected with heat pumps and this may account for the difference between appliance COP ratings and measured results.)

It is worth mentioning hot-water production at this point, since losses from pipe runs and cylinders can be very considerable. Boiler or heat pump, the DHW function can be less efficient than expected. Point-of-use electric heaters do not suffer this drawback

Out of all of the piped fossil fuels, mains gas is the best option. Methane (CH_4) is a relatively clean-burning fuel, being the most 'hydrogen rich' and 'carbon light' of the hydrocarbon fuels. There are also other atmospheric pollutants that burning fuel produces, but these are much less for gas than those of oil and wood.

Whilst the figures given for liquid and gas fuels will be fairly constant, it is more difficult to give a figure for wood. If wood is gathered locally in rural areas, it could be seen as a 'carbon neutral' fuel. Wood chip and wood pellets involve processing and transporting, so these can have a considerable impact on the overall figures, so quantifying this is very difficult. Our figures show this fuel favourably, but wood may not be ideal for certain situations, such as use in urban areas.

A question frequently asked is: what SPF (average annual COP) must be achieved to make a worthwhile environmental benefit? It is relatively easy to work out where the two values are equal (break-even), but if a saving is required, then this is more a matter of judgement to say by what magnitude the improvement should be.

The graph opposite is very useful for comparing heat pumps with conventional heating systems. The left-hand vertical scale shows figures for electric heaters (equivalent to COP1). It also shows values for gas and oil heating. The horizontal scale shows heat pumps with progressively better SPF; a SPF of 2 simply halves the electricity values, SPF 4 quarters it and so on.

This graph is very useful for comparing heat pumps with conventional heating systems.

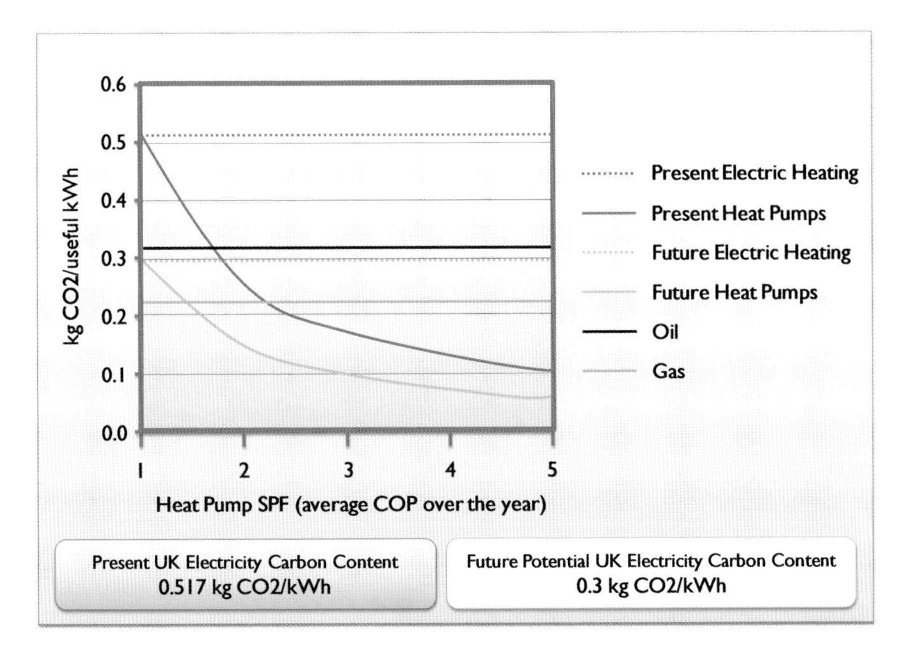

As an example: compared to the current official electricity figures of 0.517, a heat pump would need to have an SPF of about 2.3 to break-even with gas, so one might consider that a COP of 3 would show a significant benefit (+30 per cent).

For oil, the break-even SPF is only 1.7, so a SPF of 2.2 would give a similar ratio improvement, but if an SPF of 3.4 could be achieved, then this would halve the CO_2 figures. This is a very big improvement.

If we look into the future, we expect at some time to be looking at an electricity figure of 0.3kg CO_2/kWh; this makes a heat pump look far more favourable.

Environmental Impact of Refrigerants

Every heat pump (and fridge) contains a fluid to make it work. To be efficient, this fluid (the refrigerant) must have certain physical properties. Back in the 1980s, most heat pumps used

Bottle of HFC refrigerant and recovery pump.

Name	Chlorofluorocarbons	Hydrochlorofluorocarbons	Hydrofluorocarbon	Hydrocarbon	Ammonia	Carbon dioxide
Abbreviation	**CFC**	**HCFC**	**HFC**	**HC**	**NH_3**	**CO_2**
Number	R12	R22	R134A, R407C, R410A	R600A, R290	R717	R744
Ozone depleting potential **(ODP)**	1	0.05	0	0	0	0
Global Warming Potential **(GWP)**	2,400	1,700	1,500 ±15%	7	0	1
Uses	Domestic fridges	Air conditioning and heat pumps	All types of refrigeration and heat pumps	All types of refrigeration and heat pumps	Large systems	High temperature heat pumps
Status	Banned from 1998	Phased out from 2002 to 2010.	Currently the most common refrigerant.	Used in a few systems, especially smaller ones	Potential future refrigerant	New contender, shows promise for the future.

Chart of refrigerants.

CFC or HCFC refrigerants as the heat-transfer fluid. These are now known to cause serious damage to the ozone layer if released, due to the fact that they linger for many years in the upper atmosphere. Some very early heat-pumps could have caused more environmental damage than they saved, since they were notoriously 'leaky' of their working fluid.

Things have progressed dramatically since then. Systems rarely leak throughout their lifespan since joints are all welded. Gaskets are a thing of the past. Furthermore, current refrigerants no longer affect the ozone layer.

Unfortunately, the most common and the safest refrigerants have another property that is now in the forefront of our concerns. These gasses have a 'global warming potential' (GWP). This is a factor compared to CO_2's rating of 1. Many commonly used refrigerants have GWPs of several thousand times that of CO_2. That fact sounds frightening, but heat pumps only hold about one litre or so of the stuff, so this is small compared to the tonnes of CO_2 that are produced when heating the building.

The chart above lists the environmental information for refrigerants. As can be seen, the global warming potential (GWP) for CO_2 is rated at 1. The ozone depletion potential (ODP) for obsolete refrigerant R12 is rated at 1.

Let us consider a typical modern household scenario to assess the carbon savings by using a heat pump and to balance this with the risk of a refrigerant leak. As can be seen, one loss of refrigerant would do the same harm as operating the heat pump for around one year.

The graph opposite attempts to evaluate the CO_2 savings if a heat pump is fitted to replace a conventional heating method. The time period considered is ten years and the SPF assumed to be 3. If one leak were to occur during this period, the CO_2 saving would be reduced by the amount as shown by the difference between the two blocks. For gas, the CO_2 saving would be halved due to one leak over this period.

Refrigerant leaks are very rare in a modern heat-pump and few heat pumps would need major repair work during their life. However, if this were necessary, most of the refrigerant would be recovered (it is a legal requirement and refrigerant is very expensive). Most of the refrigerant would also be recovered when a unit is scrapped.

So, for many situations, the harm caused by potential leaks would be small compared to the total CO_2 numbers at stake.

Having seen that the potential impact of refrigerant loss is relatively small, it is not ideal for the planet having tonnes of refrigerants contained within heat pumps (or fridges for that matter). As can be seen on the refrigerant chart, there are alternative refrigerants, which are often referred to as 'natural' refrigerants.

Hydrocarbons, like propane, are one such contender and are used in a few smaller units and some that live out in the open. Flammability may be an issue, but such issues need not be insurmountable. Carbon dioxide itself is a potential up-and-coming refrigerant. Ironically it is the very substance that it is trying to reduce. The amount sealed into a system is tiny and, if lost, would cause insignificant harm to the atmosphere.

The total equivalent warming impact (TEWI) is an established methodology used for evaluating the environmental impact for different refrigerants. The GWP values used are debatable since they are based on an arbitrary time horizon of 100 years. None the less, whatever figures are used, they illustrate that the impact due to the occasional refrigerant leak is relatively small.

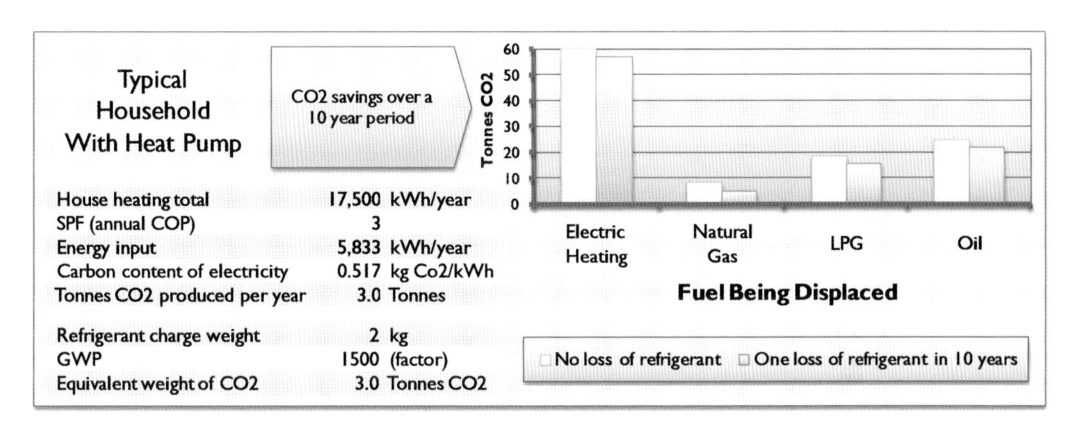

Graph comparing loss of refrigerant over ten-year period.

CHAPTER 11

ECONOMICS AND GETTING A SYSTEM INSTALLED

Comparative Running Costs of Different Fuels

In general, fuels are likely to rise at a greater rate than inflation. This is inevitable as stocks diminish and we approach 'peak oil'. In relative terms, electricity is likely to hold its own alongside gas, oil and LPG (bottled gas). This is in part due to the fact that the generating grid tends to run power stations that use the cheapest fuel available. On the other hand, we could not be without electricity for all our electronic gadgetry, so we should be prepared to pay a premium for it. In truth, we cannot say how future energy costs will pan-out, but many believe that the future will see electricity as the major form of energy, since most renewables generate electricity.

It is impossible to say how fuel costs will change, but the chart and graph shows some example typical energy costs. The figures are explained in the text below and can be adjusted to allow for variations in fuel costs over time.

	Efficiency or COP	Supplied energy unit	Example cost per Litres	Example cost per kWh	Cost of useful heat per kWh	Notes
Electric heating	100%	kWh		13p	13p	
Storage heating	80%	kWh		5.5	6.9p	(1)
Condensing boiler	88%	kWh		4.5p	5.1p	
Oil boiler	88%	litres	45p	4.4p	5.0p	(2)
Oil boiler	88%	litres	70p	6.8p	7.7p	(3)
LPG	88%	litres	55p	7.2p	8.2p	
Heat pump SPF 2.5	2.5	kWh		13p	5.2p	(4)
Heat pump SPF 3.3	3.3	kWh		13p	3.9p	"
Heat pump SPF 4	4	kWh		13p	3.3p	"
Heat pump SPF 2.5	2.5	kWh		9p	3.6p	(5)
Heat pump SPF 3.3	3.3	kWh		9p	2.7p	"
Heat pump SPF 4	4	kWh		9p	2.3p	"

Comparative example costs of fuels.

Graph comparing example costs of various fuels.

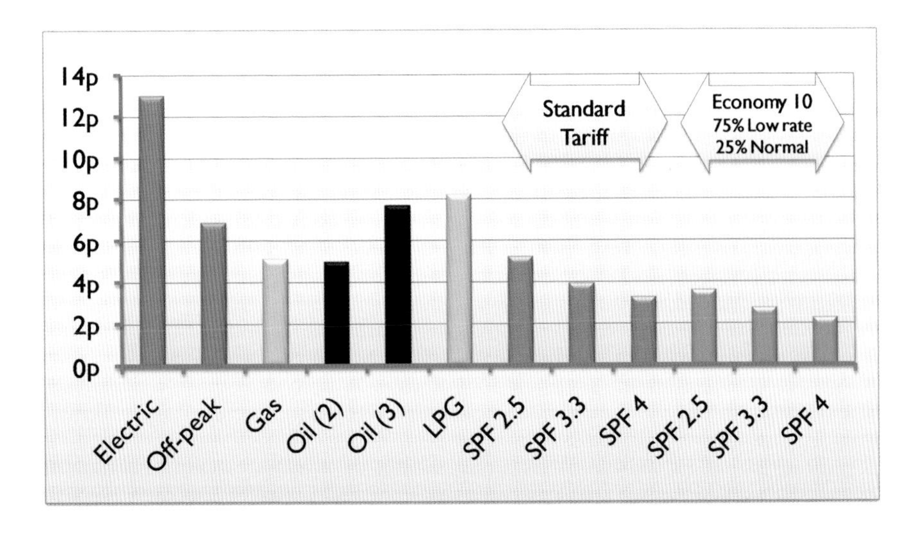

1. Storage heating often overheats the house at night, so has been given an efficiency penalty. This could be 75 per cent in an older building, or 90 per cent in well-insulated buildings.
2. Oil cost October 2010.
3. Oil cost December 2010.
4. Heat pump with various SPF values using standard electricity.
5. Heat pump with various SPF values using 75 per cent 'low' rate, Economy 10.

Electricity

Electricity is the most expensive form of energy per kWh, but since the energy demand of domestic appliances is relatively low, the price is acceptable. However, the energy required for heating is large, so electric heating is generally considered excessively expensive.

In general terms, all electricity is converted to heat, so is considered as a 100 per cent conversion. Off-peak electricity is a little more complex, since normal brick-filled storage heaters tend to emit heat all of the time and are difficult to control. Furthermore, most heat is needed in the evening when the stored heat is running out. These issues usually result in an over-heated house at night, which can be a considerable loss with older buildings. This is less of an issue with well-insulated buildings.

Mains Gas

Gas has been the cheapest heating fuel in the UK for three decades and explains the widespread adoption of gas central heating.

Gas is usually supplied in cubic metres, but since the calorific value varies all the time, the supply utilities convert this to kWh and state it as pence per kWh on gas bills. This figure relates to the energy potential of the fuel, so the boiler efficiency must be factored in.

Oil and LPG

Oil is a fuel susceptible to price variations. In late 2010, the price almost doubled within weeks of a cold snap. LPG seems to be more stable, but like oil, also has the constraint that you cannot buy unless your tank is relatively empty. It may, therefore, be difficult to buy when the price is low. Geographical location also affects the price.

Heat Pumps

Compared to direct electric heating, the running cost of a heat-pump system is simply proportion compared to the COP or SPF. For example, a heat pump with SPF 3 would have a running cost of a third that of an electric heater, so comparisons are eminently simple. To compare with other fuels, one needs to know the current cost of the fuel and the current cost of electricity.

Off-peak electricity can save a significant amount of money, but can be difficult to adopt successfully in some situations. Unlike electric storage heaters, heat pumps usually compromise and use a mixture of 'peak' and 'off-peak' electricity. The installer of the heat pump should be able to assess the viability and potential savings for your specific situation (*see* section on off-peak heating in the previous chapter).

What Will It Cost to Install?

The Renewable Heat Incentive (RHI) should dramatically change the economic viability of heat pumps in the UK. Whilst at this moment in time the final manifestation of the scheme is a little unclear, it seems likely that it will be instrumental in the rapid expansion of the industry.

The RHI will pay you for having a heat pump and the rate will relate to a 'deemed' quantity of heat that your house should need (assuming some basic energy-saving measures have been adopted first). The payment will be greater than the cost of the electricity to run the system. The reason for such a generous offer is, in part, a means to assist the country to meet its carbon-abatement targets.

It is of course difficult to suggest installation costs, since this industry is still developing. Some early adopters of the technology paid fairly high prices, as would be expected in any industry finding its feet. As operations become more streamlined, inevitably prices can drop and it would be hoped that prices will fall further. To give an indicator, a typical household air-source installation may cost between £6,000 and £10,000. A ground-source system may cost between £8,000 and £16,000.

Borehole systems are usually more expensive than horizontal trench systems – one can dig a lot of trench for the cost of a borehole. This may not apply to multiple installations, since one of the costs of making a borehole is simply getting the drilling rig and 'kit' to site. If many boreholes are required on one site, then each hole becomes cheaper.

The cost mentioned excludes the cost of the under-floor heating or radiator circuits; this can vary considerably. Under-floor heating can cost in the order of £30/m^2 and, in general, better designs (for higher COPs) will cost more to install, so an expensive system may be beneficial in the long term. Since heat-pump installations are low-carbon, they attract a reduced VAT rate of 6 per cent.

Getting a System Installed

If you have got to this point and think that a heat pump is for you, your next step will be to find a suitable installer. However, different companies can offer you very different solutions, so it is worth getting more than one opinion. Unfortunately, sifting out your best option from these may involve a considerable amount of thought, but we hope that you are now better informed. In this instance we believe that the saying 'a little knowledge is a dangerous thing' doesn't apply, since the better informed you are, the less likely you are to go wrong.

How to Find an Installer

Over the first decade of the century, the UK saw a steady tightening of regulations relating to heating installations. Whilst electricity and gas have always been tightly controlled, unusual methods like heat pumps tended to slip the net since there were no established training schemes available and no specific standards.

This has now been formalized under the Micro Generation Certification Scheme. If any installation is to attract RHI money, or any other future grants, it will need to be installed by a MCS-accredited company and the product used must also be approved. This will tend to put a stop on individuals installing systems themselves. Furthermore, the VAT on an installation is reduced to 6 per cent due to it being low-carbon, but the individual components, if purchased separately, would attract the normal higher rate of VAT.

Most customers would like an installer that is able to install the most suitable system for them, with the least disruption and at a reasonable cost. They would also expect good customer support for the odd case where things go wrong.

Local companies or companies with a local representative are usually those with the best follow-up support. Individual recommendation can be the best way to vet an installer; however, one would expect and hope any accredited company to offer a good service.

Finding a good installer is one thing, but since most installers tend to align themselves with one manufacturer, you also need to know if the product that they offer is ideally suited to your situation. For example, some manufacturer's equipment will link-in well with a boiler, others will not; some have simple controls, others are more sophisticated. The make of product may, therefore, be the most important factor to consider.

The best advice here is to approach several potential installers to see what they offer. You then need to see which one matches your needs best. If you happen to have an oil boiler that you want the heat pump to run alongside, then you might find only one of the installers is offering a proper integrated system for this.

It is always worth asking lots of questions, it is always worth getting second opinions and always worth talking to those who have lived with a system.

Another issue is the under-floor heating or radiator circuits. In some circumstances the heat pump would be installed by a completely different company to the installers of the heat-emitter circuits. Whilst there is an onus on the heat-pump installers to ensure that the under-floor is compatible, there can occasionally be issues and conflicts between the two parties. Having one company responsible for the whole system can sometimes have its advantages.

Points to Consider When Choosing a System

If you are particularly keen to save energy or reduce running costs, then you might like to consider the points on the following list.

- If radiators are to be used, will they operate at a reasonably low temperature?
- If under-floor heating has been specified, is it to the best low-temperature design practical?
- Can a solid, tile floor be used instead of wood finish?
- Is it worth specifying an 'A' energy-rated circulation pump?
- Is the heat pump as close as practical to the hot-water cylinder
- Are pipe runs in non-heated areas insulated adequately?

- Is the ground source situated in the best area of your land?
- Are radiator pipe-runs sufficient in diameter for water flow?
- Have any unnecessary mixing valves been specified?
- If a secondary return hot-water loop has been specified, are the pipes well insulated?
- Is a secondary pumped-return system (to taps) really necessary?
- Is the heat pump too big? (It is usually much smaller than a boiler.)
- Is it to small? Will it need too much back-up heating?
- Do you use a lot of hot water and like a very warm house? Will the heat pump cope?
- Has noise be considered with respect to living-rooms and bedrooms?

Although some early installations may have suffered certain shortcomings, installers are now more than aware of potential pitfalls and invariably avoid them. In many ways, this list should arguably become outdated.

CHAPTER 12

TYPICAL INSTALLATIONS CASE STUDIES

We have produced some case studies to show some real heat-pump installations. They illustrate some typical situations where the technology has been installed effectively. We have also listed running costs that the occupiers have provided. However, different people use heating systems differently and we never really know how frugal or extravagant the occupiers are. This obviously affects the energy use significantly, so our figures should be read with that thought in mind.

- Borehole system at retirement bungalow homes.
- Air-source system on a bungalow in North Wales.
- Ground-source system on a very well-insulated house in Scotland.
- Ground source with an oil boiler (bivalent).
- Air-source system in a stone-built house with woodstove back-up.

Bungalows where heat pumps have been installed. (Flintshire Council.)

Both air- and ground-source systems have been installed at some retirement bungalows in North Wales by Flintshire County Council. Dwellings are of similar size and use, so the comparisons are interesting.

Case Study 1: Ground-Source Systems on Bungalows

Outline

5kw heat output Calorex Powergen system with 70m borehole. Providing hot water and feeding radiators in reasonably well-insulated 72m^2 bungalows.

This scheme was devised to upgrade the heating systems on a row of retirement bungalows. The properties had cavity wall-insulation, thick loft-insulation and good double-glazing, so insulation levels were quite good. The scheme was to replace the existing oil boilers with a ground-source heat-pump. Under-floor heating would have been too expensive and disruptive to

Calorex heat-pump unit in old boiler room. (Flintshire Council.)

Average annual figures	
Heat pump actual electricity (kWh)	3,556
Estimated heat produced (kWh)	11,380
Old oil boiler (Litres)	1,519
Running cost	
Old boiler	£684
Heat pump	£356
Cost saving	48%
Carbon Dioxide	
Old boiler (kg / CO_2)	4,495
Heat pump (kg / CO_2)	1,839
Saving (kg / CO_2)	59%

Energy use table. (Flintshire Council.)

install. However, the insulation levels were good and therefore the reduced heat requirements meant that larger radiators (compared to those that were used with the original oil boilers) should give good results.

The controls of the system were very simple and easy to understand. The main living-room had a simple room thermostat to switch the heat pump and circulation pump on or off. When the heat pump was running, a simple thermostat on the heat pump limited the radiator water temperature to a level set by the occupier.

The picture above shows the 5kW Calorex Heat-pump unit housed in the old boiler-house/ storage shed.

A hot-water cylinder was also heated using the same system. An interesting aspect of these heat-pump units is that they are specifically designed to heat up to about 65°C. This means that the water within the cylinder can be heated up to 60°C without the need of any back-up heater. Time clocks were also fitted such that the hot-water cylinder would be heated only during specific times. This helped the energy efficiency of the water-heating mode.

Standard panel radiators are connected directly to the heat pump without a buffer cylinder. The radiators have relatively high water-content, so it takes in the region of twenty minutes to heat them from cold. This is beneficial and ensures that the heat-pump compressor does not short-cycle (turn on and off frequently), as it might tend to do otherwise. Effectively, the radiators act as the buffer cylinder.

This scheme was very successful as the electricity costs illustrated above demonstrate. It is interesting to note that the residents did take time to adapt to the heat pumps. Most occupants were worried about having a heating system that was 'on all the time' and some set the time clocks so that they only came on for a few hours in the morning and the evening.

However, it became apparent that the cosiest bungalows were the ones that were kept on constantly and the running costs of these were no greater. Since oil had previously been used on these properties, a direct comparison could be made.

The figures are based on an expected COP of 3.2, electricity at 10p/kWh and 0.517kg CO_2/kWh. Oil at 45p/ltr, 70 per cent efficiency and 0.274kg CO_2/kWh.

The above savings have been made by comparing an old boiler, whereas it might be fair to consider the heat pump against a new boiler. In this case, the heat pump would have saved about 50 per cent CO_2 compared to the 59 per cent that they recorded.

The project has proved very successful and was helped by the fact that eight systems were installed in one go. Boreholes can be expensive to install, but a row of eight are considerably cheaper per unit. Multiple installations have various advantages relating to multiples of scale and shared servicing costs and so on.

Air-source Ecodan heat-pump. (Flintshire Council.)

	kWh	Cost
Heat pump input / year	**4,259**	**£468**
Heat pump average input / day	11.7	£1.28
Heat pump mid winter average / day	31.0	£3.41
Household electricity / year	**3,381**	**£372**
Household electricity / day	9.5	£1.05

(electricity at 11p/kWh)

Cost chart. (Flintshire Council.)

Case Study 2: Air-Source System on a Bungalow

Outline

8kW heat output air-source Ecodan. Providing heat for radiators in reasonably well-insulated 85m^2 bungalows. Hot water is heated by solar and heat pump, with immersion top-up.

This air-source heat-pump was fitted to a retirement bungalow in a similar location to the ones mentioned above. The floor area is 85m^2 and just one system was installed as a trial. The building had cavity wall-insulation, 250mm of loft insulation and new double-glazed windows. The heat pump is an air-to-water 8kW Ecodan manufactured by Mitsubishi. The system feeds radiators in each room and these are approximately 1.5 times the size they would have been if a boiler had been fitted, but given the increased insulation and the more continuous-running nature of the system, this radiator sizing is relatively large and has proved adequate.

Solar is the main hot-water provider in summer, but the heat from this is insufficient for much of the year. Unlike the Calorex borehole systems, there is a maximum limit of 50°C from this heat pump, so an immersion heater is also used to automatically top-up the heat to 60°C.

The energy consumption has been monitored over the past two years and the results were recorded (above).

Whist we do not have temperature readings, we understand that the bungalow was kept adequately warm, even through early 2010 where

–9°C was recorded. The bungalow's total electricity use of 7,640kWh is quite reasonable.

The Ecodan has a variable speed inverter drive, this helps to match the heat delivered to the heat demand. This is more important with an air-source system, since it operates in greatly varying air temperatures over the seasons. The defrost mechanism on these units is well-engineered and can reverse the system when required to melt the ice. It seems that last year's low temperatures prove that this unit can cope well in extremes of temperature.

Case Study 3: Ground-Source System in a Very Low-Energy House

Outline

5kW Nibe ground-source system feeding under-floor heating in very well-insulated house. Living area 250 m^2.

One of the main criteria for this self-build project was low carbon and also longevity: this was to be a house for the future. The building itself was designed to AECB Silver Standard (very low energy). The design heat loss is very low and equates to only 30kWh/m^2/year, whilst houses built to current building regulations lose around 150kWh/m^2/year. Since the heat demand was so low, the best choice for automatic heating seemed to be a heat pump.

This type of system is eminently simple: heat is extracted from pipes buried in the ground outside and this heat is transferred to pipes embedded into the floor screed. Since the house is so well-insulated, the room temperatures naturally tend to even-up, so temperature control can be achieved very simply by the heat pump's inbuilt controller.

The heat pump was manufactured in Sweden by Nibe (pronounced: nee-bee). It comes as a neat package and has the hot-water cylinder within the same cabinet. This makes installation simple and straightforward. The under-floor heating has a tiled surface, which gives very good performance. This means that adequate heat can be achieved with very low temperatures. The owner tells us that the floor water rarely exceeds 35°C flow.

Starting the new-build; laying the under-floor heating first. (Courtesy of Steve Macken.)

ABOVE: Here is one of the trenches going in. The pipes are being protected with sand before backfilling. (Courtesy of Steve Macken.)

BELOW: The heat-pump unit with integral hot-water cylinder. (Courtesy of Steve Macken.)

The trenches were done in Swedish style and use relatively long lengths of large-bore pipe, 2 × 200m lengths of 40mm pipe in this instance. The pipes were buried at about 1m depth.

The heat pump itself is not intrusive. It sits discreetly in the utility room, with all the workings (including the hot-water cylinder) fitting neatly in the cabinet.

The illustration above shows one of the trenches going in. The pipes are being protected with sand before backfilling. (Note: photos of trenches always seem to look shallower than they really are.)

Indoors, the heat pump/hot-water cylinder gently purrs away next to the washing machine. Note the tiled floor. Such floor coverings emit heat very well and are ideal for heat-pump installations.

This unit does have an electric back-up heater. This is fitted to most heat pumps and is typical of Swedish types.

Total electricity for the heat pump over one year was almost £500 and of this, £220 was for hot-water heating. The integral electric back-up is used automatically for hot-water top-up and had run for only 3.5 per cent of total compressor run-time, so this is relatively small. The space-heating COP was measured with a heat meter and ranges from 3.2 to just over 4.

The house has performed well and the internal living space is very comfortable. The owners feel that the performance lies within their original expectations, but think they can improve matters a little by optimizing the controls.

Information

House area 250 m^2. Nibe 5kW 1640 heat-pump unit with integral 160ltr cylinder.

Running costs of the heat pump: room heating £277, hot water £219, general electricity £338.

Case Study 4: Ground-Source System with Oil Back-Up

Outline

7.5kW ground-source slinky system feeding under-floor heating and hot water. Oil boiler back-up. House: 200m^2, retrofitted with internal wall-insulation.

This house had been in the family for generations and was due for serious renovation. The owner wanted the rebuild to consider the long-term future, since any features would hopefully be passed down to future generations. Top of the list was insulation and the walls of the house were retrofitted internally with polyurethane-bonded plasterboard to the best standard practical. All windows were new high-spec argon-filled 'k' glass and the loft was insulated with Warmcell, which is a loose-fill insulation derived from paper.

The original heating system was a standard oil-fired central heating system with radiators throughout the house and it was hoped that this could be replaced by a less polluting and less expensive heating system. The heat requirements for the house were estimated at 10kW at –3°C outside.

It became clear that the available garden size was too small for a 10kW heat pump. This left a few options:

- Fit an air-source system – this was rejected on the grounds of it being obtrusive in the garden, lower efficiency in mid-winter and reduced longevity.
- Drill vertical boreholes – this was rejected due to the high installation cost.
- Fit a new high efficiency oil boiler – this was rejected on environmental grounds.

The option chosen was to fit a relatively small heat-pump that matched the available garden size and to fit a new oil boiler to cover the shortfall in heat. When this option was chosen, the heat requirements were reconsidered with the aim of reducing them as much as possible. It became evident that a sizeable proportion of the heating requirements were attributed to ventilation losses. Since the house would have new windows fitted throughout, it could be very air-tight. Indeed, some sort of mechanical ventilation would be required to maintain good internal air quality.

A passive heat-recovery ventilation system was chosen that extracted air from the kitchen, bedrooms and toilets. The air passes a part-parallel flow heat-exchanger promising 90 per cent heat recovery. This is achieved for the running cost of two relatively small fans: one to extract air and one for fresh inlet air. The fans are high efficiency DC (direct current) types, which are considerably more energy-efficient than standard AC types. Since these fans run continuously, the energy consumption is very important. The actual wattage for the ventilation unit ranges from about 30W on low setting to about 120W on boost.

The owner also wanted solar hot-water heating. This would also reduce the total heating demand for the house and so was likely to reduce the amount of heat extracted from the garden.

The actual design for the ground source was to be narrow, vertical slots 2m deep and vertically oriented slinky coils to cover the whole garden, as evenly spaced as possible. There was an access issue, since the garden access down the side of the house had limited width. Luckily excavators are now available with caterpillar-type tracks that can close together and become narrower for such situations.

The ground loops were made from three 200m lengths of 32mm outside diameter plastic

Slinkies in – ready for covering with sand.

Digging the trench.

The house, and a section of the collector trench.

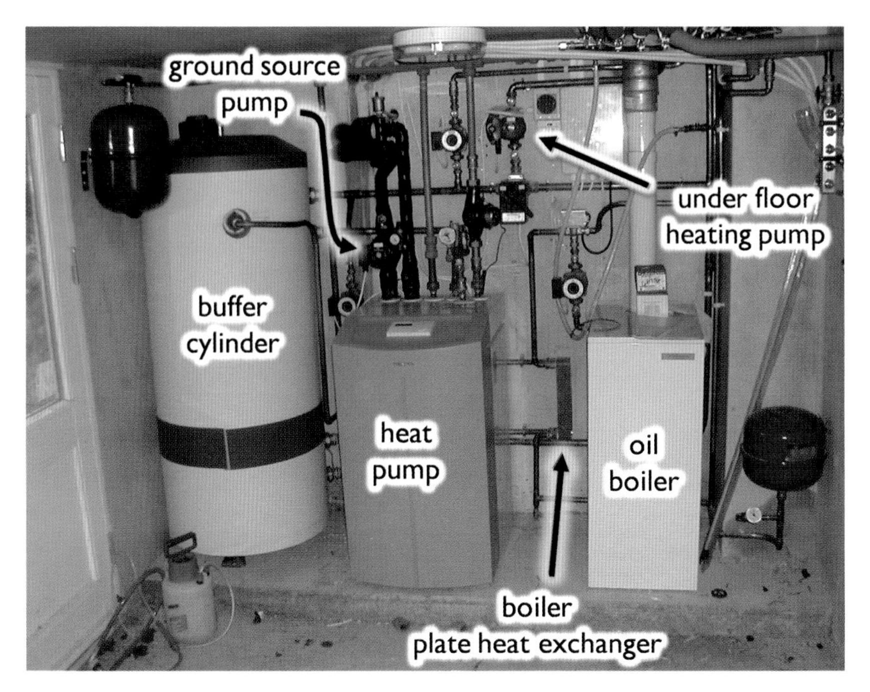

This particular installation looks complex due to its bivalent use with a boiler. Note: the pipes are not yet insulated!

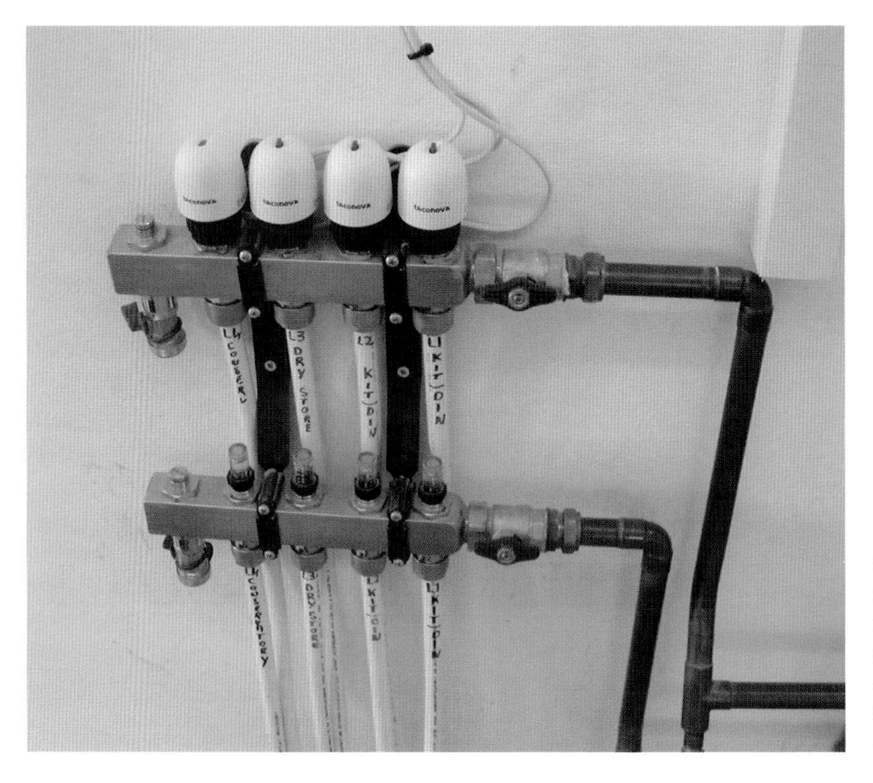

One of the under-floor manifolds. This one feeds just one room – the 'problem' suspended floor.

pipe. Each length was coiled and 'tied' into a 'slinky' and dropped into narrow trenches. Since the ground was very loose slate shale, and the wetness was unknown, the rainwater run-off from the gutters was directed on to the trenches using perforated land-drainage pipes.

The original boiler room had more than enough room for all the equipment. It was clear that the ideal strategy was to engage the boiler for the domestic hot-water heating (DHW) in winter when the heat pump's capacity was less than the total heat demand. It is better to allow the heat pump to operate at lower temperature levels where it is most efficient, i.e. for room heating.

A specialist under-floor heating consultant was engaged, since one of the rooms of the ground floor was suspended timber above the cellar. It could have been difficult to ensure that the working temperatures of the under-floor heating could be kept as low as is ideal for the heat pump.

The final under-floor design incorporated 16mm multi-layer pipe in screed above 100mm of polyurethane, with average pipe spacing of about 125mm. The 'problem' room with the suspended floor used 0.7mm thick aluminium spreader plates at the closest possible spacing practical and the joists were counter-battened at 90 degrees to accomplish this. It was decided to increase the wall insulation in this particular room and also to use a higher water flow rate within these floor pipes, since it was known that this room would be the hardest room in the house to heat.

As a safeguard, and partly for aesthetics, a wood stove was fitted to the main living room. This ensured that at least one room could be warmed, even given a power cut during a severe cold snap. We are told that the stove is almost never used.

There are no historical energy figures, but current total electricity consumption for the house is 10,500kWh/year. At 12p per unit, this costs £1,260. Oil costs only £290 per year, so a full tank has lasted three years. The total energy cost including all electricity and oil is about £1,500 per year. Remember, this is a large house with a large and active family of six, plus two dogs.

Case Study 5: Air-Source System with Wood Heating

This is an interesting installation of an air-source heat-pump on a standard stone-built house located in mid-Wales.

A Nibe air-source heat-pump was installed to replace an oil-fired heating system at this house in mid-Wales. It is a typical slate-built house with thick walls.

By modern standards this house is not very well-insulated, but many windows have been improved with secondary glazing and the loft has been insulated with four inches of rock wool. The Swedish-made heat-pump sits around the back of the house and is connected to panel radiators throughout the house. More radiators than is usual have been fitted (e.g. at least two radiators on opposite walls per room). A hot-water cylinder is located internally very close to the heat pump; this is made by the same manu-

Nibe air source installed by Llani Solar.

The stone-built house.

facturer as the heat pump and supplied as an integral part of the design.

This installation would not tick that many boxes for an 'ideal' installation due to the relatively poor insulation and use of radiators. However, the owners are very happy with it, in part because they do not wish for an overly warm house.

The system operates efficiently during the in-between times of spring and autumn. At such times, the 'weather-compensation' control automatically reduces the radiator temperature so that the energy efficiency is high. Come winter, the radiators would need to rise up to the maximum limit of the heat pump if full heating were required in this averagely un-insulated house. However, in cold periods they supplement the central heating system with efficient modern stoves, burning home-produced wood, which is in plentiful supply.

Fortunately the owners don't mind keeping the heat at a relatively low level during winter days and are content to stoke up the woodstoves when it's particularly cold and during the evenings. They also know that if they go away in the middle of winter, they will come back to a lukewarm house rather than a stone-cold one, and it will not take long to boost the heat with the fires.

The heat pump fitted is a Nibe 2005-11 that will operate down to air temperatures of –7°C and maximum water temperatures of +58°C. The following gives inputs and outputs at various temperatures:

Air 7°C, water to 35°C: power input 2.6kW, heat output 10.6kW, COP: 3.61.
Air –7°C, water to 50°C: power input 3.1kW, heat output 6.9kW, COP: 2.

Note: COP figures allow for defrost losses.

The house area is about 120m^2 but not every area is fully heated. We don't have figures for the quantity of wood used in the stoves nor for the energy generated. However, they used to spend £1,000 per year on oil and first-year figures indicate a spend of £600 per year on electricity to power the heat pump, which generates a similar level of warmth within the house. They are also saving on oil-boiler servicing costs.

The Nibe hot-water cylinder in the utility room.

CHAPTER 13

COMMON MYTHS AND MISCONCEPTIONS

'The colder the ground pipes, the more heat is extracted.'

TRUE, BUT...

Given that a colder ground coil means a larger temperature difference between the ground and the pipe, then the following example is true:

Ground 10°C, ground-pipe 5°C: heat transfer 1kW.

Ground 10°C, ground-pipe 0°C: heat transfer about 2kW.

However, the question seems to imply that 'more heat' is good. This is not necessarily so. The statement could be better posed from a different view point:

'If more heat is extracted, then the ground coils get colder.'

This leads to a further question: Is a lower ground pipe temperature good?

Answer: *No*, because it means that the heat pump would be less energy-efficient.

How else can we get a better heat transfer without increasing the temperature difference?

Answer: Have a bigger ground coil (back to our previous example):

Ground at 10°C, ground-pipe at 5°C:
heat transfer 1kW.

Now double the length of the pipe:

Ground at 10°C, ground-pipe at 5°C:
heat transfer 2kW.

In the above example, we have doubled the heat transfer and retained the same operating temperatures by increasing the pipe surface area. This is a better viewpoint to consider things from, since high source temperatures result in a better energy efficiency.

The same principles apply to the heat-exchanger coils within the hot-water storage cylinder. The larger they are, the smaller the temperature difference between the water from the heat pump and the water going to the tap. This leads to higher energy efficiencies due to the lower working temperature that the heat pump 'sees'.

'The power surge to start a compressor wastes energy.'

FALSE

When a compressor starts, it draws a high current for a fraction of a second. In energy terms this is negligible and probably equal to only about one second of running.

There is, however, an energy penalty due to stopping and starting, but this is due to the refrigerant circuit. It takes a minute of so for the system's efficiency to 'build-up' and stabilize. Also, for some systems, losses can result immediately after stopping.

'The greater the Delta T, the better the heat transfer.'

NOT NECESSARILY

The topic of temperature differences can be confusing. The Delta T (ΔT, or dt) is the difference between two temperatures and is often used to describe the difference between the 'flow' and 'return' in a system.

It may be true that if the ΔT is large, then the heat transfer is also large, but there is also another very important factor: the water flow rate.

The ΔT is dependent on two things: a heat quantity in (kW) and a flow rate (ltr/s). The result of these two factors gives a temperature rise (or ΔT).

A mathematical equation gives the relationship as follows:

$\text{kW} = \text{ltr/s} \times 4.2 \times \Delta T$, or
$\Delta T = \text{kW}/(\text{ltr/s} \times 4.2)$,
(4.2 is the specific heat capacity for water, measured in kJ/kg Kelvin).

For example, a swimming-pool heat-pump may have a heat-exchanger that takes the full pool water-flow and the ΔT may be only 0.25°C (one-quarter), but there would be no lack of heat transfer. The actual pool temperature and the source temperature of the heat pump would dictate the transfer.

The three aspects (heat, flow and ΔT) are interdependent and must all be considered.

It seems better to think that the ΔT results from a specific flow rate and a specific heat quantity, rather than considering the ΔT as the starting point.

'Under-floor heating requires a lot of power to circulate the water through all the pipes.'

FALSE

To circulate water around any circuit, pressure is required. A circulation pump generates this pressure. The flow depends on the restriction of the pipe (its diameter). The longer the pipe, the greater the total pressure drops. To overcome this, the pipe would need to have a very large diameter. However, if multiple parallel circuits are used, the pressure drop can become manageable. The 'force' required to circulate the water at an adequate rate is simply a matter of chopping the total pipe length up into a sufficient number of parallel circuits. The actual design becomes a compromise of pipe diameter and number of parallel circuits.

In summary, in a well-designed system with sufficient number of loops of circuits and large enough diameter pipe, then a standard domestic circulator should be perfectly adequate for even a fairly large house with seemingly vast quantities of pipe.

'Ice build-up on the evaporator pipes is desirable.'

NOT NECESSARILY

There is a little confusion about this topic. With respect to energy efficiency, the higher the temperature of the collector, the better the efficiency of the heat pump. So, for example, a collector temperature of +2°C is better than a temperature of –2°C. Therefore, a system that avoids ice will have a higher COP than one where ice builds up (*see* COP chart on page 140).

Confusion can result from quotes that large quantities of heat can be extracted when ice is being formed due to its latent heat. This is true, but it happens at a temperature where the COP is slightly lower. If one is considering how to get a lot of heat out of a small collector, then ice build-up can be part of the strategy. Ice build-up may be a cost-effective option from an installation-cost point of view and could make an installation economic. However, the following should be considered: ice build-up can create cavities around the pipes that, when melted, may be replaced by air, which would reduce the heat transfer. Also, densely packed clay or very dry ground would have a low water-content; rock may have none, so little or no ice would form. Geographical location also has a bearing on this topic. In cold climates, there may be no option other than to build up ice. However, in the UK, particularly in the south, collector temperatures can be kept above freezing.

'It is bad for a heat pump to run continuously without stopping.'

FALSE AND TRUE

False because, unlike some mechanical devices, a heat-pump unit can run without resting. This is not the case for many appliances. A coffee grinder, for example, would only ever be expected to run for five minutes, so it is only designed for 'intermittent' use. A heat pump is clinically clean inside and must be designed to run for many hours. After several hours it would reach steady-state equilibrium, so continuing on without rest is possible. Unlike car engines, the compressor oil never comes into contact with the air, so it remains clean.

True because a ground source loop may become exhausted of heat if the heat pump runs too much. But if the source collector is big enough, it could actually run without rest.

COPs OF GROUND SOURCE

Due to the many variables (compressor types, refrigerant types, heat-exchanger efficiencies and so on), it is almost impossible to give general performance figures. None the less, we wanted to give some charts that would be useful for reference. Actual data for specific equipment should be available from the manufacturers.

The chart below gives expected COPs at different working conditions for a typical ground-source heat-pump unit. The horizontal axis relates to the source liquid coming back from the ground source, the vertical axis is the water flow to the heating circuits. The figures are averages taken from various manufacturers and are also a merger of both high- and low-temperature units.

The green area is obviously the preferred area of operation, so any ways of shifting in that direction would be desirable.

We cannot guarantee the accuracy of these figures compared to your heat pump, but this chart may be very useful for comparing data.

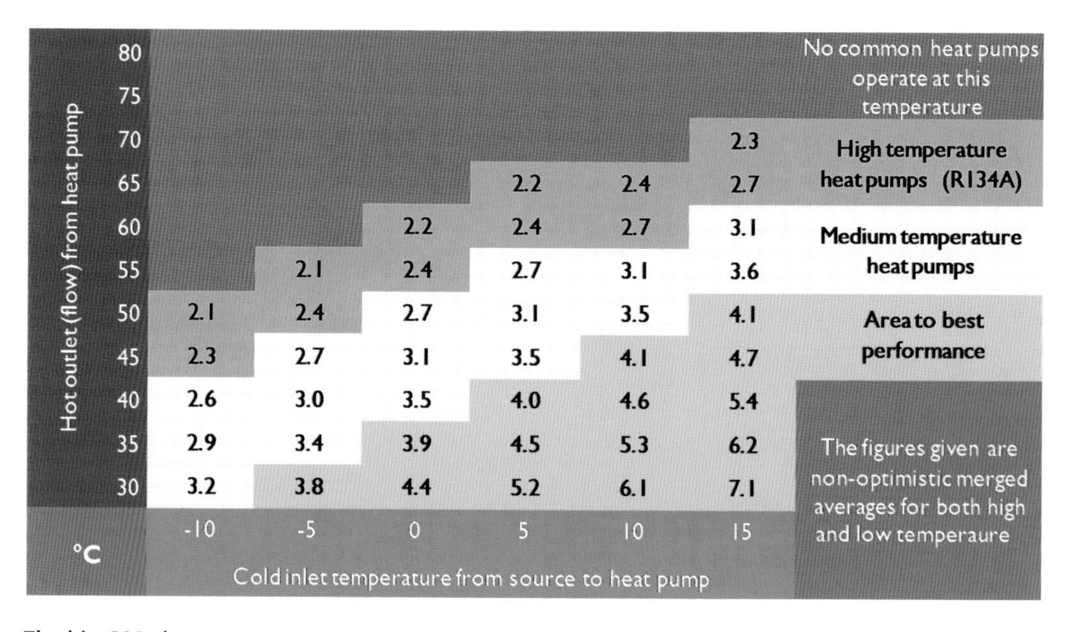

Hot outlet (flow) from heat pump °C	-10	-5	0	5	10	15
80						
75						
70						2.3
65				2.2	2.4	2.7
60			2.2	2.4	2.7	3.1
55		2.1	2.4	2.7	3.1	3.6
50	2.1	2.4	2.7	3.1	3.5	4.1
45	2.3	2.7	3.1	3.5	4.1	4.7
40	2.6	3.0	3.5	4.0	4.6	5.4
35	2.9	3.4	3.9	4.5	5.3	6.2
30	3.2	3.8	4.4	5.2	6.1	7.1

The big COP chart.

For example, you could assess the benefit of fitting larger radiators that operate at a lower temperature.

You could also use the chart to estimate the actual COP of your heat pump by reading your actual temperatures from your controller (temperature information), or with a thermometer. These values could be entered into the chart. Again, many factors could affect the actual figures, but this chart can certainly point you in the right direction towards achieving a better efficiency.

It may be important to mention again that most heat pumps display the water-return temperature back to the heat pump. However, variable-capacity inverter types indicate the water 'flow' temperature out from the heat pump. The 'flow' might be around 6°C warmer than the 'return', for example the reading on a Japanese-style air-source inverter system might be 42°C (flow), whereas the German ground source might show a setting of 36°C (return). Both are operating at about the same conditions and would correspond to 42°C on the chart.

APPENDIX II

COPs OF AIR SOURCE

The data for this graph was taken from an average of various makes of air-source heat-pump. Please be aware that the energy efficiency of different heat pumps can vary greatly. Compressor type, heat-exchanger size and refrigerant types can make a great difference. None the less, we have included this graph and warn that it is only a guide. In general, cheaper units have lower efficiency than more expensive units. The figures include any energy required for automatic defrosting, which mostly occurs below 6°C.

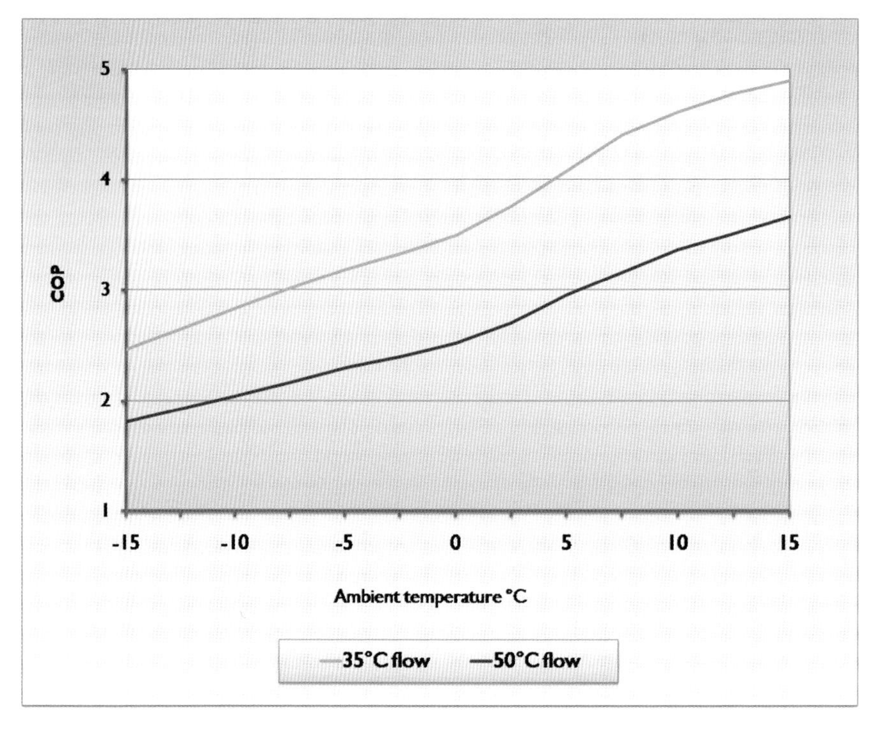

Air source performance.

REAL-TEST DATA OF AIR SOURCE

We wanted to show you some real live data from a working heat pump. The graph was taken from a small Japanese-style inverter-drive air-source heat-pump that we have monitored. Using a data-logger, we measured the water flow rate, the water temperatures (in and out) and the electricity pulses. To make a comparison, we have fitted an immersion heater immediately after the heat pump. After the first ten minutes we switched off the heat pump and switched on the heater for about four minutes. In the final few minutes there is no heating.

The heat pump was running at steady state before this 'snap shot' of data. Note the inverter was 'modulating'. However, the COP hovers between 3 and 3.5. The outside air temperature at this time was 5°C and, as the graph shows, the flow is about 42°C.

As can be seen, the heat output is about 5kW for an input of about 1.5kW, giving a COP of over 3.

At about eleven minutes, the electric heater takes over and about 2.8kW of electricity converts to 2.8kW of heat (COP 1). The final few minutes proves the sensors are calibrated.

We also tested the defrost and assessed it to reduce the COP by about 10 per cent at the worse times. However, the unit only defrosts when necessary and seems to be very accurate and economical in this matter. For much of the time the defrost occurrence is infrequent.

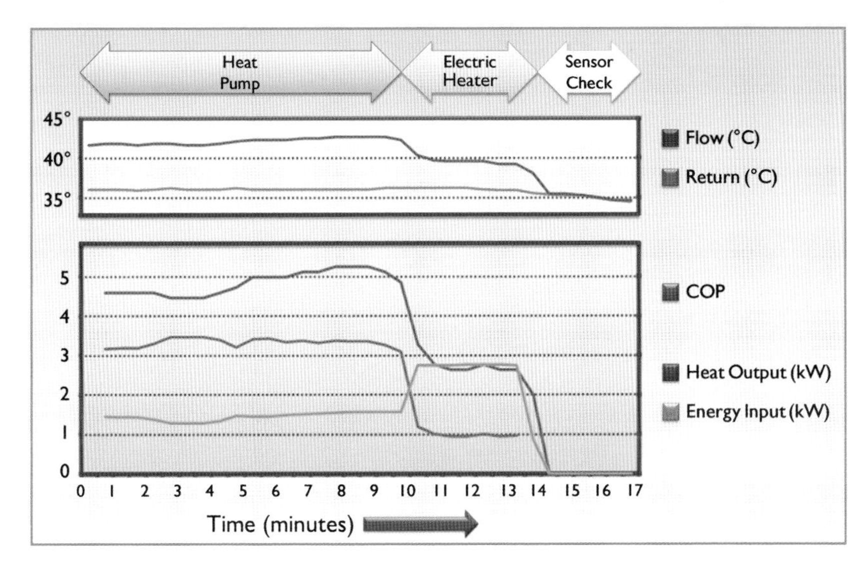

Real-life test data.

APPENDIX IV

WHAT GOES ON INSIDE A HEAT PUMP

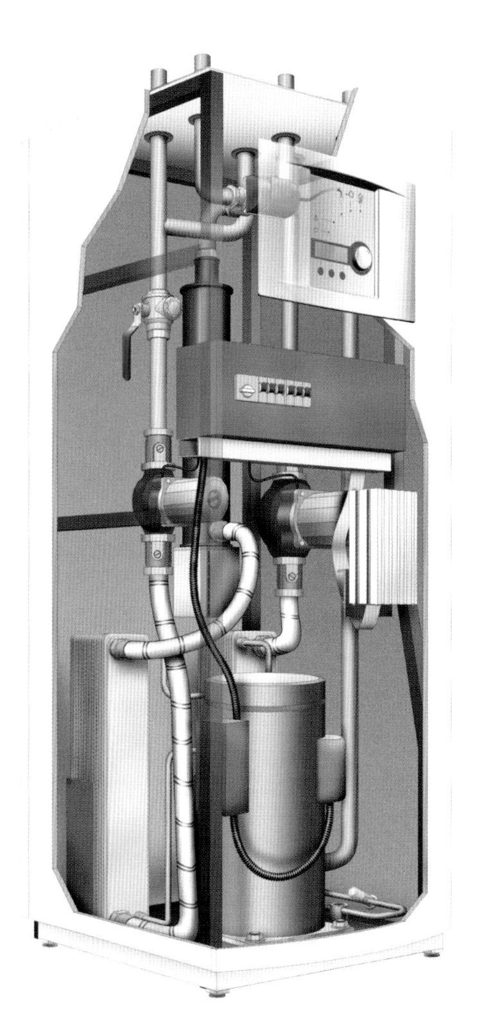

Inside a heat pump.

Let us start at first principles in simple language and then look in more scientific terms.

Consider what happens when liquids turn to vapour. We are all familiar with water boiling in a saucepan. It takes a lot of energy from the cooker ring for the pan to boil dry. A great deal of energy is required to convert water to steam. We are only familiar with the process when heat is added to the pan; however, there is another way to make a liquid boil or 'vaporize' – reduce the pressure. You can boil water at a lower temperature on a mountain, as there is less air pressure at high altitude. If you put water in a vacuum, it is effectively forced to boil and will do so at a much lower temperature. Amazingly, boiling iced water is possible if the pressure is low enough.

Let us now consider the saucepan at room temperature. If we were to seal the top of the pan with a strong lid and attach a pipe from a vacuum pump, we could remove air from above the liquid and create a vacuum. Some of the liquid would vaporize to fill the vacuum. In doing so, energy (the latent heat of evaporation) would be removed from the liquid and the liquid would cool to a temperature below the saucepan's surroundings. The cooling of gas bottles and aerosols whilst in use helps to demonstrate the same principle. If we continue to suck out the vapour, liquid continues to vaporize and heat energy will flow into the pan from the room, since the pan is colder than the room. It is the room's energy (as opposed to the cooker ring) that is now being absorbed and it is this energy that is converting the liquid to a vapour.

Vapour contains more energy than liquid and it is not too difficult to arrange things such that the vapour condenses back to a liquid. This would take place if we simply 'force' the vapour into another sealed pan. The pressure and the temperature would rise and heat would be given off. The vapour would condense as heat leaves the second pan, thus giving out the energy that was previously absorbed. In simple terms, that explains the vapour compression cycle.

That was the way that the first refrigeration experiments were performed by scientists back in the eighteenth century (well, they probably didn't use saucepans).

To make this process work continuously, we can take the liquid that has condensed on the 'hot' side of the circuit and allow it to flow back, at a controlled rate, into the low-pressure 'evaporator'. It now experiences a drop in pressure and evaporates again. So now we have a complete cycle that can continue indefinitely provided that we keep powering the compressor.

The pressure–enthalpy (PH) graph on page 146 is an excellent way to 'map' the cycle; graphs are available for any specific fluid. This one is for refrigerant R134A, which is found in some heat pumps. It shows the change of heat-energy (enthalpy) plotted against the pressure.

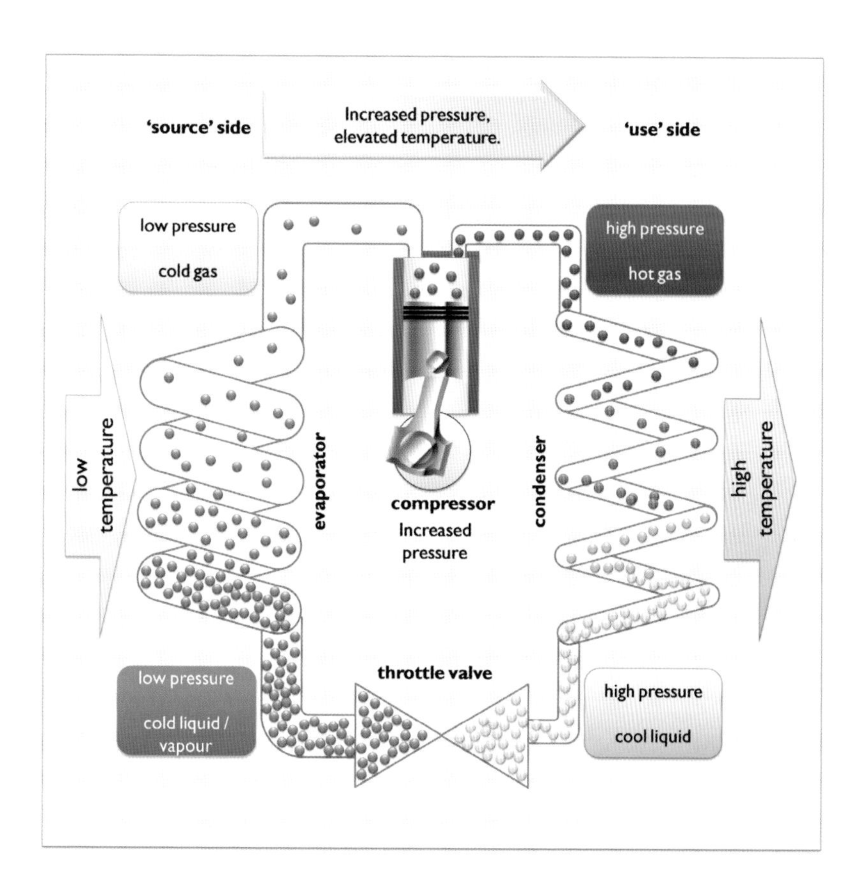

The diagram shows the vapour compression circuit.

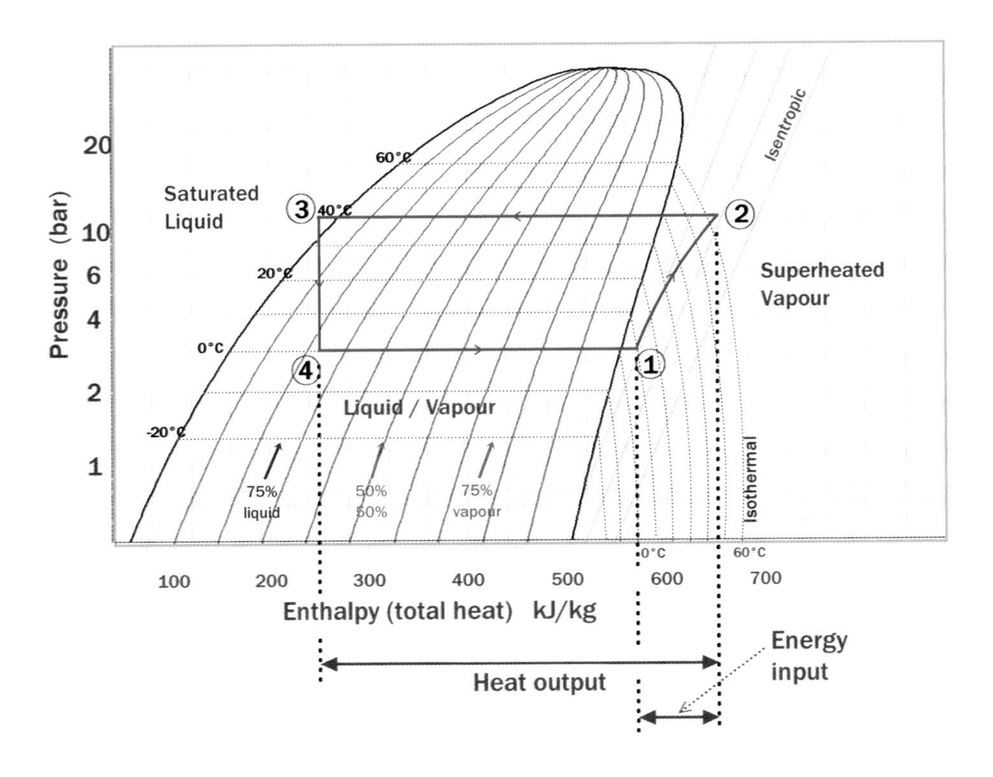

PH diagram.

To explain it, we can consider the following. Imagine a point on the left in the saturated liquid zone. If this liquid is heated (assuming unvarying pressure), we can follow a horizontal line to the right (as its energy increases). Its temperature rises as we travel to the right and it starts to boil as it reaches the left side of the 'hump'. It then vaporizes bit by bit, at constant temperature, as it traverses the liquid/vapour zone. By the time it has reached the right-hand side of the 'hump', it is 100 per cent vapour. As we continue to the right, the vapour becomes superheated. The position along the line imagined represents the energy content of the fluid.

We normally only experience things at one pressure – atmospheric – but heat pumps have a high- and a low-pressure side. Now let us see how the vapour-compression heat-pump cycle can be mapped on the chart. Let us start at the low-pressure inlet of the compressor of about (1). The vapour is compressed within the compressor and becomes high pressure as it emerges at point (2). It has also increased in temperature during the fast compression process. From point (2), the hot vapour enters the condenser and we can follow the horizontal line to the left where the vapour changes to liquid bit by bit as it traverses to point (3) at constant (high) pressure. The liquid is warm but, having moved to the left, the energy content is now low. It is also slightly 'sub-cooled', being firmly in the liquid zone. From point (3) to (4) the refrigerant experiences a pressure drop as it passes the expansion valve; this is done without a change in energy content, but due to the fact that some of it has become a vapour, it has also dropped in temperature. It is now a cold mixture of about 75 per cent liquid and 25 per cent vapour. From point (4) to point (1), the liquid/vapour mixture absorbs energy and the remaining cold liquid turns to vapour. This happens at a constant low temperature and low pressure. The enthalpy rises significantly as it traverses to the right. We are now back at the start ready for the compressor to raise the pressure again in a continuous circular process.

The energy content on the horizontal axis tells us how much energy is involved in each part of the process. The heat output is the distance from (2) to (3). The energy input is the horizontal distance from (1) to (2). Thus the ratio of these two values describes the COP of the process.

It is rather fortuitous that CO_2 has the right properties to operate as a refrigerant in the transcritical cycle, at temperatures that can match our domestic needs. This has given rise to an interesting new development, and a few products are currently in the market. The transcritical cycle differs from the conventional vapour-compression cycle described above since the pressure on the 'high' side of the system goes above the 'hump' of the PH graph. This region is above that where liquid can exist, so no condensing takes place in the high-side heat exchanger (we can no longer call it a 'condenser'). In the transcritical cycle, the high-pressure dense substance loses its heat and drops in temperature as it does so. This is in contrast to a condensing vapour that losses heat at a constant temperature. The transcritical cycle is sensitive to the water flow rate in the 'hot' heat exchanger, so the design of the heat-output side of the system is key to efficient operation. Whilst energy efficiency may not be as high as that of the conventional system, the high temperatures possible, and the benign nature of CO_2 refrigerant, may make this system worthy of development and optimization.

Inside your heat pump will be the following components:

Picture of a twin compressor Kensa unit with its cover off.

A stainless steel plate heat-exchanger.

- Evaporator.
- Condenser.
- Compressor.
- Expansion device.
- The refrigerant.
- Electrical controls.
- It may, or may not, contain circulation pumps and diverter valves.

The evaporator is sometimes almost identical to the condenser, but performs an opposite function. One is where the liquid refrigerant evaporates and cools the glycol mixture that flows around the ground loops. The other is where the compressed liquid condenses and delivers the heat to the water for its final use in radiators and so on. Formerly these heat-exchangers were often simple copper tube-in-tube devices usually coiled for compactness. These 'coaxial' heat-exchangers have now been almost exclusively replaced with the stainless plate heat-exchanger, as shown in the picture. The reason for this trend is simply due to modern mass production techniques. There are two pairs of pipe connections: one for one fluid and one for the other. The fluids do not mix, but pass in close proximity over a large area, such that heat is transferred. These multi-plate compact units are induction-brazed in an inert gas environment. They offer excellent performance and high reliability and are convenient to fit in a compact heat-pump unit.

To enable the pressure difference between the two heat-exchangers, a compressor is used. The compressor is actually a very highly developed electric motor connected directly to a mechanical compressor. These are contained in a welded steel shell and are therefore 100 per cent leak-free.

There are a few different types of compressor used in domestic heat pumps:

- Reciprocating (piston type).
- Rotary scroll.
- Rotary eccentric roller with vane.

Each may be chosen for different reasons but this detail is a little beyond the scope of this book. However, we can say that the scroll is exclusive to medium to large heat-pumps and the rotary roller-type is more suited to smaller units and common in inverter drive air-source units.

Prior to the development of the 'scroll', compressors were exclusively reciprocating (piston) types and it is incredible to think how many

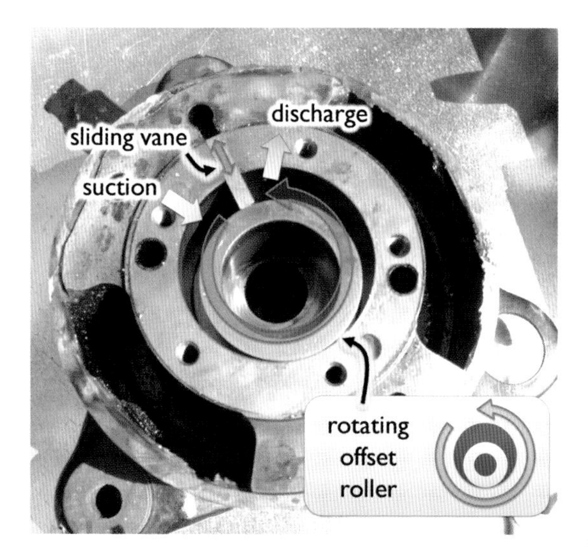

LEFT: **A cut-open small rotary compressor. This type is used in the Mitsubishi Ecodan and most small to medium air conditioners.**

BELOW: **A Scroll compressor.**

piston strokes are possible. A compressor could easily run continuously for thirteen years at 3,000rpm. That would be about 20,000,000,000 piston strokes! That is an amazing durability, made possible by the fact that the system is completely sealed. The oil, after all these years, may be as clear and honey-looking as the day it was put in.

The scroll hit the market around 1990 and promised significant energy efficiencies in the order of 20 per cent. Again, it was modern mass production techniques with very high accuracy that made this design possible. The low noise, energy efficiency and compactness made it the preferred choice.

It is worth noting that one reciprocating design, the Bristol Inertia, did put up a good contest. However, as time goes on, the scroll is continuing to be optimized. It is an evolutionary process and the most efficient designs that are cheap and practical to manufacture tend to survive.

We are all familiar with boilers automatically 'cycling' on and off to give us the heat output we need. Most heat pumps work in this manner. The compressor automatically stops and starts as dictated by the controller, thus the required heat output is achieved. It should be noted that compressors cannot be switched as frequently as the flame in a boiler. Heat pumps should not start too frequently. Generally, a compressor should not start more than once every 10–15 minutes, ideally longer. This is for several reasons: partly for wear and tear, possibly due to a risk of the windings overheating and also for energy efficiency. It takes a minute or so for the refrigerant circuit to settle down, so energy transfer immediately after start-up is poor. Also, back-transfer of refrigerant after stopping may take place in some units and this would be a small energy loss. It should be noted that the starting 'kick' draws a very high current, but only for a fraction of a second, so energy losses here are negligible.

Like modern 'modulating' boilers, some heat pumps have compressors that can vary and reduce their capacity. This is generally achieved by an electrical device that varies the speed of the electric motor by varying the electrical alternating-current frequency. This is known as an 'inverter' drive and is common with modern Japanese-style air-source units. Other methods of capacity control are possible by unloading the compressor, and this can be achieved efficiently with a scroll compressor. A two-stage heat-pump gives a part variable capacity by simply switching in one compressor or two.

Methods of capacity control are no doubt being developed all the time. There are pros and cons of both:

- Variable inverter drives are very good for direct blown-air systems (air-conditioning), since stopping and starting could result in batches of varying temperature air. A possible downside is that, whilst very reliable, they could be expensive to replace.
- Inverters are often seen as the preferred modern system; however, the on/off control can be easily accommodated with radiator and under-floor systems, where the on/off nature would be 'buffered' by the volume of water in the system. So the choice should be dictated by the need for capacity control specific to the installation.

The liquid metering device is commonly called an 'expansion valve'. High-pressure liquid goes in and low-pressure liquid (with some vapour) comes out. The term can be a little misleading and it could be argued that 'throttling' valve or 'restrictor' describes it better. The thermostatic expansion valve has a small orifice and needle that modulates and is effectively controlled by the temperature conditions in the evaporator. A simpler, liquid metering device is a small capillary pipe. This is only used in domestic fridges and air-conditioning. It is not quite as simple as first envisaged, since the control of flow is controlled automatically by the bubbles that form as the refrigerant passes down the pipe. It is actually very cunning and self-regulating. However, the device is inherently inefficient as a control device, since it partly relies on changes in pressures to regulate the flow. On the other hand it is intrinsically reliable.

A development that has led to far superior flow control is the electronic expansion valve. It is advantageous on systems that operate over a wide range of temperatures, hence its popularity with air-source systems. There are many different types and no doubt they will evolve to become cheaper and cheaper. This should drive up COPs.

De-Superheater

This device is a heat-exchanger that takes heat from the discharge pipe as it leaves the compressor. Normally this heat would find its way to the condenser and be used. However, the discharge from the compressor is 'superheated' and therefore can be many degrees hotter than the condensing refrigerant. This superheat may only be a small proportion of the total heat, but it could be worthwhile separating-out this heat.

For example, if a heat pump is producing 10kW of heat to under-floor heating at, say, 40°C, then maybe 1kW could be taken from the discharge pipe at around 60°C. In certain circumstances the superheat could go as high as 80°C. Furthermore, if a system is in reverse-mode for cooling, then the de-superheater can continue to heat water.

One might be wondering why every heat pump doesn't have one: the water plumbing becomes a little more complex and it may not be quite as straight forward to set up. But if the heat pump has an integral water cylinder, then the superheat could be utilized by simply configuring the condenser appropriately.

Sight Glass

You can actually see the refrigerant here if one is fitted. If operating correctly, this spyglass should be full of liquid, not bubbles. However, some care should be taken if diagnosing, since bubbles can form in certain conditions and this may not necessarily mean that you are short of refrigerant. If it is never full, then there could be a problem, and would manifest in a reduced heat output.

Filter-Drier

This never needs changing unless a refrigerant component is changed.

Pressure Switches

These act as safety cutouts if the pressures stray beyond normal conditions. They indirectly stop the compressor.

Refrigerants

The working fluid in a heat pump is called a refrigerant and is also used in every fridge, air-conditioner and supermarket chiller. It must have certain properties for it to be efficient at heat transfer. It should also ideally be non-corrosive, non-toxic, non-flammable and mix with oils for compressor lubrication.

In the post-war era, there was a rapid growth in the refrigerant industry and CFC gases (chlorofluorocarbons) were thought to be ideal. They were inert, non-toxic and had ideal thermal

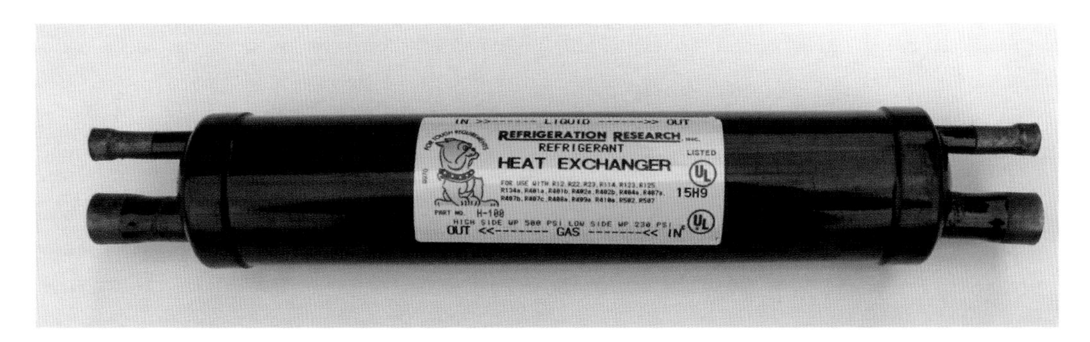

A de-superheater heat-exchanger could take many forms. This one has a copper coil inside a steel shell.

properties. They were also ideal propellants for aerosols. Sadly, there was also a downside to this seemingly perfect fluid, which was not realized or acknowledged until the early 1980s. CFC gases were discovered to destroy the ozone layer in the Earth's upper atmosphere, which is important in filtering out harmful ultra-violet rays from the sun.

Less harmful alternatives were sought and by the late 1980s the major chemical companies had developed refrigerants that did not, to our knowledge, harm the ozone layer. These gases are known as HFCs and are now standard to most refrigeration and heat-pump systems. HFCs seem to be the best refrigerants to use with existing compressor technology. Different oils were required, but otherwise equipment stayed much the same. There are now stringent rules relating to the use of refrigerants, and gases can no longer be vented to the atmosphere. It is now a legal requirement to recover and contain refrigerant when old equipment is scrapped.

There have, however, been some other contenders that promise much lower environmental impact. Hydrocarbons are one such relatively benign refrigerant. They have very good thermal properties but there is a downside: they are flammable, so some care is required with their use. That said, many domestic fridges use Hydrocarbon R600A; this is iso-butane and a typical small fridge would need about ten cigarette lighter's worth. Such a small amount is not deemed to be hazardous. Heat-pump units would tend to have a larger charge, typically 1ltr. This is seen to be a little more hazardous, so its use is generally limited to units that sit outside a house.

Hydrocarbons remain a reasonable option and flammability risks could be addressed if the need was there (remember, there is an endless gas supply on a gas cooker and this technology is commonplace and deemed safe).

For larger installations, ammonia is a possible contender. It is locally quite hazardous, but has little or no long-term effects if released in to the atmosphere.

The use of CO_2 as the refrigerant is another possibility. Ironically using a negligible amount as a working fluid of the very gas that is alleged to be causing global warming could potentially save tonnes of CO_2 over its working lifetime. This is a fairly new development and requires components that can accommodate exceptionally high pressures. The thermodynamic process is slightly different to the vapour compression cycle. It is called transcritical – the CO_2 at high pressure and high temperature goes above the 'critical' pressure, such that neither liquid nor vapour can be defined. Such systems seem well-matched to hot-water production. It is possible that this would become the refrigerant of choice in the future. At this point, all we can say is 'watch this space'.

The vast majority of heat pumps have one single compressor, but there are some variants:

- Larger units may use a 'tandem pair' of compressors. These are simply two compressors side-by-side that are linked with common oil ways. Either one or both can run, offering 50 per cent or 100 per cent capacity.
- Alternatively, a unit can have two entirely separate refrigeration circuits in one cabinet. These are potentially more expensive to buy, but if one system were to fail, it is likely that the other would still operate.
- A more complicated use of a double system is the 'cascade' where one system comes after the other. This may only make sense if high temperatures are needed. This system is very complex, so it is unlikely that this method would be viable for domestic applications.

Pipe Diameters and Lengths

We considered earlier in the book that the flow in a pipe depends on two things:

- The pressure across the pipe (ultimately caused by the circulating pump).
- The diameter or restriction of the pipe.

Now look at an example: if we increase the pipe diameter, then we need less pressure to circulate it, hence the pump consumes less energy. It can be an expensive strategy to install a large pipe, so a compromise is found between energy expended in pumping and the cost of pipe and fittings.

It would at first seem far from ideal having apparent bottlenecks at each end of the 100m-long pipe-run in our example. However, about half of the total pressure drop occurs in the small 5m sections. The other half occurs in the 80m-long large pipe. It follows that short sections of smaller pipe may be acceptable. It is a matter of calculating the total pressure drop of the system. There is an extra pressure loss due to the pipes 'sizing-up' and 'sizing-down', but this is relatively small and accounts for only around 5 per cent of the total.

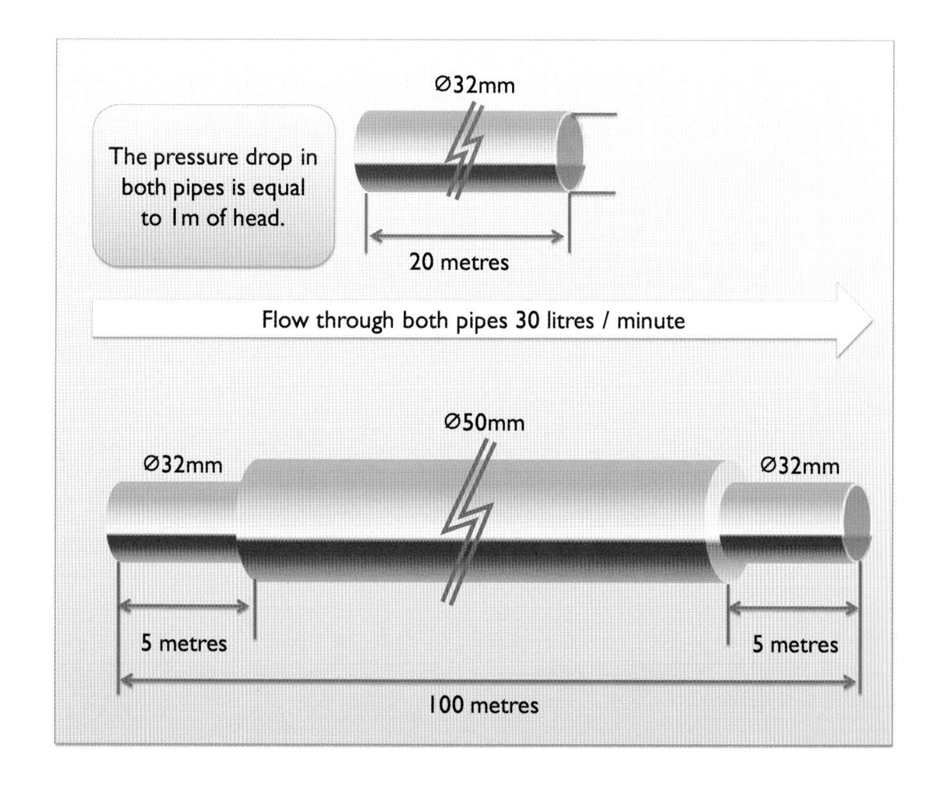

Pipe run diameters.

POWER

Power is a measurement of energy used or generated in a unit of time. It is commonly measured in Watts (W). For example, a one-bar electric heater consumes 1kW (1,000W) and so uses one unit of electrical energy every hour.

1W = 1J/s.
1kW = 3,412 British Thermal Units (Btu) per hour, so 10kW = 34,120Btu/h.
1kW = 860kcal/h.

A normal immersion heater uses about 3kW when heating and draws about 12 Amps.

Energy

1kWh (kilowatt hour) is a quantity of energy, or one unit of electricity. A 1kW heater would use 1kWh per hour of energy, or 24 units per day. Note that gas bills now also use kWh, instead of the old Therms unit.

3,600 kilojoules (kJ) = 1kWh.
3.6 megajoules (MJ) = 1kWh.

Calorific values of fuels:

Oil is about 10.25kWh/ltr.
LPG is 7.4kWh/ltr.
Mains gas about 38.5–42MJ/m^3 (this varies and is stated on gas bills) or about 10.7 to 11.7kWh/m^3.

To remember the prefix of Systeme Internationale (SI) units as they progress in multiples of 1,000:

Kilo, Mega, Giga, Tera, Peta – use this mnemonic: Klean My G T Porsche.

HEAT TRANSFER AND WATER FLOW RATES

Specific heat capacity of water: 4.2kJ/kgK.

Specific heat capacity of ice: 2.1kJ/kgK.

Latent heat of fusion of water (water to ice): 333kJ/kg.

kW = litres/second × specific heat capacity of water × temperature rise (dt).

If 10kW were extracted from water having a flow rate of 0.8ltr/s then the temperature would drop by 3°C (3K).

HEAT TRANSFER AND AIR FLOW RATES

Heat capacity of air: 0.33W/m^3K.

W = m^3/h × heat capacity of air × temperature rise (dt).

With an air flow of 305m^3/h, or 85ltr/s and 1kW of heat, the temperature would rise by 10 (K or °C).

HEAT-PUMP ENERGY

Note: heat pumps are rated by their heat output, not their input.

A 10kW heat pump with a COP of 4 can be represented by the following equations:

COP = heat output/electricity consumption.
4 = 10kW/2.5kW.
Heat delivered – electricity consumption = Heat extracted from the ground.
10kW – 2.5kW = 7.5kW.

CONVERSIONS

0°C = 32°F (freezing point of water).
10°C = 50°F.
20°C = 68°F (room temperature).
100°C = 212°F (boiling point of water).
Or, if you have a calculator:

°F –32 ÷ 9 × 5 = °C.
°C × 9 ÷ 5 + 32 = °F.
1ltr/s = 3.6m^3/h = 13.19 Gallons (UK)/minute.
1m^3 = 35.315ft^3.

DOMESTIC HOT-WATER USE OF AN AVERAGE HOME

45ltr per person per day.

So for four persons per home: 180ltr = typical household consumption.

10°C = typical mains water temperature.
55°C = typical end-use temperature.
9.5kWh/d = energy used per day.
400W = average energy input.

Glossary

Active cooling Normal heat-pump cooling, as opposed to 'passive' or 'free' cooling.

Air-conditioning Originates from the system that both cools and controls the humidity of air in a building. It is now loosely used to describe any room cooling application.

Air–air heat-pump A heat pump that uses air as the medium for both heat source and heat sink. It extracts energy from the air outside and distributes it indoors using a fan. It can also be used in reverse to cool the building.

Air–water heat-pump A heat pump that uses air as the medium for heat source and water as the medium for heat sink.

Ambient temperature Outside temperature.

Antifreeze An additive that gives water a lower freezing point. Ethylene or propylene glycol is most commonly used in heat-pump systems.

Auxiliary heating Also referred to as supplementary, back-up or top-up heating, this could be an electric element or a boiler.

Back-up heating *See* Auxiliary Heating.

Bivalent When a heat pump operates alongside a boiler or other heating device, it is said to be bivalent. There are different control strategies that are usually programmed in the heat-pump's controller.

Borehole Vertical hole drilled in the ground. A ground-source collector pipe can be installed in a borehole.

Brine Fluid used in the source collector and usually consists of a mixture of water with either ethylene or propylene glycol. Brine is not used here to describe salt water, as in the common usage.

Buffer cylinder Water cylinder or tank that acts as a very short-term store of heat. It is generally fitted to minimize short-cycling, meaning frequent stop/start of the compressor.

Calorific value (cv) Amount of heat that is potentially available when a fuel is burnt. It is expressed in kJ/kg and assumes 100 per cent conversion efficiency.

Circulator Correct term for a water pump. A central heating pump should, strictly speaking, be referred to as a domestic circulator.

Closed loop System using sealed, plastic ground-pipes, which usually contain a glycol antifreeze. It is the most common trench or borehole ground-source system.

CO_2 heat-pump System where the refrigerant used is carbon dioxide and the 'transcritical' cycle gives rise to different characteristics.

Coefficient of performance (COP) Used for measuring the efficiency of a system and found by dividing the useful heat output by the energy input, e.g. a heat pump that produces 4kW of heat for 1kW of input power has a COP of 4. (*See also* Seasonal performance factor)

Collector loop The matrix of pipes that is used to extract or dissipate heat energy from or to the external ground, bedrock or water adjacent to the premises.

Compressor The heart of a heat pump. With its integral electric motor, it compresses the gaseous refrigerant, enables a pressure difference and enables the 'up hill' heat transfer process.

Condenser Heat-exchanger on the 'hot' side of the system where refrigerant condenses.

COP *See* Coefficient of performance.

Defrost Any air-source unit used in temperatures of around 7°C and below will need an automatic defrost mechanism. This can be reverse-cycle or hot-gas. A simple off-cycle defrost mechanism may be acceptable for outside temperatures down to about 3°C.

De-superheater A device fitted to the outlet pipe of the compressor to capture a small proportion of the heat at an elevated temperature.

Delta T, ΔT, dt or DT Delta is a Greek letter (Δ) that signifies a change in something. Delta T is a difference between two temperatures and is usually denoted by 'K' rather than '°C'. For example: flow temperature = 35°C, return = 30°C, dt = 5K.

Direct expansion system (DX) A system where the refrigerant flows directly within the ground pipes. This system is less common and may have some disadvantages; however, it can promise higher efficiencies, since there is one less pump and one less heat-exchanger.

DX system Abbreviation for 'direct expansion'. (*See* Direct expansion system)

Efficiency Loosely used as 'effectiveness' but it is more accurately defined as output divided by input. Energy efficiency of a heating system is specifically the heat output divided by the energy input.

EGS Enhanced or engineered geothermal systems. Also known as hot dry rock, where water is pumped into the ground and steam comes up.

Emitter Component that 'emits' the heat into a building, e.g. radiators or under-floor heating.

Energy efficiency ratio (EER) Used to define the energy efficiency of refrigeration and air-conditioning plant. It is the same ratio as cooling COP.

Enthalpy Total heat that any solid, liquid or gas holds. It is expressed in kilojoules per kilogram (kJ/kg).

Evaporative cooling Intake air to a room passes over a wet material. The evaporation causes some cooling. Air must be relatively dry. Not effective for re-circulation.

Expansion valve A component part that controls the refrigerant flow.

Floating condensation A term that originated from the refrigeration industry and is occasionally used in relation to heat pumps. A better term to use is 'weather compensation'.

Flow Used to describe the pipe taking water out from a boiler. It could also be labelled 'outlet' from heat pump. Some confusion can arise when the term is used on the source (cold) pipes. The return pipe to the boiler is called the 'return'.

Glide Characteristic of some refrigerants that are made of mixtures. The 'glide' refers to the temperature gradient as the refrigerant changes phase.

Heat capacity Similar to 'specific heat', but based on the volume of a material rather than its weight. Can be called 'volume-based heat capacity'.

Heat-exchanger Simple component that transfers heat from one fluid to another. It could be liquid to liquid, liquid to air, air to air. Two heat-exchangers are housed within the heat pump: one for the hot side (the condenser), one for the cold side (the evaporator).

Horizontal collector Can be either coiled 'slinky' or straight pipes that are buried up to 2m deep in open ground (your garden). The pipe is usually plastic and contains a glycol antifreeze solution.

Hot-gas defrost Less common method of periodically defrosting an air source heat-exchanger.

Hysteresis Difference between switch-on and switch-off temperature. It is also called 'differential'.

Inverter Electronic device that varies the frequency, hence rotational speed, of a compressor. It is used to vary the capacity of a heat pump.

Joule (J) A unit of energy. More commonly used than calorie or British Thermal Unit.

Latent heat Energy involved when a substance changes phase, e.g. when a liquid changes to a vapour.

Mean temperature In this book, 'mean' and 'average' are interchangeable.

Mono-energetic Sometimes used to describe a heat pump that also has an integral electrical top-up heater. The heat is thus mostly heat pump but partly direct electric heating.

Open loop System where river or ground-water is pumped through a heat pump then expelled to the environment a few degrees colder.

Passive If an exchange of heat is 'passive', it is done naturally without a heat pump. If a heat pump is involved, it may be described as 'active'.

Passive Cooling Cooling without a heat pump. This is achieved by simply circulating the water from the ground directly through the under-floor heating system. It is sometimes called 'free cooling'.

PassivHaus Internationally accredited standard for very low-energy buildings. Sometimes referred to as 'Passive House'.

Phase change Changing state between solid, liquid or vapour.

Recovery time The time taken for a hot-water cylinder to be restored to its required temperature, e.g. after a bath.

Refrigerant The working fluid within the heat pump. It evaporates in one part and condenses in another. By doing so, heat is transferred from cold to hot. This fluid is sealed in and should not degrade within the life of the heat pump.

Return This term is used to describe the pipe coming back to a boiler or heat pump. This could also be labelled 'inlet'. It is the opposite pipe to the 'flow'.

Reverse-cycle defrost An air-source heat-pump usually 'reverses' to melt ice build-up on the heat-exchanger fins.

Rotary compressor Any compressor without a piston is rotary. Term commonly used to describe small 'offset-roller' compressors as used in small air-conditioning units.

Scroll compressor Compressor that was developed around 1990 and involves two 'scroll'-shaped components that oscillate relative to each other.

Seasonal performance factor (SPF) Similar to COP, but is the total heat over a year divided by the total electrical input. This also takes into account any necessary electric top-up heating load.

Secondary return hot-water loop Hot water is pumped around a loop to ensure taps run-hot immediately. Commonly used in hotels and large houses.

Sensible heat The energy change when a material changes in temperature but does not change phase.

Set-back A reduction in temperature-setting for unoccupied or night periods. It is often programmed with daily time settings.

Set point Temperature setting of a thermostat.

Short-cycling Term given when a compressor switches on and off fairly quickly. Normally you would not expect a compressor to start more than once every fifteen minutes. If it runs for less than five minutes, it could be described as 'short cycling'.

Sink The side of a heat pump where the heat is emitted or dissipated for use. Also referred to as the 'load' side of the system.

Slinky Sometimes used to describe the type of ground collector pipes that are coiled before burying in a trench. Slinky is a trade mark.

Specific heat The property of a material relating to its thermal capacity. Expressed in kJ/kgK, i.e. the amount of energy required to raise the temperature of 1kg of material by 1°C. We have used the 'heat capacity' on a volume basis (kj/m^{3}K) in this book since it is more relevant. (Note: 'K' is the same as '°C' but refers to a change in temperature rather than a specific temperature.)

Standard assessment procedure (SAP) Procedure for estimating energy use in buildings.

Standing column Type of borehole that is used as both a water supply and as a source for a heat pump by re-circulating the water around the borehole.

Steady state When a system reaches equilibrium over time.

Thermal mass Usually refers to a building or item's ability to store heat, i.e. a high thermal mass item will take a long time to heat up and also a long time to cool down. In essence, it is the same as heat capacity.

Transcritical Vapour compression cycle where the pressure rises above the 'critical' point. This transcends the point where 'liquid' or 'vapour' states can be defined.

Water–air heat-pump A heat pump that uses water as the medium for heat source and air as the medium for heat sink.

Water–water heat-pump A heat pump that uses water as the medium for heat source and also as the medium for heat sink.

Weather compensation Automatic adjustment of the heat pump's output temperature dependent on the outside temperature.

Wet heating system Heating system that circulates water as the heat transfer medium.

Abbreviations

ACH	Air changes per hour (ventilation)
ASHP	Air-source heat pump
CFC	Chlorofluorocarbon refrigerant
COP	Coefficient of performance
DHW	Domestic hot-water
EER	Energy efficiency ratio (refrigeration)
GSHP	Ground-source heat pump
GWP	Global warming potential
HC	Hydrocarbon (refrigerant or fuel)
HCFC	Hydro-chlorofluorocarbon refrigerant
HFC	Hydro-fluorocarbon refrigerant
LPG	Liquid petroleum gas (bottled gas)
MCS	Microgeneration Certification Scheme
MHRV	Mechanical heat-recovery ventilation
NRV	Non-return valve
ODP	Ozone depletion potential
RHI	Renewable heat incentive
SAP	Standard assessment procedure for energy ratings
SEER	Seasonal energy efficiency ratio
SPF	Seasonal performance factor
TEV	Thermostatic expansion valve
TEWI	'Total equivalent warming impact' for refrigerants
TRV	Thermostatic radiator valve

Useful Websites

Microgeneration Certification Scheme MCS
Currently administered by Gemserv Ltd
www.microgenerationcertification.org

Ground Source Heat Pump Association
www.gshp.org.uk
Email: info@gshp.org.uk

Heat Pump Association
www.heatpumps.org.uk
Email: info@feta.co.uk

IEA Heat Pump Centre
www.heatpumpcentre.org
Email: hpc@heatpumpcentre.org

International Ground Source Heat Pump Association (IGSHPA)
www.igshpa.okstate.edu
Email: igshpa@okstate.edu

www.heatpumps.co.uk

INDEX